D0298577

Mende Nazer is studying English and intends to become a nurse. She is an active campaigner for human rights and has spoken out internationally against slavery in Sudan. Mende received the Madrid-based Coalition Against Racism's (CECRA) International Award for European Human Rights in 2002.

Damien Lewis is an award-winning writer and filmmaker. For over fifteen years, he has directed and filmed documentaries on the front line of war, conflict and disaster zones in Asia, South America, and across Africa. Working with agencies Frontline TV and Journeyman, his films have appeared on the BBC, Channel 4, CNN, ABC and a host of other broadcasters, whilst his written work has featured in international newspapers. He has produced over a dozen films about war, slavery and related issues in the Sudan.

SLAVE

Mende Nazer's happy childhood in the remote Nuba Mountains of Sudan was cruelly cut short when raiders on horseback swept into her village. The Mujahidin hacked down terrified villagers, raped the women and abducted the children. Twelve-year-old Mende was one of them. Sold to an Arab woman in Khartoum, Mende was kept as a domestic slave, without any pay or a single day off. Her food was leftover scraps, and her bed was the floor of the garden shed. She endured this harsh and lonely existence for seven long years and was then passed on by her master to a relative in London. Eventually Mende managed to make contact with other Nuba exiles who, with British journalist and filmmaker Damien Lewis, helped her escape to freedom.

MENDE NAZER
AND
DAMIEN LEWIS

◆

SLAVE

THE TRUE STORY OF A GIRL'S LOST CHILDHOOD AND HER FIGHT FOR SURVIVAL

Complete and Unabridged

CHARNWOOD
Leicester

First published in Great Britain in 2004 by
Virago Press
London

First Charnwood Edition
published 2005
by arrangement with
Virago Press, an imprint of
Time Warner Books UK
London

British Library CIP Data

Nazer, Mende
    Slave.—Large print ed.—
    Charnwood library series
    1. Nazer, Mende 2. Women slaves—Sudan—
    Biography 3. Slaves—Sudan—Biography
    4. Women slaves—Great Britain—Biography
    5. Slaves—Great Britain—Biography
    6. Large type books
    I. Title II. Lewis, Damien
    306.3′62′092

    ISBN 1–84395–836–8

Published by
F. A. Thorpe (Publishing)
Anstey, Leicestershire

Set by Words & Graphics Ltd.
Anstey, Leicestershire
Printed and bound in Great Britain by
T. J. International Ltd., Padstow, Cornwall

This book is printed on acid-free paper

This book is dedicated to my *Umi* and *Ba*.
I miss you so very much.

Mende

For Tean, my beautiful daughter and my best friend, and for my mother, for being there in times of need.

Damien

Contents

Prologue: The Raid 1

Part One Nuba Childhood 7
    1. My Home 9
    2. Daddy and Me 29
    3. Weddings and Funerals 44
    4. The Arab School 53
    5. Snakes and Search Parties 60
    6. Spirit Wrestlers 70
    7. The Cutting Time 89
    8. My Dream 96

Part Two Into Slavery 105
    9. Allahu Akhbar! 107
    10. The Dark Forest 116
    11. To Khartoum 126
    12. Slave Traders................135
    13. Sold 149
    14. Master Rahab 157
    15. No Escape 173
    16. Blood Rites 181
    17. Death Threats................186
    18. Faith, Hope and Identity 194

19. Murderous Intent 206

20. Revenge 220

21. Rescue Me 224

22. Of Slavery and Chastity 230

23. London Bound? 240

24. They're Alive!................245

25. New Millenium, New
    Slave 251

Part Three Journey to Freedom...............259

26. Telling Lies 261

27. Nanu's Story.................270

28. Fear of Flying................281

29. False Hopes...................295

30. Suicide?......................319

31. Salvation.....................330

32. Desperately Seeking
    Asylum 354

Epilogue: Truly Free?........................376

Afterword 381

Acknowledgements................395

Helpful Addresses 399

Prologue

The Raid

The day that changed my life forever started with a beautiful dawn. I greeted the sunrise by facing east and making the first of my five daily prayers to Allah. It was the spring of 1994, at the end of the dry season. I was about twelve years old. After prayers, I got ready to go to school. It would take me an hour to walk there and an hour back again. I was studying hard because I wanted to be a doctor when I grew up. This was a big dream for a simple African girl like me. I come from the Nuba tribe, in the Nuba Mountains of Sudan, one of the remotest places on earth. I lived in a village of mud huts with grass-thatch roofs, nestling in a fold in the big hills. My tribe are all hunters and farmers and most of them are Muslims. My father had a herd of fifty cattle, which meant that, although he wasn't a rich man, he wasn't poor either.

After a day's hard study at school, I came home and did my chores. Then my mother cooked the evening meal. My father had been out in the fields getting the harvest in and my brothers had been helping him, so they were all very hungry. When we had finished eating, we went out into the yard to listen to my father's stories. I remember sitting around the fire in the

1

yard laughing and laughing. He was a very funny man, my father, a real joker. I loved all my family dearly. It was a cold night so we did not stay out for long. I went to bed as I always did, cuddling up to my father. There was a fire burning in the middle of the hut to keep us warm all night long. My little cat Uran curled up on my tummy. My mother lay on her bed, across the fire from us. Soon, we were all fast asleep. But we hadn't been sleeping long when, suddenly, there was a terrible commotion outside. I woke up, startled, to see an eerie orange light playing over the inside of the hut.

'*Ook tom gua!*' my father shouted, jumping up. 'Fire! Fire in the village!'

We ran to the doorway to see flames reaching skywards towards the far end of the village. At first, we thought that someone must have accidentally set their hut alight. It did happen quite often in our village, but then we caught sight of people running amongst the huts with flaming torches in their hands. I saw them throwing these firebrands onto hut roofs, which burst into flames. The people inside came running out, but they were attacked by these men and dragged to the ground.

'Mujahidin!' my father yelled. 'Arab raiders! The Mujahidin are in the village!'

I still didn't really understand what was happening and I was frozen with fear. Then my father grabbed me by the arm.

'*Go lore okone!? Go lore okone?*' he shouted, 'Where can we run? Where can we run?!'

He was desperately trying to see a way to

2

escape. I could feel my mother, standing close to me, trembling. I was terrified. I had my cat Uran clutched in one arm and my father's hand in the other. Then we started to run.

'Run to the hills,' my father shouted. 'Follow me! Run! Run!'

We ran through scenes from your worst nightmare — my father leading, me following and my mother right behind us. I still held my cat in one arm. There were so many huts on fire, the whole night sky was lit up with the flames. Women and children were running in all directions, crying and screaming in confusion and terror. I saw the raiders grab hold of children and pull them out of their parents' arms.

'If anyone tries to grab you, hold onto me for dear life, Mende!' my father yelled.

I saw the raiders cutting people's throats, their curved daggers glinting in the firelight. I cannot describe to you all the scenes I saw as we ran through the village. No one should ever have to witness the things I saw that night.

Through the smoke and the flames I realised that my father was heading for the nearest mountain. But, as we approached the cover of the forest and the hills, we suddenly noticed a ragged line of raiders on horseback, right in front of us. They had wild, staring eyes, long scraggy beards and they wore ripped, dirty clothes. They brandished their swords at us. They looked completely different from the men in our tribe. They had blocked the only obvious escape route. I could see terrified villagers running ahead of us towards their trap. As they caught sight of the ambush, they started screaming and turned back, trying to find some other way to escape. There was complete chaos and terror and the sound of gunfire.

As we turned to run in the opposite direction, I heard my father shouting desperately for my mother. In all the panic and the confusion, we had lost her. Now I was alone with my father, running, running. I could feel him trying to urge me to run faster, faster. But then I tripped and fell to the ground. I remember my cat jumping out of my arms. Then, as I struggled to get up, one of the Mujahidin grabbed me and started to drag me away. My father jumped on him and wrestled him to the ground. I saw my father beating the raider around the head, and he went down and didn't get up again. My father grabbed me by my arms and started to pull me away from the fighting. My legs felt as if they were being torn to pieces by the sharp stones as he dragged me away, but I didn't care about the pain. And then he hauled me to my feet again and we were running, running, running.

'Run, Mende! Run! As fast as you can!' my father shouted at me. 'If the Arabs try to take you, they'll have to kill me first!'

We sprinted back towards the other end of the village, but I was tired now, really tired. I was getting weaker by the minute. Then, quite suddenly, a big herd of cattle fleeing from the fire cannoned into us, and I went down a second time. I felt hooves pounding over me as I lay curled into a ball on the ground. I really thought that I was going to die. From a distance, I heard my father's voice crying out, 'Mende *agor!* Mende *agor!*' — 'Where are you, Mende! Where are you!' His voice sounded like it was breaking with grief. I tried to shout back and make him hear me, but my throat was choked with pain and dust. My voice came out as a rasping whisper. *'Ba! Ba! Ba!'* I croaked — 'Daddy! Daddy! Daddy!'

But my father couldn't hear me. As I lay there, petrified, with tears streaming down my face, trying to shout for my father, a man seized me from behind. As he pinned me down, with his stubbly beard pricking the back of my neck, I could smell the ugly odour of his breath. I knew that my father was somewhere nearby, searching desperately for me. I kept trying to shout for him. But the man clamped his grubby hand over my mouth. 'Shut up,' he hissed, in Arabic. 'Shut up and lie still. If you keep shouting, the other men will find you and they will kill you.' He dragged me to my feet and started to march me through the village. By the light of the burning huts, I could see that he had a curved dagger and a pistol tucked into a belt at his waist.

As I was led away, I'm sure I heard my father still shouting for me, 'Mende! Mende! Mende!' My father was the bravest man in the world. I knew that he would have tried to save me if only he could find me, even if he had to fight every Mujahidin in the village. I wanted to shout out, *'Ba! Ba!* I'm here! I can hear you.' But the raider kept his hand clamped over my mouth.

As we walked, I could see the village burning

and I could hear screams all around me. I saw Nuba women on the ground with Mujahidin on top of them, pawing at their bodies. I could smell the stench of burning, of blood and of terror. I prayed to God: 'Oh Allah, Oh Allah, please save me, please save me.' And I prayed to God to save my family too. Over and over as I was taken away to the forest, I kept praying to God that we might all be saved.

Leaving the burning village behind us, we arrived at the edge of the forest. Beneath the trees there were about thirty other children huddled together. More Mujahidin kept arriving, bringing young Nuba boys and girls with them. The raiders' clothes and knives were covered in blood and they had the look of absolute evil about them. As they arrived, I heard them chanting at the tops of their voices, '*Allahu Akhbar! Allahu Akhbar! Allahu Akhbar!*' — 'God is Great! God is Great! God is Great!'

I had no idea if any of my family had escaped, or if they had all been killed in the raid. I had no idea what would happen to me now. This is how my wonderful, happy childhood ended and how my life as a slave began.

Part One

Nuba Childhood

1

My Home

When I was born, my father chose to call me
Mende. In our Nuba language, a Mende is the
name of the gazelle — the most beautiful and
graceful animal in the Nuba Mountains. I was
my father's fifth and last child and he thought I
was the prettiest daughter ever. Our village
backed onto a huge rock that towered above all
the mud huts below. Behind this rock, the
mountains rose above us, high into the sky. In
fact, the village was ringed with mountains on all
sides. In just fifteen minutes you could walk out
of our village and lose yourself in the foothills.

Our home consisted of a rectangular compound, enclosing two mud huts facing each
other. This we called the *shal*. The *shal* was
fenced around with a wall of wooden posts
interwoven with straw. Two benches ran down
each side of the *shal*, where we would gather
around a fire in the evening and laugh and tell
stories. Around the *shal* there was a much larger
yard, the *tog*. The fence of the tog was made of
strong, straight tree branches and it was as high
as the roof of a house. I suppose the *shal* was like
a Western house, and the *tog* was like the garden
that surrounds it. Our sheep and goats lived in
the *tog*. We had to be careful that they didn't

9

break into the *shal* and steal our food.

I lived in one hut with my mother and father. There were three beds inside, one for each of us. They had bamboo frames, with a rope mattress made from the bark of the baobab tree. My father always slept by the door to protect us. There were snakes and hyenas in the forest and hills nearby and I was afraid that they would come in and get me. Every night, I would leave my own bed and cuddle up to my father where I felt safe. In the rainy season we had a fire burning in the middle of the hut to keep us warm at night. We kept a big pile of dry firewood in the middle of the hut, and when it ran out we'd have to collect damp wood from the forest. Then, the fire would struggle to burn and make the inside of the hut all smoky.

One of my earliest memories is of my father getting me a kitten. It was jet black and shiny. I called it Uran — which means 'blackie'. Uran turned out to be a good mouse-killer and she was the source of great fun for all of us. At night, when I would jump up on my father's bed to sleep, Uran would jump up on me. Then my father would wake up.

'I've already got you in my bed,' he'd say, sleepily. 'D'you think I can manage to sleep with your cat as well?'

'Yes, of course you can,' I'd reply, giggling. 'I'm sleeping with you and we're sleeping with my cat. And that's that.'

'Look. If you want to sleep with Uran, then go and sleep in your own bed,' he'd chuckle.

I would always refuse. Then my mother would

call from across the hut.

'Come here, Mende. My bed's big enough for you and me and your cat.'

'No,' I'd call back. 'I want to sleep here with my father.'

So began a game of musical beds. I would take Uran to my mother, leave her there and then run back to my father's bed. But Uran would immediately jump off my mother's bed and run back to us again. By now, my father would be laughing out loud.

'OK,' he'd sigh, 'you go and sleep with your mother and Uran stays here with me.'

'All right, *Ba*,' I'd say. I knew how this joke would end. I would go over to my mother's bed, and Uran would run back and jump up with us again. By now, the whole hut would be rocking with laughter.

'So, whatever we do, Uran wants to sleep with you,' my father would say. Then he'd fetch my small bed from across the hut and place it beside his. I would jump up onto my bed, Uran would jump up on top of me and my father would sleep next to both of us. Like that, everyone was happy.

Three tall, conical grain stores, *durs*, stood to one side of our yard. Each had one small entrance, high up in the wall, which was just the width of a man's body. The only way in was to climb up a ladder and dive in, twisting yourself through the entrance hole as you did so. It was designed like this so that no rats or goats could get in. The *dur* kept the grain dry so it would last us from one harvest season to the next. When we needed some more grain, my father would jump into the *dur*. He would scoop up a gourd-full and pass it up to my brother, Babo, who would stand at the entrance, perched on a ladder. I would wait down below to take it from him.

My oldest sister, Shokan, lived in a neighbouring compound with her husband and children, as did my other sister, Kunyant. My brothers, Babo and Kwandsharan, lived outside the family compound, in the *holua*, the men's house. Each family had its own *holua*, where the unmarried boys would eat and sleep together. At mealtimes, my father would go out to the *holua* to eat with the men.

My father would call out to all our male relatives to come and join him: 'Come and eat with us! Come and drink tea!' My uncles and aunts all lived within easy shouting distance of our home. In our tradition, it is very important that you do not eat alone. You share any meal with whoever is around at the time. It may be a family member, a village neighbour, a visitor from another tribe or even a foreigner. It doesn't matter. Anyone who is in hearing distance is welcome. Maybe my mother would have roasted sorghum and peanuts on the fire and ground this into a delicious paste. Or she might have cooked *kal*, a sorghum mash boiled with water and milk, or *waj*, a curried stew of vegetables and meat.

I lived in a very close-knit community. We had few secrets and there was little need for privacy. When I was very young, I would just go to the toilet behind our yard. But when I was around six, I started going to a special patch of bush, which was the grown-ups' toilet. I would crouch down behind a bush with the grass brushing my bottom and grab the nearest leaf to clean myself. When it was the wet season, the leaves were too tough to pull off the tree. Then I would take a handful of dry raffia palm leaves with me, but this presented another problem. Raffia leaves have very sharp edges and you could end up with some cuts in very awkward places. One morning, when I was still very small, I went to relieve myself in the bush, accompanied by my friend Kehko. She went to one tree and I went to another. We had just crouched down, when Kehko shouted over to me.

'I can hear something moving, Mende. What d'you think it is?'

'It's probably just a mouse,' I called back.

But suddenly, out came a huge snake. Kehko saw it a moment before I did and she started screaming. Then I saw it too, slithering through the bush. Kehko jumped up and started running with all her pee-pee going down her legs. It would have been very funny were we not so scared. My situation was even worse and as I was straining to finish, the snake was slithering towards me. There was nothing for it. In a flash, I jumped up out of the undergrowth and started to run. I did a very uncomfortable short sprint, with my bum stuck out behind me. When we were far enough away from the snake, we stopped and both collapsed with laughter. After this, Kehko and I decided we would never go back to that part of the bush again.

Behind our house we had a garden where we

grew maize, and vegetables like beans and pumpkin. In October, the rains would come and the maize would swell up fat and juicy. My favourite treat was fresh maize cobs roasted over the fire, with home-made butter. When we'd eaten all the food in the garden, we'd send the goats in to eat up all the leftover stalks and leaves.

Every day, we girls had to go to the mountains to fetch water and firewood. We'd walk for as much as two hours on little paths that wound through the forest. Because the hills were full of snakes and wild animals, we'd always try to get some of the boys to go with us to protect us. Sometimes, when we arrived at the water hole with our clay pots, there would be girls from another village there too. Then there might be an argument about who would get to fill up first. Pretty quickly, we'd start to call each other names: 'You're ugly! You're lazy! You're a liar!' Then someone would start a fight. It was all only in fun really. But I'd always call for my brother Babo to save me. 'Mende, come and stand behind me,' he'd say. 'Now, if any of you want to touch Mende, you'll have to get past me first.'

When the rains finally came, after the long hot, dry season, all the children would run outside and dance for joy, singing the rain song: '*Are coucoure, Are konduk ducre*' — 'The rain is coming, Too much rain'. We'd wave our hands above our heads and dance around in the warm, balmy rain. It was a time of such relief, because the rains meant that we would have a good harvest and no one would go hungry that year.

When I was about six, for the first time in my life the rains failed. Our crops wilted and died. We started running out of food. Week by week, the situation was getting worse. People were very hungry and getting desperate. Soon, the children were looking thin and sickly and some of the old people started dying of starvation. I can remember that I had never felt so hungry in all my life.

Then, one day, I saw an amazing sight — a huge cloud of dust billowing up from the old track that wound up from the valley floor. As I watched, I saw a line of gleaming white trucks emerging from the dust. Once or twice before, I had seen an old truck chugging its way up into our village, but I'd never seen anything like this shining convoy before. I could see that it was headed for the market place in the centre of our village. I rushed down there and saw two men getting out of the lead vehicle. To my amazement I saw that these men had pale, white skins. It was the first time in my life that I'd ever seen a *Hawaja*, a white man. I stood there with the other village children, staring at the *Hawajas* from a distance and wondering where on earth they might have come from. To us they looked like ghosts.

They walked up the line of trucks and began to direct the drivers where to unload. The young Nuba men from our village rushed over to help carry the big sacks, drums of cooking oil, medicines and blankets into an empty building nearby. Each family was entitled to one blanket, one sack of lentils, one tin of oil and some sorghum seeds for planting the following year. My father joined the queue, whilst we just stood and stared and stared at the *Hawajas*. Eventually we headed for home, with my father carrying the sack of lentils, my mother carrying the oil and me carrying the big blanket.

'These *Hawajas* are very good people,' my father said, smiling, as we walked back to our hut. 'They come from far, far away because they know the rains have failed and we're hungry. But the Arabs don't help us — even though they share the same country with us.'

All that year, convoys of trucks snaked up the steep mountain pass to bring us more aid. It turned out that it was being sent by America, so everyone kept talking about what a good man President Bush (the father of the present US president) was to help us like this. One woman in our village even decided to name her son 'Bush'. He had been born in the midst of the famine. There was then a rash of copycat naming, so that soon there was a string of little boys named Bush in our village. Then some of the women decided they wanted to call their daughters after Bush's wife, but no one could find out her name. Another woman composed a song in praise of President Bush. It quickly became very popular and you could hear the women singing away as they worked. I can't remember the words exactly, but it went something like this:

Bush, Bush, Bush, Bush,
Bush is very kind,
He helps the Nuba,
With lentils and oil,
If it wasn't for Bush,
We'd all die,
Bush, Bush, Bush, Bush.

One of the worst things about the drought was that lots of our livestock died. In the Nuba Mountains, cows are very important — they are the sign of a man's wealth. You would hear people say, 'Hmmm . . . That man is a very rich man. Look how many cows he has.' My father had maybe fifty or sixty cows in all. Some of the other men had even more, maybe as many as one hundred cows. During the famine, lots of our cows died. It took my father years to build up his herd again.

Normally, it was Babo's responsibility, as the youngest boy, to look after our cattle, but when he started going to school, my father employed a boy from a neighbouring village to do it instead. He was about thirteen years old and named Ajeka. Ajeka — who we called Ali — carried a spear and an *ondo* — a musical instrument made from a gourd and three wire strings. All he wore was a string of beads around his waist. Ali would take the cows into the fields or the forest to graze, and stroll around all day long, playing gently to himself on his *ondo*. After one year, my father would give Ali one cow. That was his wages for the year.

My father's herd of cows was kept about ten

17

minutes away from our house in an enclosure called a *coh*. It was made of huge tree branches driven into the ground. There was a big *coh* for the adult cows and the calves had their own smaller enclosure, a *cohnih* — which means literally, 'house of the small cows'. Before sunrise, Ali and my brothers would get up and go to the cattle enclosure. They would take the hungry calves over to their mothers so they could start suckling. As the milk began to flow the boys would take the calves away again and start milking the cows themselves. The boys would leave a little milk for the calves and carry the rest home to my mother.

Sometimes, we would drink the milk immediately — delicious and fresh and still warm. Or we would put it on the fire to make sorghum porridge. Or I might be sent out with a bowl of fresh milk into the yard, where there was a gourd hanging by a rope from a post in the ground with a fork at the top. I would pour the milk into a small hole at the top of the gourd and seal it with a cork. Then I would shake it backwards and forwards, to churn the milk. I would shake for five minutes and then rest, shake and rest, shake and rest, until I had separated out the buttermilk and the curds. From this we made butter and yoghurt.

People used to say that I looked exactly like my mother. She was very slim and she was very, very beautiful. But my hair was like my father's — much softer and longer than my mother's. In my earliest memories, my mother used to walk about completely naked. For the first eight years or so of my life, no one in our village wore any clothes to speak of. Then my mother took to wearing a short, colourful woven cloth wrapped around her hips. Or when it was cold she might wear a blanket wrapped around her shoulders. I never knew my mother's age, but she looked about ten years younger than my father. In our tribe, a man always married a much younger woman.

My mother had decorative scars all over her body. When my mother was still a child, my grandmother had spent hours with a sharp stone cutting her skin to make beautiful, geometric patterns. My grandmother had chosen to cut spirals and whorls into my mother's breasts and long rows of straight lines on my mother's abdomen. I thought these scars made my mother look very beautiful. Scars are *kell* in our Nuba language — signs of beauty. Both the men and the women used to have them. My mother had the most beautiful scar on one side of her face — like a three-headed arrow. My grandmother had cut her until the blood had started pouring down her cheek.

'I saw the blood dripping onto the earth, Mende,' my mother told me, touching the scar with her fingertips. 'But we were taught to be brave, so I didn't complain.'

I had four older brothers and sisters, but none had had the scarring done to them. My mother told me that it was an old tradition that had been stopped before we were born. She was sad about this, but she understood why these old traditions had to come to an end. She always wore a

19

necklace of black and white beads around her neck, and around her waist she wore a wide band made of strings of white, red, yellow and black beads. In Nuba culture, the beads each tribe wears are very distinct and identify one tribe from another. My mother wore these beads to show that she was from our tribe, the Karko (a subtribe of the Nuba). If strangers came to our village, we would know immediately if they were from our tribe, just by looking at their beads and their scars.

Although my mother always wore her hair in braids, she hardly ever allowed me to braid her hair because I wasn't very good at it. A friend who lived nearby usually did it for her. This woman had spent a long time learning how to braid hair in the Nuba tradition. She was really like the hairdresser of our tribe, but no one ever paid her for it. She just did it as a favour and that's how we all treated each other. If you could help someone, you would.

Each girl had a different hairstyle for different occasions — for the coming of the rains, for harvest time, for the wrestling time or for the boys' circumcision ceremony. My mother told me that, in her day, the boys had been circumcised at seventeen or eighteen years old to mark their transition to manhood, but my brothers were circumcised when they were much younger, around ten or eleven. The traditions were changing, and it was now seen as much safer to circumcise boys at a younger age.

My father had a beautiful, kind face. He was not tall for a Nuba, but he was fit and lithe and

20

strong. His features looked fine, almost European, but his skin was very black. All he ever wore was a short strip of cloth wrapped around his waist and a white skull cap. My father's hands were hard and callused. Sometimes, after rolling baobab tree bark all day long to make rope to sell in the market place, his hands would bleed. He had deep fissures and cracks in the soles of his feet from walking barefoot over sharp stones and rocks in the hills. He had a short beard, just like stubble really. He kept his jet-black hair cropped close to his head. But it grew very quickly and when it did it was soft, unlike most Nuba hair which is hard and wiry.

Many of the men in our village had several wives. My Uncle Jerongir and my Uncle Foneshir both had two wives. But my father only ever had one wife. I would still have loved him, even if he had married ten wives. I don't know if my mother would have liked it, but she wouldn't have had a say in it. That's our tradition. My father loved my mother very much. He used to say to us, 'Your mother is such a good woman, she's like ten wives to me.'

Life in our home was very peaceful. My father and mother never argued. The only fights I ever had with my brothers and sisters were in play. My father was always joking with our neighbours and inviting them in to eat with us. While he was boisterous, my mother was very quiet and reserved. Everyone liked and respected her. She didn't join in the village gossip. People said that while my mother was like an angel, my father was like a very loveable, but naughty, devil.

My father had a huge hunting spear with a long, whippy wooden shaft and a sharp metal tip. When he went hunting in the mountains he would take his spear, a long stick, an axe and a gourd full of drinking water. He would carry an enormous cow's horn with him too. Often, he might just kill a rabbit or a small, pheasant-like bird, but sometimes, he might kill a *shukul* — a big forest deer. Occasionally, he might even catch a hyena. If he had killed a large animal, he would blow on his cow horn, echoing from hill to hill. We would hear it in the village and get very excited. Then the men would set off to help him carry back the dead animal.

★　★　★

When I was about six years old, I became very worried about my cat Uran. She was so fat that I thought she was about to burst. '*Umi*, why is Uran getting so fat?' I asked my mother. 'I think she's eating too many mice.'

'She's not fat because she eats too much,' said my mother, laughing. 'She's pregnant — she's going to have babies.'

I was so shocked. How had Uran become pregnant, I asked my mother?

'Well, Uran got pregnant by eating too many mice,' my mother said, immediately contradicting herself. I think this was just a convenient way for her not to have to explain the facts of life to me at such an early age.

'*Umi*,' I wailed, 'I don't understand. Is Uran going to give birth to mice then? We brought her

22

here so she could get rid of all the mice.'

My mother sat down on her wooden stool and pulled me over to her. 'Listen, Mende. Uran may eat mice, but she'll give birth to baby cats. You wait and see.'

I still didn't understand, but I was happy that Uran was going to have kittens. I picked her up and took her over to my mother. 'When will she have them?' I asked her.

'I don't know exactly,' she said, feeling Uran's tummy. 'But by the way her tummy feels, I'd say pretty soon.'

I was so excited. One morning, a week later, I went to check on Uran and found her curled up with four gorgeous little kittens. They were black with white patches. She was lying there gazing up at me, looking very proud of herself. Uran really was my best friend. I ran out into the yard, caught a goat, milked it and rushed back with a gourd-full of milk for Uran. I spent all day lying on the ground next to her. I held the kittens and stroked them. Later, I ran to tell my friends and they came over to play with the kittens too. As they grew, they started to jump all over me and play with my fingers and ears. They became the highlight of my life. Then, one morning, my mother said that she needed to have a little talk with me.

'One of our neighbours has asked if they can have a kitten to live in their house,' she told me. 'So we can give them one of Uran's. Won't that be nice?'

I couldn't believe what she was saying. 'You want to give Uran's children away?' I wailed.

'How can you? Why don't you give your own children away, if that's what you want to do?'

'Don't be angry with me,' my mother told me, gently. 'If we keep all these kittens, Uran will soon have another five and then we'll have ten cats and where do you think all the milk will come from to feed them all?'

'We have cows and goats. We can drink the cows' milk and the cats can drink the goats' milk.'

'And where do you think they're all going to live? Should we build a fence and keep Uran and all her children outside, like we do the cows? Would you like that?'

'Why can't we all live together in our hut? Cats are only small and there's lots of room.'

But my mother was adamant. We would have to give Uran's kittens away. I was so upset that my mother didn't know what to do. Finally, she said, 'Listen, Mende, for the time being they can all stay here with us, all right? Now, will you stop crying?'

I was so relieved I ran over to Uran to tell her the good news — that her kittens could stay. But of course my mother had tricked me. One morning, a few days later, I woke up to discover that all the kittens had gone. I rushed around the hut in a complete panic looking everywhere for them. Then I ran outside and searched the yard. Eventually, I sat down and burst into tears. '*Umi*,' I cried, 'I can't find the kittens anywhere. Where've they gone?'

My mother pretended to look surprised. 'Really?' she said. 'Where can they have got to?'

She began to search the hut with me. After about five minutes, she gave up. 'Maybe Uran took them into the garden,' she said. 'Have you tried there?'

I was about to rush off and search the garden, when my mother told me that I must have some breakfast first. I told her I would eat when I had found the kittens. I set off with Uran in tow. I was rather annoyed that my mother wasn't helping me. An hour later, I was still searching around the yard, when one of my friends came running over. She told me that she was overjoyed because — guess what? — they had been given one of Uran's kittens. Suddenly, I realised that my mother had tricked me. I couldn't believe that she could be so cruel. I ran back into our hut. 'Why did you give Uran's children away? How could you do it?' I shouted at her, stamping my feet. 'How could you be so mean? You lied to me.'

My mother sat me down and tried to explain that Uran would have more kittens and that she wouldn't send them away next time. But I was inconsolable. I was worried that Uran couldn't have any more kittens because she had eaten all the fat mice and only thin ones were left. I was so sad for days after that. But as the kittens grew up I could see them playing happily around the village and I soon forgave my mother.

★ ★ ★

Because I was the youngest child and my father's last daughter, I think I was probably a bit spoilt.

Shokan was about thirteen years older than me. Her name means 'no hair', because when she was born she was completely bald. I don't think she ever went to school, and by the time I was born she was already married and had left home. I went to visit her often, as the path to the forest wound past her house and then past Kunyant's house too. I could call out from our hut, 'Shokan, where are you?' She would hear me and shout back from her house, 'Over here, Mende, over here.' Kunyant must have been around seven years older than me. By contrast, her name means 'lots of hair', because she was born with a thick fuzz. I remember everyone saying that Kunyant was very beautiful, but not very clever. She did go to school, but not for very long. She too got married when she was about thirteen.

My eldest brother was called Kwandsharan, meaning 'short boy', as he was so small when he was born. He was always laughing and making jokes and he was very handsome. Kwandsharan hoped to go away to study and become an officer in the army. I liked him but I never understood why he wanted to leave the village and become a soldier. My other brother, Babo, was just two years older than me, so he was the nearest to me in age. His name in our language means 'baby' and he was my mother's favourite. He was tall and slim and thoughtful and very clever, and he always came first in his class at school. He used to tell me that he wanted to be a trader, working in the market. Out of all my brothers and sisters he was my favourite. Wherever he was in the village, I was always at his side.

The only time Babo ever left me behind was when he went to the forest to hunt birds. He would shoot them using a slingshot made from raffia palm, which fired small pebbles. Or sometimes he would use a wooden catapult. If we were lucky, he'd get a big pigeon. When he got home, he'd give it to me to put on the fire to singe off all the feathers. Then he would gut it and we'd cook it in an iron pan over the fire, with some water, onions and salt. It was a delicious treat.

Babo used to play with me all the time. One of our favourite games was called *Kak*, the stone game. We would take eight pebbles the size of large marbles, sit down on the ground facing each other, and lay the stones out in a line between us. Babo would always let me go first. I had to throw one of the stones up in the air, grab another off the ground and catch the falling stone before it landed — all with the same hand. When I had caught all eight stones, I had to start all over again, but now I had to grab two stones at once, then three, four and so on. If I managed to catch all the stones and finish the sequence, I'd shout, '*Kak!*' Of course, if I dropped a stone, that was my go over with. Babo and I would play the stone game for hours on end.

But my favourite game was *omot nwaid* — the moon game. We could only play it when there was a full moon lighting the whole of the village and the surrounding mountains with silver moonlight. Twenty or thirty children would gather in the centre of the village. First, we'd build a big stone circle. Then, one of us would throw a flat disc of cow's bone (usually one of its vertebrae) spinning through the air as far as we could. We'd all go running after it, screaming and laughing and falling over each other in the rush to be first to find it.

If I found the bone, I'd keep very quiet and try to run back into the stone circle without anyone catching me. But as soon as the rest saw that I had it, they'd shout, 'Quick! Quick! Get Mende! Stop her!' If I reached the stone circle without being caught, I would dance around and shout, *'Eyee langaa! Eyee langaa!'* — 'I've made it! I've made it!' I was then the winner and I got to throw the bone. If they caught me, I was out. If we'd been allowed to, we would have played *omot nwaid* all night long. But after a couple of hours or so, our parents would call us in. 'Come on, Mende!' my mother would shout. 'Come home now. It's time to sleep.'

2

Daddy and Me

One day, just after the start of the rains, my father asked me to go with him to the sorghum fields. Sorghum is our staple crop. I was only about six years old at the time. But I knew that the fields were a very long way away, down on the plain where the soils was more fertile.

'I'm going there for a few days to plant our sorghum,' he explained. 'Then I have to come back to the village. So, I want you to stay there while I'm gone and chase the birds away. Otherwise, they'll eat all the seeds we've just planted. I'll only be away for one day and then I'll come back for you. OK?'

'Yes! Yes!' I said, dancing up and down. 'I'd love to go with you, *Ba*. But please, *Ba*, can I take Uran with me?'

'Uran will get lost in the forest, Mende, and then she might get eaten. So she's much better off staying here in the village, isn't she?'

Despite having to leave Uran behind, I was so happy. It was the first time that my father had taken me with him. I missed him when he was away and I especially missed his stories. The night before we left, my mother packed food for us and pots and pans for cooking. At first light the next morning, we slung all the provisions in sacks over the donkey's back. Then my father jumped onto the donkey and lifted me up in front of him. As we set off, everyone was waving goodbye. I felt very important and very special.

'When are you coming back, Mende?' my friend Kehko shouted.

'Never,' I shouted over my shoulder. 'I'm going to spend all my life in the fields with my father. Bye-bye.'

'Who will play with you then?' Kehko shouted after us.

'No-one,' I replied, haughtily. 'I'm not going for playing. I have a very important job to do. I have to keep our fields safe from the birds.'

Before long, the forests and the hills that we passed through were new and strange to me. My father was well armed with his spear and his axe and a stout stick, so I wasn't afraid. As we rode along, I chatted away.

'Before we left the village, you said that I'd have to stay in the fields when you go. But what will I do if the ghosts come?'

My father seemed to think about this for a while. 'Good point,' he said, eventually. 'I should have asked Babo to come too. The forests are full of ghosts.'

'They are? Well I'm not staying there alone then. You'll have to take me back home with you.'

'If I take you home with me, who will scare all the birds off the fields?'

'The ghosts can scare the birds away just as well as I can,' I said, starting to get upset.

'I'm not so sure, Mende,' said my father

slowly, shaking his head. 'I think you'll do a much better job.'

I started crying loudly and kicking my feet into the donkey's sides. 'Well, you can't expect me to stay there alone with the ghosts, can you?' I wailed.

'Don't kick the donkey like that,' my father said, trying not to laugh. 'If you do, he'll start to run so fast that we'll fall off.'

'I don't care. Anything's better than being left alone in the fields with the ghosts.'

My father couldn't keep a straight face any longer. 'I'm teasing you, Mende,' he said. 'There aren't any ghosts in the forests. Look around you. Do you see any ghosts here? No.'

Gradually, I stopped crying. My father tried to cheer me up, but I didn't answer him for ages. I was in a sulk. 'You don't love me,' I eventually snapped. 'You want me to stay all alone with the ghosts. If they touch me or even breathe on me I'll die!'

'I've told you, I was only joking.'

'Well, you wait and see, I'm not staying in that place alone. I'm coming back with you to the village.'

'All right. We'll wait and see, shall we,' my father said, chuckling.

We must have looked a very strange couple, shouting and laughing and crying our way through the forest. The longer we travelled, the more strange the surroundings looked. Soon, the forest was thick all around us. It was steamy and humid. The trees were dripping wet from the recent rains. In places, there were the gullies of seasonal riverbeds snaking through the huge trees. For a few days after the rains, these would be transformed into raging torrents. All the rest of the year they would be dry.

Finally we reached one of these gullies, full of deep, turbulent water, which was blocking our path. My father went to check the current and decided that it was too dangerous to cross. We would have to wait until it had died down a little. An hour or so later, he thought we should give it a try. He tied the donkey to a tree and then put me up on his shoulders. He told me to hold on very tightly with both hands. Then, very slowly, he waded out into the rushing torrent. He had a long stick in either hand and as he inched across, he used them to test the depth and the strength of the current ahead. From up on his shoulders, the sound of the raging water was deafening. As he waded in deeper, the water surged up around my father's chest and then started to swirl around my bare feet.

'Hold on tight, Mende!' he shouted. 'Hold on tight!'

'How can I hold onto you?' I yelled back. I didn't want my father to see how scared I really was. 'I'm only small. Why can't you hold onto me? Or do you want me to be washed away?'

My father couldn't stop himself from bursting into laughter. 'Do you want us to fall into the river?' he shouted up at me.

'Of course not,' I yelled back.

'OK, so how can I hold onto you and these sticks at the same time?'

'I don't know! But you must hold onto me

32

tightly. I'm only small. Don't you care if I fall in?'

'How many arms do I have?' he shouted in reply. But I was giggling so much by now that I couldn't answer. 'How many arms do I have?' he shouted, even louder. 'How many arms do I have? You going to answer me, Mende?'

'*Ore, Ba*' — 'Two, Daddy' — I finally blurted out. 'Two arms!'

'Yes. Two arms. So, how can I hold onto you and the sticks at the same time?'

'I don't care,' I shouted back. 'But don't you dare drop me! Walk slowly. And don't step into a big hole or we'll both drown!'

'You are a crazy, crazy girl,' my father shouted up at me. 'Why do I have to have you as a daughter? You're just the biggest bundle of trouble ever.'

By the time we'd reached the middle of the river, we were laughing so much that I'd forgotten all my fear. When we finally got to the far bank, my father took me down from his shoulders and collapsed on the ground, panting with the exertion and with laughter. Then he turned back to fetch the donkey.

'Don't go near the river,' he warned me, serious for a moment. 'It's very dangerous. Stay away from the water.'

Soon, my father was pulling the donkey by its reins down the opposite riverbank. But it was very stubborn and refused to set foot in the raging water. It was braying in panic, 'Eeeh-aaw! Eeeh-aaw! Eeeh-aaw!' My father stood in the river trying to pull the donkey in while it pulled

33

in the opposite direction. From where I was sitting it looked so funny. 'What're you laughing at?' my father shouted, in mock anger. 'You think it's funny, do you? If the donkey falls in, all the food gets wet and the sorghum flour gets swept away downstream. Then what'll we have to eat? We'll starve! Or we'll have to go back to the village and everyone will laugh at us.'

Finally, after much pulling and cursing, my father dragged the donkey across. Then, panting and soaking wet, he sat down and gave me a big hug. This first river was the most difficult to cross. We were still high up in the hills and the water was deep and fierce. As we descended towards the plains, each river became a little easier. By late afternoon, we reached the edge of the forest. Before us lay a vast, treeless plain stretching as far as the eye could see in all directions. I was used to the mountains and I felt isolated and vulnerable in this huge, vast emptiness.

'I don't like it here,' I said. 'It's flat and empty. We'll get lost.'

'I know. I don't like it much either,' my father answered. 'But this is where the soil is fertile.'

My father had made a small, rectangular shelter from dry sorghum stalks at the edge of his fields. Inside, there was a fireplace with four big stones to balance a cooking pot. On either side of the fire, there were raffia beds. At the far end, away from the door, there was a big bed of sorghum straw for sitting on and telling stories in the evening.

We took all our things into the hut and made

ourselves at home. Then my father lit a fire to warm us up after the long, wet journey and to boil some sweet tea. He took off the blanket that he'd been wearing around his shoulders and put it to dry hanging from the roof of the hut. All I was wearing was a pair of knickers, so I took them off and followed his example. After we ate some of the food that *Umi* had prepared for us, we were ready for bed. My father settled down on one of the small raffia beds next to the fire and I jumped up next to him. It had been an exhausting journey and we were soon fast asleep.

★　★　★

The next morning my father woke me up with a breakfast of sorghum porridge with milk. Then we went out to start work. My father started by digging holes in the soil with a long, heavy stick tipped with metal. I followed behind him popping a couple of seeds into each hole and stamping down the earth with my bare feet. The soil was wet from the rains and very soft. My father sang as he worked. To left and right, I could see other Nuba people doing the same as us.

Then, on the morning of the third day, after we'd eaten breakfast, my father sat me down for a talk.

'Today, I've got to go back to the village,' he said, gently.

'I'm not staying here without you,' I retorted.

'Yes. You are,' he replied, calmly. 'You're staying here just like we agreed — to keep the birds off the fields.'

'I'm too afraid,' I whimpered. 'I can't stay here alone.'

'Look at me, Mende,' he said sternly. 'You know that's why I brought you here in the first place . . . '

Before he could finish, I butted in. 'But you didn't tell me about the wild animals and the ghosts before we came, did you? You only told me that on the way here.'

'Wait, I haven't finished. Now listen to me.' He was serious now, which was unusual for him. 'I explained to you why I wanted you to come here with me. Now, you'll only be here on your own for one day, and then I'll come back. I was only teasing you about the ghosts and the wild animals. Surely you know that?'

'I know,' I said, bursting into tears. 'But I don't think jokes about wild animals and ghosts are funny.'

'So, what do you want me to do? There's no way you can come back with me. I need you to stay here and watch out for the birds. When the sun sets you can run across to stay with Uncle Jerongir. His fields are just nearby.'

By now I was getting hysterical. 'I'm not going to watch out for any stupid birds,' I shrieked. 'I'll leave the birds to eat all the seeds. You see if I don't.'

'OK,' my father retorted. 'You let the birds eat all the seeds and you see what happens when I get back.'

With that, he jumped on his donkey, kicked its flanks and set off at a trot towards the forest. I started running after him, shouting at the top of my voice through my tears.

'*Ba! Ba!* Don't leave me. Take me with you. Take me back to the village. You can't leave me here. I'll die!'

My father was really getting angry now. 'Go back, Mende!' he shouted at me. 'Go on! Go back.'

But I just kept running after him. As he kicked harder and the donkey ran faster, I ran faster too. Finally, my father stopped. When I caught up with him, he leaned down and scooped me up with one arm. For a second, I was so happy because I thought he was going to take me with him — until he turned the donkey around and trotted back the way we had come.

'Don't think you're coming back to the village, because you're not,' he told me, sternly. 'You're going back to look after the fields.'

All the way back down the path I cried and kicked my father in the shins. But he was losing patience with me. This was costing him precious time and he had a long journey ahead of him. Back at the hut, he took me on his lap under a tree.

'Mende,' he said gently, stroking my hair. 'Please listen to me. You heard what I said. If you come back with me, the birds will dig up the seeds and we'll have to do all this work again. Then our sorghum might never be ready in time. Is that really want you want?'

'No,' I said quietly, hanging my head.

'So, you must stay here and be brave. I'll come back tomorrow, just like I promised.'

'OK, *Ba*.'

'Smile for me, this time when I leave,' he said, grinning at me. As he climbed on his donkey I stopped crying and attempted a smile.

'Goodbye, see you tomorrow,' he called as he trotted off up the path.

As he disappeared around a corner in the path through the forest, I suddenly felt very alone and very afraid. I knew that I couldn't run after him again, so I sat under the tree throwing rocks at the birds. 'Go away, you stupid birds,' I kept shouting. 'Go away. Go away!' But all day long, I kept imagining that I could hear animals moving in the shadows in the nearby forest.

At sunset, I hurried over to my Uncle Jerongir's fields. I ran so fast that my feet didn't touch the ground. He gave me some goat's milk and some sorghum porridge. After that, I was so tired that I went straight to sleep. The next morning I set off at the crack of dawn for my father's fields again. All morning, I chased the birds away, with half an eye on the path behind me, watching for my father. I waited and waited but he didn't come. In the early afternoon, I spotted a woman from our village walking down the path towards me. 'Why hasn't my father come back yet?' I called out to the woman, in a near panic. 'He promised he'd be back this morning.'

'Oh, he told me to tell you that he can't make it,' she answered, 'so he'll be back here tomorrow.'

My first thought was that my father had tricked me. Then I realised that something must have happened to delay him. I had no choice but to wait for him. So I carried on throwing stones and shouting at the birds. But around mid-afternoon, I heard a horrible cry from just within the forest behind me, echoing through the trees. I spun around. 'Aooowww. Aooowww.' There it was again! It sent a chill up my spine. I knew this sound very well. It was the call of the wild dog, an animal with a fearsome reputation. They hunt in packs and will attack anything, being particularly fond of young Nuba children. I kept turning my head from side to side to try to see where the howls were coming from. I could feel my whole body shaking with fear.

Suddenly, I saw a movement amongst the trees, and out stepped a wild dog. I watched transfixed as it jumped over the fence into our field. I knew the rest of the pack would be somewhere close by. I was scared that if I made a move he would hear me and come after me. But I also knew that if I stayed where I was, he would eventually smell me out. Finally, terror forced me to run and the only thing that I could think of doing was heading for the big tree in the middle of the field.

When at last I reached the tree I jumped up into the lowest branches and quickly climbed to the top. I'd spent so much of my time playing in the trees back at the village that it was easy for me. I could feel my legs shaking uncontrollably; I was still scared that the dogs had heard me or seen me. Although I knew they couldn't climb trees, I imagined them waiting for me to fall out when I dropped off to sleep.

I turned around and caught sight of the wild dog stalking slowly across the field towards me, its belly to the ground. Then, when it was quite close, it suddenly pounced. I heard a bird making a sickening, squawking sound, as the wild dog sank its teeth into its neck, holding it down with its paws. It was a big *Shengokor* — a forest chicken. Then the wild dog ran off, jumped the fence and disappeared into the forest with the bird in its mouth. That could have been me, I thought.

It was a long time before I could pluck up courage to come down from the tree. When I finally did, I set off running as fast as I could to my uncle's. I didn't care anymore if the birds ate all the seeds that we'd planted. When I caught sight of Uncle Jerongir I ran up to him and threw myself into his arms. I didn't cry, because he was my Uncle Jerongir, not my father. But he could see that I was upset.

'What's happened, Mende?' he asked. 'What's wrong?'

'Uncle Jerongir, the wild animals came! The wild animals came.'

'They didn't come for you, Mende. They came for the birds!'

'But Uncle, I was so scared I ran and I climbed up a tree!'

Uncle Jerongir burst into laughter. When he'd recovered a little, he glanced over at the shadow that a nearby tree cast on the ground. This was the way we told the time — by looking at the shadow a tree casts as the sun moves around during the day.

'Well, it's getting late,' said my uncle, chuckling. 'There's no need to go back to the fields now. All the birds will have gone to sleep anyway. You've had a big fright, eh? Stay here now, and then you can go back tomorrow morning.'

★   ★   ★

I went into Uncle Jerongir's hut and drank some goat's milk. I was too upset to eat, so I went straight to bed. All night long, I kept having nightmares about wild animals attacking me in my bed. The next morning, Uncle Jerongir came with me to my father's fields to check that there were no wild animals there. Once he'd gone, I spent an hour or so watching out for the birds, watching out for the wild dogs and watching out for my father. At last I heard a welcome call from the forest.

'Mende! Mende! Mende!' It was my father.

I was so relieved. I caught sight of him, leading the donkey laden with supplies, coming along the path towards me. I was just about to run up and hug him when I remembered how angry I was with him. So I stopped and hung my head. 'I'm not going to say 'hello' to you,' I shouted. 'I told you the wild animals were going to come!' Then I burst into tears. 'I told you the wild animals were going to come and try to eat me. If I hadn't climbed the tree to save myself you wouldn't find me here now.'

'I don't believe you, Mende,' my father said. 'There weren't any wild animals. You're only

41

saying this to make me feel guilty about not coming back yesterday.'

'If you don't believe me, go and ask Uncle Jerongir. He knows I'm telling the truth. Or come with me and I'll show you the blood on the ground.'

Suddenly, my father looked really worried. 'Whose blood?' he asked.

'My blood,' I told him, pointing at my left arm. 'The animal bit me here, on my arm.'

I was wrapped in a small blanket because it was still quite chilly. My father jumped off the donkey and went to inspect my arm, but I tore away from him, pretending that he had hurt me. I ran across the field, my father chasing after me. As I looked back at him, I noticed that he had forgotten to tether the donkey, which was wandering off into the forest. My father caught up with me as we reached the place where the wild dog had killed the bird. He caught hold of me by the shoulders and spun me around to face him.

'Mende, stop fooling around and tell me what happened. Look, your mother and all the others have come to see you, too.'

I looked where he was pointing and I saw our whole family coming down the path towards me. I was so happy to see them. But I had not given up on my joke yet. 'Look, there's the blood,' I said, pointing at the ground. My father glanced down. There was a tiny pool of dried blood and a big pile of feathers. I hadn't figured that the feathers would give me away. My father laughed and laughed until the tears came streaming down his face. Finally, he managed to catch his breath.

'So, Mende, since when have you been a bird?' he said. 'Come on now, show me your feathers! You'll be flying back home to the village, will you?'

Then we hugged each other and made up. 'I tricked you because you didn't come yesterday,' I told him.

'I'm sorry, but I had some important things to do. Now, go and say hello to your mother and your brothers and sisters. They've come all this way just to see you.'

That evening, my father shot a *Shengokor* with his bow-and-arrow. We plucked and gutted it and cooked the meat over the fire. We had a big family feast together. We stayed in the fields a week or more that time. My father killed lots of rabbits too. Rabbit stew was just about my favourite meal. But from that day on, if ever my father asked me to go to the fields with him, I would at first refuse. I'd say that he would just leave me there to be eaten by wild animals. And then we would laugh and laugh and remember that day.

3

Weddings and Funerals

Shortly after my fright with the wild dog, I had another surprise. One day, a man called Musa came to talk with my father about marrying my sister Kunyant. He had been engaged to her a few months after her birth, but they had never met before. The men all disappeared into the *holua*, the men's house, to discuss the wedding details. My mother made some food and Babo took it out to them. After they'd been talking for around three hours, Musa left and my father came in to discuss it with my mother.

'Musa came to sort out his marriage to Kunyant,' my father said.

'So what did he say?'

'He said that he thinks the time is right for them to be married now. Then he talked about how many cows and goats he would pay us and we agreed on what was a fair price.'

In our tribe, the groom has to pay the bride's family a dowry — usually a number of cows and goats and some sacks of sorghum. This is the 'bride price', the amount he pays to marry their daughter.

When the day of Kunyant and Musa's wedding came around, I decided I would watch very closely and learn as much as I could. After all, one day I was going to be married too. Everyone from the village was invited. Around mid-morning, people started to arrive. The groom's family came last, carrying big bowls of dates and sacks of sugar on their heads, as gifts for our family. They also brought with them Kunyant's wedding gown — a beautiful blue and yellow robe. Then all the girls went into one hut to prepare Kunyant for the wedding. I tried to go with them, but they shut the door on me and told me I was too young to join them.

Kunyant's friends spent hours preparing her, and when she came out of the hut she looked so beautiful. Her whole body was glistening black with oil. They had stripped all the hair from her legs and her arms and she had black paint around her eyes and eyebrows. She was wearing a bead tunic, a bead skirt and beads around her wrists and ankles. I watched in awe as she went to join her husband on the bed — which had been pulled outside to use as a wedding bench. I can remember thinking to myself, 'This beautiful woman can't really be my sister Kunyant, can it?'

A man had came to play the *ond*. All the girls and boys started singing and clapping as they stood in a ring around the newlyweds. Then everyone cheered as Kunyant and Musa danced together, smiling and laughing at each other. The party lasted all day and all night. But around late evening time, Kunyant put on her beautiful blue and yellow wedding robe and she and Kunyant retired to their hut. Some time later I must have fallen asleep, as I was carried off to bed by my father.

After the marriage, Kunyant and her husband moved in to live with us. In our tribe, the newlyweds live with the bride's family for the first year. A few weeks before the wedding, Musa had come over to our yard to see where he could build a new mud hut for himself and Kunyant. A few days later, he returned with a bunch of his friends. First, they built a circular wooden frame, tied together with strips of bark. Then they built a conical frame for the roof and placed this on top. They used dry sorghum stalks to thatch the walls and the roof. Normally, this would then be plastered over with clay or mud. But they didn't bother because the hut was only going to be used for one year.

After Kunyant's marriage my father went to sleep in the men's house for one month, as our house was full of Kunyant's girl friends. They came to help cook, clean, wash clothes and get water for the newlyweds. The day after the wedding, I was sleeping late. But I woke with a start to a loud crying from outside: 'Aye, Aye Aye, Aye!' At first, I was a bit scared; I didn't know what was happening and, as my father wasn't there, I couldn't jump up on his bed for safety. I could hear the shouting getting louder and louder.

'*Umi,*' I asked, nervously, 'what's all that noise?'

'Your aunts are making the '*illil*' for Kunyant,' she said, smiling. 'One day, when you're married, your aunts will do it for you too.' I was to learn later that I, too, was engaged to be married and had been since birth, as is the tradition in our tribe. My fiancé, a man called Juba, came from a distant village, called Juba, and I had never met him before.

I was about to ask some more questions about the *illil*, but my mother told me to come with her and see for myself. I followed her outside and we walked across to where all the noise was coming from. To one side of Musa and Kunyant's hut there was a crowd of women. They were chanting, and pointing at a sheet that was hung on the fence. My mother had spent the previous week weaving Kunyant and Musa a beautiful new raffia mattress. The night before the wedding, she had put a special white marriage sheet on their marriage bed. Now it was hung on the fence and there was a large red stain halfway down it, which looked to me like blood. What could it mean? I thought with horror that maybe Kunyant had died in the night. I looked around, but everyone seemed so happy that she couldn't be dead, could she?

'Come on, Mende,' my mother said, 'come and see.' She took me by the hand and led me closer to the fence. I stood beneath the bloodstained sheet and looked up at my mother. 'What's this, *Umi*?' I whispered.

'Just take a good look and when you get married you'll know what it is,' she said. 'Your aunts will be happy with you too, when they find this on your sheets.'

I was really worried about Kunyant and I wanted to see her so much, but the door to their hut was shut. My mother told me that Kunyant and Musa were inside and that I wasn't allowed to see her. As the day wore on, I got more and more concerned.

'I'm scared Kunyant is dead,' I finally told my mother. 'Can't I go and see her? Please.'

'No, you can't. It's not allowed,' my mother told me.

'Why can't I go and see her, *Umi*?' I pleaded with her now and began to cry. 'She's my sister.'

'When Kunyant comes out, then you can see her,' my mother promised.

Just before sunset, I saw Musa leave to go to the men's house. My mother went across to Kunyant's hut and I jumped up and trotted along behind her. No one was going to stop me seeing my big sister a moment longer. My mother bent down and spoke gently through the door.

'Kunyant, how are you? Come out into the *shal* and talk with us.'

There was no reply. I couldn't bear it any longer. I could see that the door to the hut was slightly ajar and quick as a flash I slipped around my mother and ran inside. She tried to grab hold of me, but I was too quick. I looked up and saw Kunyant lying on her side on the bed. She was crying softly to herself. She was only thirteen years old or so, and looked far too small to be married, really. I rushed over to the bedside. She was wearing a *gurbab*, a colourful wrap tied at one shoulder. I tugged at the thin cotton. 'Kunyant. Kunyant, are you OK? Come out and talk to us in the yard.'

'Mende, I can't. I can't move,' she sobbed,

gently. 'Just sit down here next to me and hold my hand.'

I didn't know what was wrong with Kunyant, so I called my mother. When we tried to get her to sit up on the bed, it was too painful for her. We tried to do everything we could to comfort her, but she just kept crying. I was really shocked. The day after her wedding when my big sister was supposed to be so happy she was sobbing and in agony.

'Does it hurt?' my mother asked, giving her a hug. 'Please stop crying. After one or two weeks you won't feel any more pain. You'll be fine.'

Kunyant stayed in the hut all that first week. My mother made her food and I took this in to her. Kunyant's best friend, Mardiah, stayed with her all week too. Mardiah was the same age as Kunyant and she too was about to get married. Kunyant spent most of her time talking quietly with Mardiah. At first I tried to listen, but Mardiah scolded me and chased me away.

'Go and sit with your mother, so we can talk,' she shouted at me.

'So whose sister is she anyway?' I retorted. 'Is it my sister or your sister that just got married? She's my sister and I want to be with her.'

Mardiah started laughing and I could see that even Kunyant was smiling. 'Mende, you don't understand anything,' Mardiah said. 'Now go and play with the children your age.'

Just then my mother heard all the commotion and called me over. 'What's the matter now?' she asked.

'Mardiah told me to go away and play, but I

want to stay with my sister.'

Then my mother put me on her lap. 'Look outside,' she said, stroking my hair. 'All your friends are missing you. Mardiah's right, go and play with them.'

So I went out to play. But I still didn't understand what had happened to Kunyant and where all the blood had come from. Someone must have hurt or injured her. I could only think that that person was her husband, Musa. I was very frustrated that no one would bother to explain anything to me.

After about five weeks Kunyant was up and about again, fetching water and going to the fields. I was so happy to see her looking better. At last, she seemed to be enjoying being married. Gradually, I forgot all my worries about the bloody sheets and everything.

A few months later, I was surprised to see Kunyant's tummy starting to get big and round. After my experiences with Uran, I had an idea what might be going on. But I went to ask my mother, just to be sure.

'Kunyant has a baby in her tummy,' my mother told me.

'What, just like Uran when she had the kittens?'

'Sort of. But she'll probably have only one baby. Not four, like Uran.'

Over the next few months, Kunyant often seemed so happy and proud to be pregnant; then she would let me rest my head on her big, round tummy. At other times she was too shy to come out of her hut even. 'I don't want *Ba* to see me with this big tummy,' she'd say. 'I'm too embarrassed.'

Then, one day, she started to feel spasms of pain. My mother said it was time for Kunyant to give birth. Our aunts came into the hut to help her. All the men, including Musa, were banished to the men's house. I was sent outside to play, but I didn't want to, so I just went and sat outside Kunyant's hut. As the evening drew on, I could hear her rhythmic cries from inside the compound and my aunts urging her to push and be strong. As soon as I heard the baby cry, I jumped up and ran over to the men's house.

'The baby's born, Musa! The baby's born!' I shouted.

'Is it a girl or a boy, Mende?' Musa asked, as he came rushing out.

'I don't know. I just heard it crying.'

Musa and I ran over to Kunyant's hut. When I caught sight of the baby, it was so tiny and so beautiful. Kunyant reached out weakly and took it in her arms, smiling and crying at the same time. 'My baby. My baby. My little baby girl,' she cried. The baby had her eyes closed. Kunyant kissed and hugged her and stroked her tiny head of soft hair. Then Kunyant passed the tiny baby over to Musa. Musa took the baby and held her up for all of us to see. 'This is my first baby,' he said, proudly. 'Let there be many, many more.'

Then my mother cradled the baby in her lap, took some sesame oil that she had made that morning and oiled the baby's tummy-button and the remains of the umbilical cord. As I watched all of this new life unfolding in Kunyant and

Musa's hut, I was so happy.

'I'm going to carry this baby everywhere I go,' I said. 'She's so lovely.'

'No you aren't. You'll fall over,' said Kunyant, smiling weakly. 'So shut up. You're not taking my baby anywhere.'

But a few minutes later, I noticed that my mother was looking worried. She had passed the baby back to Kunyant to suckle, yet the baby didn't seem to want to take her breast. As the minutes ticked by, the baby began to take shallower and shallower breaths. Within minutes, she was dead. Poor Kunyant broke down and wept and I was crying with her. Musa looked devastated and I could see his tears glistening in the firelight. But the older women didn't seem too upset. I think they had seen so many of their own babies die in childbirth that they were quite used to it.

'Don't worry, Kunyant. Don't cry,' said my mother, trying to comfort her. 'Your baby has gone to be a bird of paradise. 'You'll have another soon, *Inshallah* — God-willing.'

My mother took the baby's body, washed it, wrapped it in a tiny white burial shroud and took it away. After the baby was buried, she was all but forgotten. There was no funeral ceremony and it was almost as if she had never existed.

'Why did the baby have to die?' I asked my mother later, in a sad little voice.

'Allah decided that she should be born and He decided she should die,' she said calmly. 'It's His will.'

4

The Arab School

Shortly after Kunyant's baby died I started going to school. I was about eight years old by now. My first day at school was a new adventure for me. I had to wear school uniform: a green dress, which a man in the village market had made on his sewing machine, and some leather sandals which my father had made for me. So I went to school wearing my first ever pair of shoes and my first ever dress. Having run around all but naked for the first eight years of my life, it was very exciting. As I'd never worn clothes before I felt very proud of my smart uniform.

It was my best friend Kehko's first day at school too. The night before, we didn't sleep at all, we were so excited. It took us about an hour to walk to school, carrying our packed lunches with us. On that first day, I took milky sorghum porridge. On other days, I took maize, yoghurt and nuts. For the first year, school started at eight o'clock and finished just after midday. So we had all afternoon back at the village to do our normal chores — fetching water and firewood. By the second year we were expected to stay at school all day, so my father would go instead, to collect the water and firewood on his donkey.

The school consisted of six buildings with

strong stone walls and thatched roofs. They were the first buildings I'd ever seen that weren't made of mud. The teachers also had houses made of stone, with separate rooms and a kitchen. There was no electric power in the Nuba Mountains, so they used kerosene lamps at night. The school was surrounded by a tall wooden fence and it had a neat grass border. All we were taught that first week at school was how to keep everything clean and tidy.

The classrooms were very basic, with wooden desks and long benches. The teacher did have a blackboard and chalk, but there was no glass in the windows. When the weather was hot, which it usually was, the only ventilation was the breeze from outside. And we had to share books, most of which were very old. At the back of the school there was a toilet of sorts — a pit over which there was a wooden cover with a hole. The toilet smelled so bad, most of the girls would not use it unless forced to. There were lots of flies and maggots. We would hold on until lunchtime and then rush off to relieve ourselves in the forest.

We had no Nuba teachers — they were all Arabs. The woman who taught me Arabic was called Fatimah. She was very tall and she wore a beautiful white robe and veil. My Koran teacher was called Miriam and she looked of mixed Arab origin. An Arab man called Amruba taught us gymnastics and exercises outside in the school yard. The headmaster, a man called Osman, really cared about the school and even had his own children attending lessons there. One of his children, a girl called Taysir, was in my class.

We started off learning all twenty-eight letters of the Arabic alphabet by heart; then we learned how to count in Arabic. Then we started to read the Koran, the Holy Book in Islam. This is all we learned for the first year. Sometimes, the teachers would tell us to bring an axe to school, and we'd be sent into the forest to cut wood. We might have to build a new fence, or maybe the school roof would need repairing. We all enjoyed the chance to have a day off studying. We also knew that if we didn't keep the fences intact, the animals would wander into the school. The cows would eat all the grass and the goats would eat all the schoolbooks. Goats eat anything.

It was a government-run school and there were no school fees to pay, but the teachers were always asking for money, saying they needed it to buy pens, books or chalk. We rarely saw any evidence of what they'd spent it on. If we didn't give them the money, they would beat us and send us home. Sometimes, I wasn't able to return to school for a week or more, because I had been told not to return until I had the money.

'These teachers are always asking for money,' my father would say, shaking his head. 'What do they use it for?'

But my father did want me to do well at school, so he would spend all week making baobab bark rope to sell in the village market. He would cut the bark from one side of the baobab tree one year, and from the opposite side the next, so as not to kill it. He would roll the bark on his thigh to make the twine for the rope.

In a good week, my father would manage to make two ropes, which would sell for the equivalent of one dollar in local currency. Then I could return to school and give the teachers the money they had demanded. If there was any money left over, we'd buy some onions, sugar, oil and tea.

At the end of the first year, we had two exams. I was amazed to discover that in the first exam, my friend Kehko came first and I came second in our class. I even beat Taysir, the headmaster's daughter. Her family came from El Obeid, a big city far away from the Nuba Mountains. I couldn't understand how a little village girl like me could beat her: I was just the daughter of a poor Nuba farmer. After the exams, we had a special school assembly. I felt so proud as I walked up to collect my exam certificate, which showed that I had come second in our year.

When I took my school report home to my parents, they couldn't read it because they were illiterate. I had to read it for them and translate the Arabic into Nuba. At the end, my teacher had written, 'You are a very clever little girl, may Allah help you achieve your dreams.' She had added a message for my father: 'You have a very intelligent daughter. You must keep her at school and encourage her in her studies.'

I soon realised, though, there was a sinister side to the school, too. During my first week at school, I was shocked when our teacher told us, 'You must stop speaking Nuba. You must learn Arabic instead. Nuba is very stupid because no one can understand it. Arabic is a far superior language.' We knew very little Arabic at first, but if we tried to answer the teachers in Nuba we were immediately punished. If we were lucky, the teacher would just grab our cheek and twist it or slap us around the face. But they each carried a long switch and if they whipped you on the bottom or across the back it was very painful.

Then the teachers told us that we were not allowed to use our Nuba names anymore: we were all to be given Arabic names instead. I was renamed Zainab. My best friend Kehko was to be called Fatiyah. Then we were told that we were not even allowed to speak Nuba amongst ourselves during break and we had to call each other by these Arabic names at all times.

The teachers appointed one child in each class to act as class policeman and report anyone who disobeyed these orders. Our teacher made Mohamed the class policeman. He was the cleverest boy in our class, but he wasn't as clever as Kehko or me. We always beat him in the exams. The teacher made a special fuss of Mohamed and made him think he was very important. From that moment on I began to hate him.

Kehko and I and a boy called Anur formed a gang. We were always playing tricks and making an uproar if the teacher was out of the class. I didn't like Mohamed from the start, as he tried to stop us having fun. And he kept reporting us to the teacher when we spoke Nuba. In no time, war broke out between Mohamed and me. He knew that I was cleverer than he was, and he wanted me to help him with his class work. But whenever he asked me anything, I wouldn't answer him.

'I don't understand you. Don't speak to me,' was all that I would say.

'Why don't you like me?' Mohamed asked me one day.

'Because you are Nuba and I am Nuba and you let the teachers tell you that we can't speak Nuba and then you report us if we do. You are stupid. You don't understand anything.'

'But I've been ordered to do this,' said Mohamed, in a hurt voice. 'I don't have any choice. So why are you being nasty to me?'

'I know you have,' I retorted. 'But why can't you just keep quiet?'

'Well, maybe I can,' replied Mohamed, uncertainly. 'But if you have to talk Nuba in class, do it quietly and then I won't have to report you. Or do it when the teachers aren't around. And be careful in the schoolyard. All the other classes have their own policemen.'

From this time onwards, I tried to be nicer to Mohamed. I realised that he was in a difficult position. In my third year at school, I started learning geography, history, science and art. My favourite subject was science, because I liked learning about the beauty of nature. I would go home in the evening and tell my father all about the new things that I'd learned. I think he'd probably heard the same things from my older sisters and brothers before me, but he pretended to be interested anyway.

I tried to study hard as I really wanted to do well at school. At the same time, I realised that the way the Arab teachers were treating us was wrong. They behaved as if we weren't as good as they were. Sometimes, it felt like they were treating us almost as if we were savages.

5

Snakes and Search Parties

We weren't savages at all. We were proud of our traditions. In the Nuba Mountains, men prided themselves on being warriors. They were strong and fearless. When we girls went into the forest, we would usually carry an axe with us, but it was for cutting wood, not for self-defence. If we saw a snake for example, we would start shouting to raise the alarm. A man would always come running to help. It didn't matter if he was from our village or not, because every Nuba man prides himself on his bravery. He'd take a stick and, if it was a small snake, he'd beat it to death. If it was a big snake, he'd go and search for a rock. Then he'd approach it slowly, while we watched from a safe distance, and crush it to death. There were snakes that were as tall as a man and as thick as his thigh, and lots of smaller ones that were very fast. In the rainy season, there were even more snakes around than usual. They were actually very beautiful, if you could risk getting a close look at them.

I saw a lot of snakebite victims, but one really sticks in my memory. I was only about eight years old, and it was the first time that I saw someone die. My mother went with her Aunt Nhe to cut raffia in the forest. After an hour or so, my mother had tied up a big bundle of raffia to take back to the village. She'd arranged to meet Nhe at the huge baobab tree, a favourite meeting place because you could sit under the branches in the cool shade. My mother waited there for a long time until she started to become anxious.

'Nhe! Nhe! Nhe!' she began calling through the trees. 'Nhe! Where are you?'

But the only answer was her own voice echoing back through the forest. She went to look for Nhe, but couldn't find her anywhere. By now, her water gourd was almost empty and so there was nothing for it but to return to the village. From the big baobab tree to the village usually took an hour, but my mother did it in just over thirty minutes. When she threw her raffia down in the yard, I heard the crash of the bundle and I ran out to meet her. Immediately, I could see that something was wrong.

'Has Nhe come back yet?' she asked me.

'No,' I said, 'I thought she was with you.'

'Yes, she was. But I waited for her by the big baobab tree and she didn't come. I thought she must have come back to the village.'

My mother was looking really worried now. I built the fire up with a handful of dry sorghum stalks, and started to make her a strong coffee with sugar. By the time it was ready, my father had appeared.

'Something serious must have happened,' my father said, after my mother finished telling him her story. 'Nhe wouldn't go off alone into the forest, especially as you arranged to meet at the tree. And she can't be lost. Nhe knows the forest like the back of her hand. Maybe she's been bitten by a snake. That part of the forest is full of them.'

Then my mother said something that I didn't understand. 'Maybe the Militia captured her.' The Militia? Who were the Militia, I wondered.

'Maybe,' my father said, nodding his head slowly. 'But they haven't been seen around here for ages now, let alone attacked anyone.' He got up to fetch his axe and his spear and a long, stout fighting stick. 'We'd better be prepared for anything though,' he added, going off to fetch his old rifle that he kept in the men's house.

'What's the Militia, *Umi*?' I asked my mother.

'The Militia? They're very bad people. Arab raiders who come to attack us. We're worried that maybe they attacked Nhe. Whenever there's been war or fighting in the past, it's because the Militia have come. But don't worry, Mende. Your father will protect you.'

The search party was being assembled, so I didn't have time to ask any more questions. As the crowd gathered, it was starting to look more like a war party. My father was carrying his old gun and he had a bullet belt around his waist. All my uncles had come to join him and they had their guns and spears too.

'Nhe went to the forest to cut raffia,' my father explained, standing on a stool so everyone could see him. 'But she hasn't returned, so she must be in trouble. It's probably a snake or maybe she's just fallen and hurt herself. But there's also a chance that it might be the Militia. So, keep your eyes and ears open and be careful.'

My father tried to stop me coming along. But I kicked up such a stink about being left behind with no-one to protect me from the Militia that eventually he relented. When we arrived at the big baobab tree, we all started shouting. 'Nhe! Nhe! Where are you?' We strained our ears for an answer, but there was none.

'Where was the last place you saw her?' my father asked my mother.

'I left her over there,' she said, pointing.

My father told me that I had to wait at the baobab tree, as it was too dangerous for me to go into the forest with them. I knew better than to kick up a fuss this time. After a while, I heard my mother shouting: 'I've found her! Nhe's here! She's still alive.'

I rushed over to where my mother's voice was coming from. Nhe was lying on the ground on her back. She was having horrible spasms, her feet and arms twitching and her head jerking backwards and forwards. She was groaning, rhythmically, 'Erhh, Erhh, Erhh . . . '

My father knelt down beside her. 'What's happened? Tell us what's happened! Speak to us, Nhe!' But either Nhe couldn't hear him or she wasn't able to reply.

I'd always thought that Nhe was a very beautiful woman, but her face had now swollen up, like a balloon. At first, I didn't even recognise her. As I watched helplessly, I started to cry. My father was checking all over her body. And then he found what he was looking for — two puncture marks from a huge bite on her forearm.

Part of one fang was broken off in her skin, which had swollen and was turning blotchy black.

'*Kung anyam!*' — 'A snakebite' — my father said. 'That's what I feared.'

I could see that my father had started to cry too. Of course, he was very brave, but he was also a gentle and sensitive person and he now feared that Nhe was going to die. He started to search in the bush all around us, and eventually found a large hole in the ground. It was the snake's burrow. He took a big stick and poked around inside but he couldn't feel the end. So, he took his gun, pushed it into the hole and, 'Bang!' there was an enormous explosion as his ancient rifle went off. The hole filled with smoke and I could smell the spicy tang of gunpowder on the air.

My father tried to force some drops of water through Nhe's lips, but her jaws were locked solid. 'I can't get her to drink,' he said, looking up at us, desperately. 'Maybe if we take her back to the village we can force some water into her mouth with a spoon.'

My father and some of the other men left at a run to fetch a bed from the village to use as a makeshift stretcher. When they returned, they laid Nhe gently on the bed. Four men lifted her up onto their shoulders and they set off back to the village. From time to time, they changed the carrying team, as it was exhausting work. When they finally reached our house, they put her down in the yard and my father started to prepare some medicine. He took some forest leaves that he kept in our hut and boiled them up into a soggy mash. Then he smeared this over the snakebite and the worst of the swelling.

'Nhe? Nhe, can you feel this? Can you hear me?' my father kept repeating.

But there was no reply. She just kept groaning, 'Erhh, Erhh, Erhh . . . '

Everyone in our tribe knew how to make traditional medicines. My father had already started to teach me which leaves in the forest would cure which illnesses. He tried to force Nhe to drink some liquid from a spoon, but he couldn't get her mouth open. As the afternoon wore on, her whole body began to swell. When my father touched her, his fingers just disappeared into her flesh, like a sponge. By evening, Nhe's face was so puffed up that her eyes had completely disappeared.

As night fell, she began to bleed. First, from her mouth, and then from her eyes, her nostrils, her ears and from her genitals. She even started to bleed from under her fingernails. Soon, she was sweating blood too. It was so horrible that I couldn't watch any more. It was clear that Nhe didn't have long to live. As dawn approached, she stopped making the rhythmic groaning noises and a deathly silence fell. 'Nhe is about to die,' my father said, looking up from where he sat at her side. A few minutes later she was dead.

Then the mourning commenced. The women started crying and moaning and the men began firing their guns into the air. The women took Nhe inside the hut to wash her. Then they wrapped her from head to toe in a white funeral shroud. Four young men took her body away because they knew that my father was too exhausted and too traumatised to help. As they carried her into the hills, they kept shifting the load, as they had a long way to go. Their destination was the *tilling*, the place of the dead. None of the women were allowed to go to the burial ceremony. It was the men's job to lay Nhe to rest.

After the burial, the whole village came together to build a new shelter made of wooden posts and thatched over with fresh sorghum leaves. All that day, the men stayed in the shelter, and the women prepared food. A funeral feast followed that lasted for three days. On the third day, the men killed some goats by slitting their throats and the women cooked *mulla* — goat stew — with *ngera* — sorghum pancakes. The final meal was a quiet affair, with people praying to Allah to take Nhe up to Paradise.

* * *

I was born a Muslim and nearly all the people in our village were Muslims. In Islam, a good person goes to join Allah in Paradise after death. That's what I believed had happened to Nhe. When I was young, my father taught me to pray five times a day, facing east towards Mecca — the birthplace of the Prophet Mohammed. The first prayer, *Subr*, took place at dawn. The second, *Duhur*, was around midday, then there was *Assur*, around mid-afternoon. The fourth prayer, *Mahgreb*, came just before dinner, and the last prayer, *Aisha*, was just before bed.

Our family tried to keep to the five daily prayer times, even if we were out in the forest or working in the fields. When we prayed together as a family, my father would stand in front of my mother and me. At the end of the prayers, we would bow down and touch our foreheads to the ground, in supplication to Allah. My father told me that if I did not pray I would be sent into the fires of Hell, which was a very scary prospect. Occasionally, my father would go to the village mosque to pray with the other men in the village. The mosque was just like a normal mud hut, only a little bigger. There was a part-time village Imam, or Muslim holy man, who led the men in prayer.

My favourite time was the Muslim festival of *Eid*, which in the Western world is a bit like Christmas. For the month before *Eid*, everyone would fast from sunrise until sunset and then break fast with a big feast in the evening. During this time, we'd wear our best beads and make ourselves look very beautiful. When the month was up, there was a day-long festival to celebrate the end of *Eid*. This was held in the yard of the *Kujur* — the village shaman, or medicine man. The Imam would sit at the front with the first row of the faithful — all the old men. Behind them, the younger men and boys would pray. Behind them came the women, and we girls would sit at the back.

The *Kujur* was from a time and a religion before Islam came to the Nuba Mountains. One day, my father told me all about the 'old

67

religion'. He said that in the time of his father's father, they treated the *Kujur* as a true Holy Man. If there was anything to decide in the village, they always asked the *Kujur* first. They believed he was the man through whom the Gods spoke to the Nuba. At this time, there was not one God, but many Gods: the God of the Hills, the God of the Sun, the God of the Moon, the God of the Rain, the God of the Forest and the God of the Wind. Then Islam came and replaced the old religion, and the *Kujur* became less important.

But the old religion had not really been forgotten in our village. One day, when there had been no rain for many weeks, an old woman went around to all the houses announcing that she was going to 'talk to the *Kujur* about the rains'. She said that each woman should be ready the next morning with a handful of seeds to be blessed by the *Kujur*. Early the next day, I watched the old women going to the *Kujur*'s house. They spent about two hours there and I could hear the *Kujur* shouting and mumbling his prayers and his spells. And then, quite suddenly, it started to rain.

People came running out of their huts and gazed up at the sky in disbelief. Along with the other children, I started to play and dance and sing the rain song. I spotted the old women coming out of the *Kujur*'s house. I don't think the old women really wanted to pray to the new God, to Allah. They still believed in the old ways. Having shown the rest of the village that the *Kujur* could still make it rain, they looked very smug. They walked through the village, swinging their big hips and ignoring everyone completely. I was confused. I knew that I was a Muslim and that we did not believe in the *Kujur* or the old religion. But I had now seen proof that the *Kujur* could make it rain. I went to ask my father for an explanation.

'*Ba*, did the *Kujur* really make it rain?'

'Yes, the *Kujur*'s made it rain,' my father said, smiling at me. Then he added, 'But of course the *Kujur* could only do this with the help of Allah.'

So, while my village was nominally Muslim, in truth both religions coexisted peacefully side-by-side. I thought that my father's answer was a very clever one. He had never been to school, but I used to think that he was very wise.

6

Spirit Wrestlers

My favourite time of the year was when we celebrated the harvest. All the Nuba tribes would come together for a series of big wrestling matches. The exact time to start the wrestling matches was decided by the *Kujur*, who consulted the positions of the stars and the moon. I wasn't allowed to go to the wrestling until I was about nine years old, as my mother said I was too young. I'll never forget that first time I went. It was the time for our tribe, the Karko, to host the wrestling. All the other tribes would come to our lands to fight. After the matches, we would invite them back to eat in our village. I hoped that my parents would make enough money in the village market so that we could afford to make sweet rice for all our guests. For us, this was a real luxury — eaten hot, milky and sweet, just like rice pudding.

As the day of the wrestling approached, my mother started to make me some new bead designs to wear, using a needle and thread. We had a gourd bowl full of beads at home, most of which had been in our family for generations. Luckily, she only had to make them for me because Kunyant and Shokan were married and wouldn't be going to the wrestling. The night before the wrestling match, I was so excited that I couldn't sleep. As soon as I saw the sun start to lighten the horizon, I jumped up and went to fetch water with my friends. Normally, we would walk at a leisurely pace to the water hole and back again; this morning, we ran all the way.

When I got back to the house I rushed in to prepare myself. My mother started by oiling my body until it was soft and glistening all over. I had chosen to wear red, yellow, blue and white beads — my favourite colours. First, I put two simple strings of beads around my waist, then I slipped string after string of beads around my wrists until they stretched halfway up my arm. I wore a special bead design high up on each of my arms, just below my shoulders, and my mother spent ages weaving thick wads of beads into my hair. I wore a wide band of red and white beads crossing over each shoulder and down each breast, like a pair of sashes. I had another, very wide, white and yellow band hanging vertically down my back from my neck to my thighs.

Then my mother had a wonderful surprise for me. She had made me something that she'd managed to keep a complete secret. She must have worked on it night after night by firelight, after I had gone to sleep. I was so happy when she took it out of its hiding place and proudly presented it to me. I looked it over, turning it around and around. I was sure it was the most beautiful thing in the whole world. It was a wide band of red, white and yellow beads that I wore around my waist, with many strings of beads

71

hanging off it, almost like a bead miniskirt.

We had no mirror so I couldn't see how I looked, but my mother told me that I was very beautiful. By now, the men were blowing great blasts on their cow horns and I could feel the excitement building in the village. The wrestling would pit our Karko men against all the surrounding Nuba tribes: the Fenee, the Shimii, the Keimii, the Maelii and the Kunuk.

From a very early age, almost every Nuba boy wants to be a wrestler. They start play-wrestling before they can even walk. When my father was a young man, he had been a great wrestling champion, a *kuul*. But Kwandsharan, my eldest brother, had always hated it. For a while, my father had tried to encourage him but he just wasn't interested. When Babo came along it was a different story. He was determined to grow up and wrestle for our tribe. My first time at the wrestling was also the first time that Babo was going to fight — he'd just been made one of the juniors in the Karko team. For many weeks, Babo had been practise-fighting with the other boys in the village, my father giving instructions.

'No, not like that!' he'd shout, stepping forward to show them. 'If you want to throw him, get in like this, put your leg here, then flip him over like that.' Crash, went one of the boys onto the ground. When I'd finished my morning chores, I would watch the boys practise, and would shout encouragement to Babo from the sidelines.

'Keep your legs back, Babo,' I'd yell, at the top of my voice. 'Keep them back!' Then, 'You'd better be careful,' I'd shout to Babo's opponent. 'My big brother's very strong and he'll beat you!' If the boy managed to get Babo into a wrestling hold, I'd go wild. 'What're you trying to do,' I'd shout, 'break my brother's neck? You'd better watch out. If you hurt Babo, my father will beat you. We'll tell your parents that you were cheating.'

'This is a fair fight between me and Babo,' the boy would shout back, angrily, 'but you want to go and tell your father. Can't Babo defend himself, then?'

'Of course he can! You're just a bad wrestler.' I suppose I was just trying to make the boy angry and distract him long enough for Babo to get the better of him. Eventually, Babo would have to stop me. 'No, Mende,' he'd say. 'Stop interfering. It's a fair fight.'

On the morning of the match itself, as I was getting ready in all my finery, Babo was preparing to fight for our tribe. When I was ready, I came out of the hut and heard him shouting from across the yard. 'Hey, look at Mende! She's very beautiful. Is this really my little sister, Mende? She's the most beautiful girl in the village.'

'Yes, it is,' I shouted back. 'And today you'll be the best wrestler and I will clap and sing for you!'

My friends came running over to get me and we admired each other. They were all looking so lovely in their beads and their oil. But I didn't think anyone had designs as wonderful as my own. I said goodbye to my mother and father

73

and left with the other girls. Our route followed a path that wound up into the mountains. After three or four hours, we were in parts of our tribal area that I had never seen before. By now, there was a huge crowd all walking in the same direction. The older girls in our group carried gourds on their heads full of hot soup for the wrestlers. We were all so excited. We wondered if our tribe would win. We talked about all the food we'd prepared back at home. Then we caught sight of some girls from another tribe.

'Look! Look at those girls!' I shouted to my friends. 'Look at their hair. Isn't it beautiful? I want my hair done like that for the next wrestling match.'

'But you can't, Mende,' said Kehko, laughing. 'That's the Shimii's style. Everyone will think you're Shimii, not Karko.'

'I don't care,' I said, tossing my head at her and rattling my beads as I did so. 'I'm going to ask my mum to do it like that anyway. If she refuses, I'm going to run off and join the Shimii.'

When we finally arrived at our destination, an extraordinary sight met our eyes — vast crowds of people were gathered as far as we could see. The wrestling was being held on a flat plain, surrounded by hills on three sides. It was a very beautiful setting. From every direction came the sound of cow horns and the singing of wrestling songs. The wrestlers were gathering in the centre of the plain. They were completely naked and their bodies were daubed from head to toe in a white paint made of ashes. From a distance, they looked grey and ghostly, with even their hair matted white with ashes.

As I got closer, I could see that the wrestlers had strange geometric patterns painted in jet black over their white body paint. They also had scars on their bodies, which showed up as raised black lines under the white paint, tracing figures of animals, birds and snakes, or of warriors. The wrestlers of one tribe were dressed like huge, fierce eagles. They had giant pairs of birds' wings attached to their backs and towering feather headdresses. They looked ready to take flight and attack their opponents on the wrestling field. There was something of the wild about the wrestlers and something of the dead too.

Each fighter wore a gourd, filled with small stones, hanging down over his buttocks. When he stamped his feet, the stones in the gourd rattled like an eerie drum. They topped off their ghostly appearances with fantastic headdresses made of wood, cloth, animal skins and feathers. I knew this was how Nuba warriors dressed when they went off to war, to strike fear in the hearts of their enemies. Now I could understand why.

Gradually, we girls shoved our way to the very front of the crowd. By the time we got there, the wrestlers had begun running around the ring, their stone-filled gourds rattling out a staccato rhythm as they did so. They were carrying spears, which they clashed against animal-skin shields. As they ran, they began a deep, guttural chanting that was answered by the men in the crowd, who were beating out a deafening percussion on drums.

Clouds of dust rose into the hot air as the

runners pounded past, barely a few feet away. I could almost touch their bunched, glistening muscles. I was deafened by the drumming, the clash of spear on shield, bare feet pounding the hot earth, whistles shrieking, cow horns blowing and the bells on the wrestlers' ankles ringing wildly. My nostrils were full of the sticky smell of sweat, mixed with the sweet aroma of the soup and the dry bite of the dust. All around me, there were the cries of a thousand excited young girls and a thousand men, whipping the wrestlers into a frenzy of physical power.

But there was also some semblance of order amidst all the noise and confusion. The mountains formed a natural amphitheatre for the wrestlers running in the centre, surrounded by the crowd. Young men with spears and sticks stood facing outwards to keep the crowd at bay. If anyone pushed too far forward, these 'stewards' would shove them back again. Some of the wrestlers were now starting to choose their opponents. A wrestler would step forward and call out a challenge to the man he wanted to fight. The challenger would then stand in front of his chosen opponent, pick up a handful of sand and let it run slowly between the fingers of both hands — the traditional Nuba challenge to fight. '*Heya! Heya!*' — 'Let's fight, let's fight' — he would cry out.

Soon, all across the wrestling ring, pairs of fighters were squaring up to one another. They crouched, bent double at the waist with their hands almost on the ground, swaying backwards and forwards and flexing their muscles. For maybe ten minutes or so they stayed like this, each man trying to size up his opponent's strengths and weaknesses. Usually, a wrestler would choose to fight with a man of a similar age and build, but if a smaller man did find a big man challenging him, a more suitable fighter from his team could take over the challenge. These were the unwritten wrestling rules.

There must have been over fifty wrestlers from our tribe and similar numbers from the other five tribes. Altogether, about three hundred men were fighting. A wrestler won by throwing his opponent to the ground. At the end of the day, one tribe would be the overall winner: the man with the most throws would win on behalf of his tribe. If two men from different tribes had the same number of throws, then they had to fight each other in a final bout. We Nuba wrestled to reaffirm our traditions, to strengthen our sense of community, to celebrate the harvest — and for the sheer fun of it. There were no prizes and no one ever fought for money or personal gain. Having said that, the winning wrestler would be lavished with attention. Girls would run forward, take the beads from around their necks and place them over the winner's head.

As the first round got underway, I couldn't see Babo anywhere. I presumed he wasn't fighting yet but, at the last minute, I caught sight of him in the distance. With my friends, I fought my way over to where he was. I could see that his opponent was strong and he looked older than Babo too. But I wasn't worried. After they'd been fighting for five minutes or so, my brother suddenly whipped his opponent up over his shoulder and threw him to the ground. We all jumped for joy and started chanting, '*Bire! Bire! Bire!*' — this means 'one' in our language — because it was Babo's first throw. Then we waited for the next challenger to come. When he walked out of the opposing team's ranks, my heart sank. He was only a little taller than Babo, but he was so stocky and sturdy that he dwarfed him. I knew that Babo was lithe and strong, but I didn't think there was any way that he could win this match.

'No! No, Babo!' I shouted out. 'Don't fight him! He's much bigger than you are. He's too fat! Choose someone your own size. Thin, like you are!'

'Stop him! Stop him, Mende!' my friends begged me. 'He's going to get badly hurt if you don't.' My brother was clearly very popular with the girls in our village.

When Babo heard all our commotion, he just smiled over at us. 'Don't worry,' he said coolly. 'I'll win.'

'But you can't fight that fat man, Babo!' I urged loudly. 'Remember what *Umi* said! You're only allowed to fight a thin man your own size!'

At this, the crowd burst into laughter. 'Don't worry,' repeated Babo again, a little more firmly this time. 'I'll beat him!'

When they started wrestling, I simply couldn't watch. I put my hands over my eyes, peeping out now and again between my fingers. 'I can't watch! I'm too scared!' I shouted at my friends. 'Tell me what's happening! Tell me what's happening!' 'Shut up, Mende,' they replied, laughing. 'Nothing's happened. Stop hiding. Why don't you watch and enjoy the match.'

For twenty minutes or so Babo and his opponent were locked together in combat. As I watched, I found myself shadowing Babo's every move. If he bent low, I found myself bending low to the ground with him. 'Be careful! Be strong!' I kept shouting, but I don't know if he heard me. So many times the fat man looked about to throw Babo, but somehow my brother always recovered. And then, suddenly, Babo grabbed the fat man held by the legs, lifted him up in the air over his shoulder and Blam! — Babo had thrown him to the ground. There was a second's stunned silence. I don't think anyone could quite believe what had happened. Then everyone rushed forward towards Babo, cheering and shouting.

'Ore! Ore! Ore! Ore!' — 'Two! Two! Two!' the crowd chanted.

'My brother's so strong! He's so brave! He's thrown the fat man!' I cried out as I danced around him. 'He's the champion!'

Then the whole Karko tribe broke into a victory song:

Babo, cherio — condore shine,
Mende net — condore shine,
Kunyant net — condore shine,
Kwandsharan net — condore shine,
Shokan net — condore shine,
Babo kuul — Hussain do.

Babo, a youth — in the wrestling ring,
Mende's brother — in the wrestling ring,
Kunyant's brother — in the wrestling ring,
Kwandsharan's brother — in the wrestling ring,
Shokan's brother — in the wrestling ring.
Babo the champion — the son of Nazer.

After the song ended, I ran over to Babo and took my beads from around my neck. Babo bowed his head, exhausted but smiling, so I could place them around his neck. I was so happy and so proud of him that tears of joy were streaming down my cheeks. Lots of other girls were also giving Babo their beads. Then he was picked up by his second and carried in victory parade around the wrestling ring. The whole Karko team kept swapping him from shoulder to shoulder, as everyone wanted a turn at carrying him.

The wrestling lasted for another two hours or so, but Babo was too exhausted to fight again. I was so caught up in his victory that I failed to notice which was the winning tribe at the end. When it was all finally over, the wrestlers shook hands and some apologised to their opponents for throwing them too hard or hurting them. I was walking amongst them, holding Babo's hand. I heard one wrestler say to another, 'Hey, you are very strong, you threw me down!' They had their arms around each other's shoulders and they were laughing. Then the fat man came over and put an arm around Babo. I was glad to see that he was fine, as he had fallen heavily.

'You know, you are very fat,' said Babo, smiling at him. 'I thought you were going to throw me.'

'So did I,' said the fat man, laughing. 'But now I'm going to train hard so I'll be thin like you. Next time, I'll beat you.' Then he lifted Babo up off the ground. 'Look,' he said, grinning. 'You are so light I can lift you with just one arm. How is it that you managed to beat me? Come on. What's the secret?'

'Well, I don't think I fought that well,' said Babo, slowly. 'I can do much better than that, but you made a big mistake. Of course I'm not going to tell you what it was.'

'Please, Babo, tell me how you managed to throw me.'

'If I tell you the secret, then you'll throw me next time.'

The fat man pleaded so much that eventually Babo relented. 'OK, listen,' he said. 'When you tried to trip me, you stepped forward and exposed your legs and that was your undoing. I kicked your legs out from under you and then you went over my shoulder and down.'

'OK,' said the fat man, chuckling to himself. 'Now I've tricked you into telling me, I'm going to use this against you next time.'

'Fine. But what you don't realise is this: in my village, there lives a very great *kuul*, one of the greatest champions in our tribe. I'll make sure that he teaches me many more wrestling secrets before we next meet.'

Of course, Babo meant my father, but he didn't let on. The fat man's name was Shadal.

81

Before leaving, Babo asked Shadal to come and visit him soon in our village.

On the way home, whenever we saw any girls from the other tribes, we took them by the arm. 'Come on, come with us,' we'd say. 'Come to our house to eat.' Although they were from different tribes, they all spoke the same language as us, the Kaakbii language. There were some regional variations, which made it all the more fun to chat with them. As Babo was walking back to the village with the other Karko wrestlers, these girls had no idea that he was my brother.

'Did you see what happened today?' one of them said, her eyes wide with wonder. 'A thin boy beat a really fat man! I was so amazed that I gave him my beads.'

'Oh yes, we saw it!' said my friends, laughing and pointing at me. 'The thin man is called Babo and this is his sister.'

'He's your brother!' they exclaimed, turning to look at me. 'Really, he's a very, very good wrestler. He's going to be a great *kuul*.'

Everyone was so hungry, but I didn't tell the girls what was waiting for them at home. I wanted to surprise them with the fact that we had sweet rice. Just as the sun started to set over the forest we reached the outskirts of the village. 'The wrestling group is coming back!' people shouted, running out to greet us. 'Welcome! Welcome!'

We went first to my house. The girls worried it might be rude to start eating right away. 'Don't be shy. Go and eat,' I urged them. 'Treat this like your own home. Maybe one day I'll come to your village, and then I'll be your guest.' When we had finished the sweet rice, we went to each of my friends' houses in turn. We ate a little more at each, until we were all stuffed. Then we went to the *Kujur*'s house. He came out, wearing a huge rainbow-coloured robe and draped in beads. On his head he wore a floppy felt hat and he was carrying a walking stick. His eyes had turned up inside his head and he was shaking and shuddering. Then he started to speak in the language of possession by the spirits. We were all a little afraid of the *Kujur*, so we sat quietly, not wanting to attract his attention. Some of the elders of our tribe understood the *Kujur*'s language.

'This year, the rain is going to come very, very good,' one of them translated. 'No one is going to go hungry. But, in a few days' time, there will be a death in the village. Be careful not to leave your fires burning unattended in your huts. This is very dangerous and I see bad things happening if you do.'

After that it was time for the girls to go. We said our goodbyes at the edge of the village and, together with the adults from their tribe, they started their journey home. They would walk all through the night, with the moon to light their way. Later, when Babo came home and sat me on his lap and gave me a big cuddle, I told him how proud I was of him.

'The thin man is always stronger than the fat man, Mende, because there's nothing inside the fat man,' he told me, smiling. 'The fat man's like a balloon. One pin and he'll burst. But I heard what you were shouting: 'Don't fight this fat man! *Umi* said you should only fight a thin man!'' Babo mimicked me, laughing. 'Everyone heard, including all the girls, and I was really embarrassed.'

One month later, Shadal came to visit Babo. My mother made a lovely meal and Babo and my father took Shadal to the *holua* to eat with them. After they'd eaten, Shadal told Babo that he'd found out the secret of Babo's wrestling prowess: his father was a famous *kuul*. Even in Shadal's tribe, the Keimii, my father was still renowned as a great wrestler. They spent many hours listening to my father's wrestling stories and they went on to become the best of friends.

★　★　★

A few months after the wrestling match, we had another visitor. One of my father's best friends was a man called Corba, from the Shimii tribe. In their youth, they had both been great *kuuls*, or wrestling champions, and had often fought against each other. It was a cold evening, so we all sat inside the hut around the fire, listening to their wrestling stories. At one stage, my father asked Corba about another wrestler in the Shimii tribe who was a good friend of theirs. A sad expression passed over Corba's face. He told my father that this man had been killed in a recent attack on a Shimii village.

'He was killed too? I didn't know,' my father said, staring into the fire. 'This war. It's a very bad thing.'

I had often heard talk of 'the war'. But I just thought it was something far, far away — especially as our village seemed so quiet and so peaceful.

'It's very sad,' Corba continued. 'So many people from our tribe were killed.'

My father and his friend were silent for a while. Then I noticed that my father was crying. I jumped up and wiped away the tears from his eyes with my hand. '*Ba*, why are you crying?' I asked him. 'What's the matter? What's wrong?'

My father remained silent for some moments, just stroking my hair, then he spoke: 'Mende, you don't want to know about this. When they attacked the Shimii, they killed some of our best friends.'

'*Ba*, tell me what happened.'

'Do you really want to know?' he asked, quietly. He then asked Corba to tell the story about the attack on the Shimii village, but my father's friend wouldn't talk about it. The memories were still too fresh in his mind. So it was left up to my father to tell the story.

'One day, about two years ago, the Arabs came secretly into a Shimii village at night, when everyone was sleeping. They came into the huts and cut the throats of all the men and women. They came silently, in the darkness, and they killed silently with their knives. Then they set fire to the huts, with all the bodies still inside.

'The fire was seen by the neighbouring Shimii villagers, who all came running to help. They didn't know the Arabs had attacked. They just thought some huts had caught fire. They didn't

85

know that the Arabs were hiding in the forest with their guns. As they ran in to save the village, the Arabs opened fire on them. Hundreds of Shimii were killed. Then the Arabs captured the young women and the children. Many of the girls were raped. The Arabs forced themselves on the Shimii girls — even very little girls, younger than you are, Mende.

'It's unbelievable,' my father continued, tears streaming down his face. 'All the girls your age that weren't killed were taken away to be *Dho*, to be *Abids*, to be slaves. So, even if the girl's family survived the raid, they would never see their daughter again.'

I had started crying quietly too. 'Why didn't their fathers go looking for them?' I asked my father, tearfully. 'Why did they just leave them with the Arabs?'

'Where would their fathers start? The Arabs took the girls very, very far away. They took them to work for them and to be their property and in some cases even to make them their wives.'

My father told me that when they had heard about the massacre, all the people in our tribe had been very scared that we would be attacked too. The Shimii were our neighbours. But so far, my father said, we have been lucky.

'When they realised that the Arabs were hiding in the trees, a group of Shimii warriors launched a counter-attack with their guns and their spears,' my father continued. 'The Arabs were taken by surprise, and they fled. By dawn, the battle was over. Those Shimii who survived looked around the burned-out village. There were hundreds of people who had been butchered with knives, just like they were animals.

'There were men whose wives had been killed or abducted. There was one little Shimii boy whose whole family had been killed. The Shimii elders assembled a war party to go after the Arabs. We Nuba can run very fast, and we can travel for a very long time. When they caught up with the Arabs the next day, they attacked them. But the Arabs had modern guns that could fire lots of bullets all at the same time. The Shimii only had spears and a few old rifles from the *Hawaja* times. It was no contest.

'No one has forgotten this day,' said my father, looking up at me. 'But don't think this is the first time it's happened, Mende. In the past, there has been so much fighting and so many people killed or captured by the Arab raiders.' Then, looking at me directly, he said: 'Mende, there is no justice here. We were the first people in Sudan. The Arabs came from far away and took our lands and ruled over us and they became rich men. Now, they come and kill us, because they want to exterminate all the black people. But with Allah's help, we will stay in Sudan. And the day will come when there will be equality between Nuba and Arab alike.'

For as long as I could remember, our area had been peaceful. The war hadn't seemed to touch us at all. Occasionally, I had seen the odd man in army uniform come to visit his family in our village. But there was no fighting. Sometimes, I did see aircraft flying over. I'd look up at them, shading my eyes, wondering where they were going. I didn't know at the time that they were also part of the war — high-level bombers flying off to attack people in South Sudan or other parts of the Nuba Mountains. I didn't know at the time that they bombed villages and schools and churches and hospitals.

I was no older than nine years old when my father told me this story. What he had said was frightening. I felt like he'd been shielding me from the truth for a long time, but I knew that if the Arabs did come to attack our village, my father would fight them. Just like the Shimii warriors had done, he would try to save his family and his tribe.

7

The Cutting Time

It wasn't until I was about eleven years old that I finally learned what the blood on Kunyant's wedding sheet had really meant. One day, my mother told me that I was to be circumcised. In our tradition, circumcision marks the transition from childhood to adulthood. Boys were circumcised when they were around twelve years old or so and the girls even earlier.

I asked my mother to explain to me what circumcision was. She took me into the hut and shut the door. She sat me down on the bed and asked me to open my legs. Then she showed me where they would cut me and sew me up again, leaving only a tiny hole. I was terrified. It sounded so horrible and so painful. I told my mother that I didn't want it done. All that month, whenever she tried to talk about it, I started crying. When my father found out how upset I was, he took me on his lap and stroked my hair and my eyebrows gently.

'Don't cry, Mende. All the girls in the village your age will have it done, so you're not alone.'

My mother sat down next to us and held my hand. '*Ba* is right, Mende. It's healthy for you too. And if you don't do it, then you can't be married.'

Eventually, I was convinced that it was the best thing to do. I trusted my parents and so I decided to try to get it over with as quickly as possible. My mother went to see the circumcision woman and arranged for me to be cut in three days' time. But some of my friends, the older ones who had already been circumcised, told me that it was terrible, that I shouldn't have it done. I went back home in tears. My mother asked me what was wrong.

'I don't want to have this done,' I sobbed. 'Do I have to? The other girls said it's horrible. Please, don't make me do it.'

'Don't believe what they said,' my mother told me. 'Don't worry. I'll make sure the woman does it especially gently for you.'

The woman who does the circumcision in our village is also the midwife, although she spends most of her time working in her fields. Three days later, just before dawn, she arrived at our house. Kunyant and Shokan came over too. My father went to the men's house because it was my cutting time. The woman sat me down on a small wooden stool, pushing my legs apart as far as they would go. She scooped out a hole in the bare earth beneath me. I was numb with terror as she got out an old razor blade and washed it in some water. Then, without a word, she crouched down between my legs.

I could feel her take hold of me. I let out a blood-curdling scream: with a swift downward cut of the blade she had sliced into my flesh. I was crying and kicking and trying to fight free.

The pain was worse than anything I could ever have imagined.

'No! No! *Umi! Umi!* Make her stop!' I screamed. But my sisters and my mother held me down and forced my legs apart, so the woman could continue cutting away. 'I'm sorry, I'm sorry, I'm sorry,' my mother mouthed at me silently, with tears in her eyes.

I felt blood gushing down my thighs onto the ground. I felt the woman taking hold of my flesh, slicing it off and dropping it into the hole in the ground that she had made. I felt as if I was dying. My father must have heard my screaming, as he broke all the rules of our tribe and came running into the hut. He sat down and held me tight and kept repeating in my ear, 'Please don't cry, Mende. I know it hurts. Please be brave and don't cry.'

But the worst was far from over yet. The woman then reached down and I felt her grab hold of something and start sawing with the razor blade. The pain was even worse than before, if that was possible. I was screaming and bucking and trying to shake her off, but I was held down so tightly I couldn't escape. Finally, her arms covered in blood, she pulled something else out of me, and threw it down into the hole. I remember that she had a satisfied look on her face, as if everything was going very well.

'Put some water on the fire to boil,' the circumcision woman said coldly, turning around to my mother.

As I lay there panting and sobbing and trembling, I saw that she had started threading some thick cotton through a needle. Then, she dunked the needle in the pan of boiling water. After a few seconds, she removed it and bent back down between my legs.

'No!' I screamed, fighting to get free. 'No! No! No!'

My cries were ignored. Again I was held down tightly as she began to sew up the raw remains of my flesh. I cannot describe the pain I felt. Through a haze of shock and agony, I remember thinking vaguely, 'My mother promised me that it wouldn't hurt. She lied to me. She lied to me. She lied to me.'

When the woman had finished, I was all but delirious with shock and pain. The circumcision woman filled in the hole in the ground with earth and trod it down with her foot. Where my vagina had been there was now only a tiny little opening, about the size of the end of my little finger. Everything else had gone. The whole horrific process must have taken over an hour. After the cutting, the circumcision woman was paid half a sack of sorghum by my parents.

Immediately after she left, my aunts came and did the *illil* for me. 'Aye, Aye, Aye, Aye,' they chanted, as they danced around me. Then all our relatives came and there was a big feast to celebrate. My mother tried to get the children to sing and dance for me to make me forget my pain and my loss, but I was barely aware of their presence. For three days I lay in a kind of half-coma. I couldn't sleep because of the pain, but I couldn't come to my senses properly either. My parents also couldn't sleep, because I was in so much agony that I couldn't stop crying. I think they tried to comfort me and make up for the part they'd played in my butchery. But I can't remember much. The second day, the pain was even worse. Any movement was agony. I think I must have been suffering from an infection.

'Why did you do this to me?' I asked my mother, during the occasional lucid moment. 'You lied to me. You said it would be OK. That it wouldn't hurt. You lied to me.'

'It will make you more healthy. It will make you clean. And it will keep you a virgin,' my mother kept repeating. I could tell that she didn't really believe what she was saying.

The first thing I can remember clearly was going to try to have a wee on the third day. I couldn't crouch down because of the pain, so my mother had to support me standing up. But as soon as the first drops started coming out, there was a stinging, burning sensation down between my legs. I was crying and shaking and holding onto my mother.

'I can't pee-pee,' I whimpered. 'It hurts too much.' My mother helped me back inside the hut. Then she bathed me in warm tea. As she trickled it over me, it made me want to wee, and I was just able to dribble some out.

As I lay recovering, I had ample time to think about what had happened. There was little difference, from all that I had seen, between circumcision and marriage. With both, you bled and you were in agony and unable to get up from your bed. So I decided, there and then, that I

93

didn't want to get married. I had been tricked into circumcision. I would not be tricked into marriage.

I was angry with my mother and my father, and my sisters Kunyant and Shokan too. They had told me it was a good thing to get circumcised. They had promised me that it wouldn't hurt. When I had tried to make the woman stop, they had all held me down. But most of all, I was angry with the circumcision woman. She had butchered me without any attempt to be gentle or even one word of kindness. After a week, she came back to our house. When she appeared, I refused to talk to her. She had come to remove the stitches, but I refused to let her near me.

'Don't you touch me!' I screamed at her. 'Don't you dare touch me! Get away from me! Get away from me!'

She seemed a little shocked by my reaction. She tried to explain that she had come to remove my stitches and that she wouldn't hurt me.

'Just like you didn't hurt me last time,' I retorted. 'You're not touching me. My mother's going to take the stitches out, not you.' I could see my mother standing to one side, squirming with embarrassment. But I just didn't care. I didn't want that cruel woman anywhere near me. Finally, the circumcision woman realised that she'd need to get my sisters and my mother to hold me down again, just to get a look at me. My mother apologised to her for my behaviour. 'Don't worry. I'll take the stitches out myself. Leave it to me.'

All that week, my mother soaked my stitches in warm tea and oil, to try to soften them. But each time she tried to start removing them, I had to tell her to stop. My mother was very gentle and caring. If it was too painful, she would soak the stitches some more. Then, after an hour or so, she'd try again. It was three weeks before we'd completely finished. Both my mother and my father looked very sad and guilty during this time.

Some of the girls in our tribe died after their circumcision, due to infections. Still more died in childbirth, because their vaginal opening was too narrow to allow them to give birth properly, but it was even more common for the baby to die in childbirth, for the same reason. That's probably why Kunyant's first baby died. It took me at least two months to forgive my parents for allowing me to be circumcised. I knew that they allowed it to be done to me because they feared that if I wasn't circumcised, I would never be married. No Nuba man will marry a Nuba girl unless she is 'narrow' — which proves she is a virgin. My parents really, really believed they were doing the best for me.

8

My Dream

By now, I was doing really well at school. I was around eleven years old and I had aspirations beyond just staying in the village. I had decided that I wanted to be a doctor. I knew it would take a miracle to keep me in school long enough and then I would have to be sent away to a big city to study medicine. But I prayed to Allah for that miracle.

One day, I broached the subject with my father. '*Ba*, when I'm older, I think I'd like to be a doctor,' I said. 'You can't keep going hunting and working the fields when you're old. You'll be too tired. If I can become a doctor, then I'll be able to earn enough money to look after you in your old age. That's my dream, anyway. What do you think?'

My father said that he would do everything he could to help me achieve my dream. I told him that I had decided that I wanted to become a doctor because of what happened to my brother Babo. One day, he had become very ill. He had terrible pain in his stomach and he could only urinate blood and mucus. There was no doctor in our village. The only option was to go to the *Kujur*, or try to heal Babo at home. If someone became really sick, they could be taken to the nearest big town, Dilling. But it was at least a day's walk from the village and my father and mother were away harvesting in the fields. So there was no one to take Babo to hospital.

By the third day he was so ill that my grandmother decided to set off on foot to Dilling, with Babo on the donkey. My oldest brother, Kwandsharan, and my grandfather decided to go with her, as it was such a long journey. I was in tears. My favourite brother Babo was already so exhausted from the illness that he was in no fit shape to make the journey. I tried to talk my grandmother into letting me go with them, but she told me that I was too small. So I walked as far as the end of the village with them, and then watched as they disappeared into the hills.

Two days later, and there was no news. It seemed that there had been so much rain that the path to Dilling was now almost completely impassable. On the third day, a man finally made it through. He arrived at our house exhausted, and covered in mud from head to toe. By now, my mother was back from the fields. She made him some food while he told us the news. Babo had started bleeding uncontrollably from his nose. He was deathly white, due to loss of blood. The doctors had said that he was very ill. That evening, my father returned home and when my mother told him the news, he decided to go directly to Dilling. All of us — my mother, Kunyant, Shokan and me — wanted to go with him, but my father said that we had to stay and help with the harvest.

'*Ba*, please let me come,' I wailed. 'Don't leave me behind. You can't! Babo's my best friend! How can you leave me here when he's sick in hospital?'

'Look, you can't go,' my mother told me. 'It's too far and there are too many rivers to cross. It's impossible. I know he's your brother and that you love him. We all want to go. But you'll just have to stay here with us and help with the harvest.'

But I wouldn't listen. The more I was told that I couldn't go, the more trouble I made. Finally, my father relented. 'Amnur,' he said to my mother, 'let her go. If we leave her behind, she'll cry so much maybe she'll get sick too. We'll take her with us. I will ask Uncle Jerongir if we can borrow his donkey.'

The next morning, very early, we set off. Uncle Jerongir had not only lent us his donkey, but he had decided to come with us too. It turned out to be the worst journey ever. The wind was blowing a gale, driving the rain into our faces and beating the trees down flat to the ground. The donkey kept getting bogged in the mud, so he couldn't carry me. The worst thing was the rivers, which had become raging torrents. Some of them were so deep that the water was over my head. When my turn came to cross, my uncle held onto one of my arms and my father the other, and they literally carried me across.

We had left home at six in the morning, but by eight that evening we still hadn't reached Dilling. Then we came to a river that was so swollen with the rains that we knew we couldn't cross. From where we were, we could even see the lights of Dilling, yet we had no choice but to bed down for the night. We chose a spot high on the riverbank, under a tree. I was so tired, I put my head in my father's lap and drifted off to sleep.

By sunrise the next morning, the storm had passed and the river had dropped low enough for us to cross. An hour later we arrived in Dilling. This was the first time I had ever been to a town. As I walked down the main street, I looked around me in amazement. Nearly all the houses were made of stone, with shiny galvanised iron roofs. The road that we were walking on was made of a hard, black substance. My father explained to me that it was to drive cars up and down on. Most of the people were Arabs and they were all wearing fine clothes. I couldn't imagine that there could be a bigger or smarter town anywhere in the world.

My father had been to Dilling once or twice before, to visit the big market, so he led us straight to the hospital. There, an Arab man guarding the hospital entrance told us that we had to buy a ticket before we could go in. My father told the guard that he didn't have the money, but that we he had walked all day and all night to get there. My father's Arabic was poor, and the guard told my father he couldn't understand a word he was saying. I was so angry because I knew that he was deliberately insulting my father to his face. 'Well, just you try speaking Nuba!' I thought to myself. 'We'll see who looks stupid then.'

I had to translate for my father from Nuba into Arabic, as he repeated the story over again. My Arabic was pretty good by now and there was no way the guard could pretend to misunderstand me. He looked very self-important and huffed and puffed for a while. Eventually, he said that he would allow only my father in. Uncle Jerongir and I would have to stay outside until we found the money for all our entrance tickets. I couldn't believe that after such a terrible journey I would be prevented from seeing Babo. As I sat down on the hospital steps, hot tears of rage poured down my cheeks.

A crowd of people gathered to ask me what the matter was. I told them that my brother was inside the hospital and probably dying, but that the hospital guard would not let me in. As I blurted out my tearful story, I pointed at the guard, and I think he must have been very embarrassed. He came out of his room and asked me why I was crying. Of course, he already knew. He was just trying to look good in front of everyone. With a big show of kindness, he opened the door and let my Uncle Jerongir and me in. I didn't stop for a moment to thank him. I just rushed inside to find Babo.

My brother was lying on a bed with a needle in his arm and a bag of what looked like water above his head. He looked so ill. I ran over to him, but then I saw that his eyes were half open, with only the whites showing. I tried to hug him, but he didn't respond. For one terrible moment I thought he was dead. But my older brother, Kwandsharan, who was sitting beside him, must have guessed what I was thinking. 'Don't worry, Mende,' he said. 'Babo's just sleeping.'

'If he's only sleeping, why are his eyes half open?' I asked in a panic.

Kwandsharan told me that Babo always slept with his eyes open. By now, an Arab doctor had arrived and he told us that Babo had a very virulent strain of dysentery. By the time he'd reached hospital, they thought it was too late to save him. On the first day they had put him on the drip. They had fought for three days to keep him alive, but now he was recovering well. I stayed there hugging Babo for as long as I could. It didn't look to me like he was better. His skin was dry and pale and his mouth was all scaly, like a fish.

Later, when Babo woke up, we managed to walk him out into the hospital yard to get some fresh air. The first thing he told us was that he wanted to go home. He said that the hospital smelled bad and that he hated being around all these sick people. But the doctors said it was far too soon to take him home. That night, we slept on the ground in the hospital yard. Before going to sleep, my father had a little chat with me: 'You know, Mende, it must have been Allah's will that you did come with us this time. If you hadn't, we couldn't have convinced the guard to let us in.'

Three days later, Babo was well enough to leave the hospital. So we put him on the donkey and travelled back to the village. It was a tough journey for Babo, as he was still weak from the dysentery. As it was, he had almost died. I realised there and then that if there had been a doctor in our village, Babo would have been saved the awful journey to Dilling. It was obvious that we had to have our own Nuba doctor in the village. And that's when I first thought about becoming a doctor myself.

After talking to my father about it, I made up my mind that that was what I really wanted to do. So I redoubled my efforts at school. By now, I was in year five and we had started to learn English. We learned the alphabet first and then simple words like 'Hat', 'Cat' and 'Dog'. English was the language of the *Hawajas* — so it seemed to me to be a very exotic and exciting thing to be learning.

I kept talking to my father about becoming a doctor. I knew that I'd need all of his support if I was to stand any chance of achieving my dream. 'If you succeed, you'll be able to cure the sick people,' he'd say to me. 'It's a good thing to do with your life.' I knew that he meant that I should come back and be a doctor in our village.

After the village school, I would have to attend the secondary school at El Obeid, a city far, far away. Only my oldest brother had been away to this school. It would cost my father a lot to send me there. I knew that he would have to sell at least one of his cows for every year that I would be at this school. It was a massive outlay for him. But my father supported and encouraged me in my dream without ever questioning it.

I was about twelve years old when I started year six at school. By then, I was learning eight subjects: Arabic, English, Geography, History, Science, Maths, Art and the Koran. I was doing

102

even better at school by now and Kehko and I were joint first in the school exams. The class policeman, Mohamed, usually came third. By now we all knew that getting a good education was the key to achieving our dreams, so we were all studying really hard. But six months later, the nightmare descended on our village.

Part Two

Into Slavery

9

Allahu Akhbar!

It was the end of the dry season, that beautiful time of year when the sun beats down from a wide, cloudless African sky. I was about twelve years old by now, and I was attending school in year six. At this time of year we always had gymnastics and exercises first thing in the morning, when it was still relatively cool. After break, we had Arabic and then our lessons in the Koran. I was especially looking forward to English, as it was one of my favourite subjects. That day, we studied English sentence structures: 'The bird flew over the tree'; 'The cat jumped over the dog.' After English, we had Geography and Science and then the bell rang for the end of lessons. I set off home with my best friend, Kehko. As we walked, we played a game. I would hit her and then run into the trees to escape and she'd chase after me. Finally we would collapse against each other with laughter.

When I got home, I dumped my school things in the corner of the hut and Uran came and rubbed her tail against me. I checked to see if she had any milk and then patted my lap, and she jumped into it. Then I started my chores. First, I cleaned the hut, then I swept the yard and did the washing up. Then Kehko came round and we went off to collect water. By the time we got back, everyone had come home; they'd been in the fields, as it was harvest time. I gave the water to my mother and went to milk the goats. When I had a gourd full of frothy milk, I drank some myself as I was thirsty from the long walk and I put the rest in Uran's bowl.

After dinner, I sat around the fire with my mother, my brother Babo, Ali and our uncles. It was a cloudless sky and a cold night. My father was telling the story of why the Nuba never hunt monkeys. Although I had heard it many times before, my father never failed to make each retelling very funny. Lots of black, hairy monkeys lived in the forest around our village, but we never hunted them. My father said that the reason they looked so human was that they had once really been people, but they had been bad during their lives and so Allah decided to turn them into monkeys. And that's why we never killed them and ate them. After the story, Babo and Ali disappeared into the men's house to sleep, and we retired to our hut. We talked for a little while, but it was already past eight and my parents had had a hard day in the fields. So I got up onto my father's bed and soon we were all fast asleep.

Deep in the night, I woke up with a start. I sat bolt upright in bed and I could see that my father and my mother were awake too. We were all straining our ears, trying to work out what had woken us. We could hear the faint, muffled noise of shouting in the distance. My father got up quietly and went to the door. He unlocked the wooden latch and stuck his head outside. My mother and I crept over to join him. We could see flames and hear frightened shouting. The far end of the village was on fire.

Often during harvest time, the fires people kept inside their huts would catch the dry thatch and set it alight. Harvest time was called *Karangit* — the cold time: it was the chilliest, most windy time of the year. Whenever there was a fire, everyone in the village would run to help. Now, as we hurried into the yard, we caught sight of people running away from the fire towards us. Immediately, my father knew that something was wrong. They were still a long way off and we couldn't make sense of what they were shouting. Then we caught sight of people dashing through the village with flaming torches in their hands. I watched as one of them thrust a firebrand into the thatched roof of a hut and it burst into flames. As the people inside came rushing out, these men pounced on them, dragged them to the ground and stabbed them with their knives.

'Mujahidin!' my father yelled. 'Arab raiders! The Mujahidin are in the village!'

I still didn't really understand what was happening, but my father grabbed me by the arm, and we started to run. As we did so, my father suddenly remembered Babo and Ali. 'Babo! Ali!' he cried, as he looked over at the men's house and back at the fast-approaching raiding party. I could see he was torn between his desire to warn them and the need to escape. Then he made up his mind. 'Come on! Run!

109

Run!' he shouted, as he urged us on. 'They'll have to save themselves.'

My mother had started to cry and I was sobbing violently. Yet we had no choice but to flee. I clutched onto my parents' hands and started running, but the raiders were every-where, dragging people from their huts. There was no sound of gunfire yet; the raiders were just quietly killing people as if they were animals, with a knife across the throat. I saw one father try to save his daughter, but a raider grabbed him from behind and stabbed him. I could feel my father's grip tighten on my hand as he urged me to run faster.

Through the smoke and the flames, I could see that my father was trying to make a dash for the nearest mountains. It felt as though we had been running for a lifetime when, at last, the line of trees at the base of the hills came into sight. If we could just get there, we'd be able to escape into the forest. But suddenly, my father stopped dead in his tracks. 'Mujahidin!' he yelled, pointing towards the hills. 'Mujahidin!' Up ahead, on the edge of the forest, there was a long line of raiders on horseback blocking our escape route. People from the village were running towards their trap. 'Mujahidin!' my father screamed, trying to warn them. 'Mujahidin!' And then the long line of ragged men on horseback let out a chilling battle cry and charged towards us.

We turned and ran in the opposite direction, as the deafening sound of gunfire broke out behind us. There was complete panic and terror as the crowd fought to escape and take cover. In all the chaos, I suddenly lost hold of my mother's hand. For a few seconds, my father was calling desperately for her: 'Amnur! Amnur! Amnur!' But there was no reply. 'There's nothing we can do,' he yelled. 'Come on, Mende! Run! Run! We have to keep running!'

So we ran back into the village, along the way we had just come. I could feel waves of exhaustion washing over me now. My legs were growing tired and heavy. My lungs were gasping at the cold night air. Then my father caught sight of a herd of stampeding cattle bearing down on us. He tried to lead us safely through the fear-crazed, charging herd, but suddenly one of them barrelled right into me and I went sprawling to the ground. I lay curled up in a ball, feeling hooves pounding over me. Now I'd lost my father as well and I thought I was going to die.

After what seemed like an age, the stampede passed, and somehow I was still alive. I lay there in the dust, whimpering and petrified, with tears streaming down my face. I prayed that somehow my father would find me but, instead, a man grabbed me from behind and pinned me down to the ground. A group of Mujahidin raiders had come to steal our stampeding cattle, and one of these men had now captured me.

I kept trying to shout for my father, who I knew must be somewhere nearby, but the man clamped his grubby hand tightly over my mouth. I was expecting to be beaten or worse, but instead he picked me up off the ground. I looked around at him. 'Come on,' he hissed. 'I want to help you. Come with me and I'll keep you safe and return you to your family. Otherwise, the others will find you and kill you. Now come on.'

I saw him turn and whisper to one of the other men with him, close in his ear. Then the two of them started laughing. They were Arabs and they wore dirty clothing. I could see by the light of the flames that they each had a curved dagger and a pistol tucked into the belt at their waist. Then I was marched away through the burning village.

After what seemed like an eternity, we reached the forest. Around thirty other boys and girls were sitting there under the trees. Despite the fact that they looked so shocked and so traumatised, I was so happy to see them. I recognised many of the boys and girls from my village. At least I was no longer alone.

'Stay here until the other raiders have all gone,' the man said to me. 'You'll be safe here.'

I sat down and looked around me. There were horses tethered in the forest nearby, and four men were standing guard over us. They looked similar to the man who had brought me here. I kept thinking about my father and my mother and Babo. I wondered if I would ever see them again. More and more children kept being brought to join us. Many were beside them-selves, sobbing with grief. Others sat silently, with big, haunted eyes. The youngest were around eight years old and the oldest, like me, were around twelve. The sound of fighting still filtered through the trees, but it sounded far away and muted now.

We waited there until it was almost morning. There was a girl I knew well who lived near me in the village. Her name was Sharan and she was only about eight. She was wailing loudly, and I was scared that the guards would get angry. So I made her come and sit beside me to quieten her down. I tried to comfort her as she kept crying for her mother.

A little boy started to sob out his story. His whole family had fled to escape the flames, but in the confusion, his little sister of eighteen months was left behind in the burning hut. The first another boy knew of the raid was when the Mujahidin threw open the door of his hut. He saw his mother try to hide his twin baby sisters, but the raiders grabbed her and cut her throat. Then they killed the two babies. The boy was hiding under his bed. Those were the last things he saw before the raiders dragged him out and took him away.

By the end of the night, I had listened to so many terrible stories. I thought back over the story that my father had told me about the attack on the Shimii tribe. During the raid on our village, I had seen girls pinned to the ground with the raiders on top of them. I knew that these girls were being raped. I tried to curl up into a ball and make myself look as small as possible, so as to avoid the attention of the guards. But, thinking back on it now, if they had just raped me that night and left me behind in the forest, that would have been a good thing compared to what really happened to me.

Just as dawn began to light the sky above the trees, a long line of men came marching out of the gloom from the direction of the village. As they went past, I could see that all of them were carrying knives. Some had small pistols and others had bigger guns. Many had blood all up their wrists, others blood smeared around their belts where they carried their daggers. And others had blood all over their loins. They looked crazed with violence and evil.

I searched the long line of faces for the man who had brought me here. When I finally saw him, I looked him directly in the eye. But he just looked back at me and I could see that he was laughing. He lifted his hand and gave me a small, cruel wave.

The men filed past into the forest behind us. There must have been around one hundred or so. They formed into ranks five-deep, facing back down the hill towards us. I prayed that the mountain would collapse and kill them all. The man who had been leading now stood in front of them and began to bark orders. I could not hear exactly what he said, but they all replied in a thunderous chant, 'Allahu Akhbar! Allahu Akhbar! Allahu Akhbar!' — 'God is Great! God is Great! God is Great!' Over and over they shouted this, the chant echoing around the valley.

I was surprised and I was scared. My father used to say 'Allahu Akhbar' when he killed a goat or a chicken in the village. If you did not commend the animal to Allah by saying this, it would not be *halal*, or holy to eat. But why were

114

these men now shouting, '*Allahu Akhbar*', after burning our village, raping and killing? Did they think it was *halal* to do this? We were Muslims, just like them. So how could they think this?

For around one hour we sat, waiting in the dawn shadows as they chanted their victory cries. When they had finished, they came charging back down the hill towards us. Those who were the quickest seized the oldest girls in the group. Then they started to take the younger girls and then, finally, the boys. A man came and grabbed Sharan. She cried out that she wanted to stay with me, but the man just slung her up onto his horse like a sack and rode off with her into the forest.

10

The Dark Forest

The man who had originally captured me came and grabbed me and pulled me over to his horse. He asked me my name. I didn't want to tell him, but I was too frightened to resist. I was slung into the saddle and then he jumped up behind me. The horse was huge, much bigger than my father's donkey. As we set off, I grabbed hold of the saddle and held on for dear life. Mustering up all my courage, I shouted back over my shoulder, 'Where are we going? You said you'd take me back to my family.'

'Once we're away from here,' he grinned, wolfishly, 'I'll tell you where we're going.'

Our route took us through dense forest, away from any Nuba settlements. I could see other raiders on horseback flashing past us in the trees. We hadn't been riding for long when the man started to try to touch me all over. I felt him grab my breasts — not that I really had any breasts to speak of, as I was only twelve years old. He squeezed me hard and I couldn't push him off as I was holding tightly onto the saddle.

'Stop! You're hurting me,' I cried out. 'Please stop it.'

'Hey! I'm only trying to hold you safe, in case the horse stumbles,' he yelled back.

'I'm holding the saddle. I don't need your help.'

We were following a stony riverbed that wound through the forest. It was very uneven and dangerous, he explained, and he had to hold onto me tightly, to protect me. My breasts were small and tender, and he kept pawing at them. Then, as we rode deeper into the forest, he pushed his hand down between my legs. I felt a stabbing pain and I cried out, but he wouldn't stop. When I was younger, my mother had told me that I must not let any man touch my body before I was married. If I did, I would burn in the fires of Hell. But as I sat there clutching desperately onto the saddle with both hands, I couldn't defend myself. So I started to cry.

After around two hours of this, I told the man that I wanted to stop to pee-pee. By now, the sunlight was filtering down through the trees and I was desperate to go. He reined in his horse and lifted me down to the ground. I went off behind a tree. But, before I'd even started to go, I realised that he'd crept up on me. I felt him watching and I could hear his heavy breathing behind me. I was so petrified, I couldn't even look around to see what he was doing. And then he jumped on me. I screamed out as I collapsed onto my side and he wrestled me over onto my back.

I was pinned down and I couldn't breathe as he pushed himself onto me. As he tried to force his tongue into my mouth, I felt like vomiting. I tried to keep my jaw clamped together, but he bit hard into my lip instead, until I could taste the blood. Then he started to force my legs apart. Each time I tried to push them together again, he hit me hard around the face. I felt him slip his hand down there and try to force his fingers inside me. I felt my flesh tearing, because I was so narrow. I was in complete agony. I tried to push him off and clamp my legs shut again. But he just kept beating me.

Then he got his body on top of me, forced my thighs apart and I could feel him pushing something between my legs. He was a big man and I could smell his sweaty body all over me. He was trying to force himself inside me, but because of my circumcision he couldn't seem to manage it. And then suddenly, he just let out a long moan and collapsed on top of me. He lay there, panting, for what seemed like an eternity, before rolling off to one side. He stayed on the forest floor for some time, with his eyes closed, breathing heavily. I curled up into a ball, crying and whimpering to myself.

His clothes were stained between his legs. I didn't know what had happened. I wondered if he had wet himself, but he was a big, grown man. I hoped and prayed that he was having a heart attack or something and that he was going to die. I was in so much pain that I couldn't move; I just lay there in tears and in agony, feeling my life had come to an end. When I had felt him thrusting something between my legs, I had thought that it must be his knife or his gun and that he was trying to kill me. I didn't know how I had managed to survive.

By now, some of the other raiders were riding

past, and when they saw us they stopped. Maybe they thought their man was in trouble. Or maybe they wanted to try to rape me as well. The man sat up and signalled to them and they rode on. Then he started to brush himself off where he had messed his trousers. When he pulled me to my feet walking was agony, but he shoved me back on the horse and we set off through the forest again.

We hadn't been riding for five minutes before he started squeezing my breasts all over again. He grabbed me by the chin, and forced my head around so he could kiss me. I can remember his face against mine, and the pain of my swollen lip. I can remember how disgusting it was, and the taste of the blood in my mouth again. And I can remember his foul hands on me, and the tears streaming down my cheeks.

'Why are you crying? This is good!' he kept saying.

As he tried to kiss me again, I bit him hard on the lip, in a desperate effort to get him to stop. But instead of pulling away, he forced me even closer to him.

'Yes! That's good,' he moaned in my ear. 'But don't bite me so hard. Kiss me.'

I begged him to stop. But he just kept saying that soon I would start to enjoy it. For four or five hours we rode on like this, with me trying to fight him off the whole time. After a while, I really needed to go to pee-pee again, but I didn't want to give him any excuse to stop.

Finally, we arrived at a clearing in the trees where the rest of the raiders were waiting. Many of the other girls were crying. In fact, some of them seemed to be in much more pain than me. 'I can't go to the toilet, it hurts so much,' one of the girls sobbed to me. 'That man, he cut me down here.'

Then I caught sight of Sharan, who came running over to me. In a frightened whisper, she told me how the man who carried her on his horse had tried to kiss her and touch her too. She was only eight years old. I could hear the raiders talking and laughing in Arabic and pointing at different girls. Then one shouted over to 'my' raider: 'Attif, how about you? How was the journey, then? Did you have a good time?'

'Ehhh,' whistled Attif. 'I enjoyed it so much, I wish it could go on for ever and ever!'

When all of the Mujahidin were assembled, we rode on and reached a large town. We skirted around the the borders of the town and came to a camp made up of twenty or more khaki green tents, arranged in rows. We approached the camp in a long line, and were met at the gates by a group of men in military uniforms. The leader of the raiding party stopped to talk to them. 'Everything was fine,' he told them, smiling. 'It went exactly according to plan.'

As the raiders rode past the soldiers on guard at the front gate into the camp, they shouted greetings to one other.

'How was the ride, brother?' a soldier shouted over, laughing. 'Was it good for you?'

'Oh yes, brother. We had a very, very good journey!' a raider shouted back.

'In fact, brother, we wished it could have

lasted ten days,' another of the raiders joined in. 'These girls were difficult to open. You know, these Nuba girls are just like Arab girls. They're circumcised too.'

'So, you've learned something new, eh, brother?' the soldier replied, laughing. 'But you know these girls are so small, it's going to be difficult whichever way.'

Once inside the camp, we were split up: girls into one tent, boys in another. After half an hour or so, a soldier came and left us some bread, lentil stew and some roasted peanuts. But we were all too exhausted and too traumatised to eat. I lay down on the floor of the tent to try to sleep, but the pain that I was feeling was almost as bad as when I was circumcised. By now, everyone knew that we would not be seeing our families again. Sharan came and snuggled up to me on the floor.

'This man, he was trying to eat my mouth, like it was meat,' she whimpered. Then some of the other girls started to talk about what had happened to them on the ride. Many of them had been raped, even some as young as nine and ten years old. They were in so much pain. But we were all too young to really understand what had happened. 'He tried to force something hard inside me,' I told the others, tearfully, 'but he wasn't able to. So he pushed his hand down there. It was so painful, I thought he was going to kill me.'

That first evening, there was a guard on duty who seemed to feel a little sympathy for us. 'Don't cry,' he said. 'You're very lucky. You're all

121

going to a very good place. There's nothing to worry about. Now, get some rest.' By now, it was late evening and we tried to sleep. But all night long we kept waking each other with our nightmares and screaming.

★   ★   ★

For the first few days we weren't allowed out of the tent. The Nuba boys who'd been captured with us stayed in their tent too. On the third day, a man came into the tent dressed in what I now know is an officer's uniform. He brought with him an Arab man dressed in a *Jalabia*, a long traditional robe. This man walked around the tent looking at all the girls. He pointed at three or four, and told the officer that these were the ones he wanted. About an hour later, a soldier came and took these girls away. We didn't know that they were going for good so no one hugged or said goodbye. But they never returned.

The next day, after sunset, the guard gave us two hours to get some fresh air. The boys who'd been captured with us were also let out. The guard told us we could play, but no one was in the mood. I caught sight of Ajok, a friend from my village. Sharan and I went to sit with him. Sharan had attached herself to me very closely by now. I asked Ajok where some of the boys had gone, as there seemed to be fewer of them.

'They were taken away yesterday,' said Ajok, in a low voice.

'Some girls were taken away too. Where d'you think they've gone?'

Ajok said that he didn't know, but he didn't think they'd be coming back again. Just before we were ordered back into the tent, Ajok asked me: 'What happened to your lip? Did you fall off the horse?'

'No. I didn't fall,' I said. 'The man on the horse bit me.'

'Why? Did you try to fight him?' asked Ajok, in surprise.

'But he wanted to kill me! He tried to stab me,' I told Ajok.

Just then we were sent in to sleep. The next day, the guard asked us if we wanted to go to the bathroom to wash. It was such a wonderful thought, the idea of getting ourselves clean. But we were scared that it might be a trick, and that the soldiers would jump us. So we went in a group of older girls who were brave enough to risk it. The bathroom turned out to be another, smaller tent. We stood on a wooden platform, took water from a big stone sink and poured it over ourselves. It felt so good to wash the touch of those men off our bodies. For the first time in days, we felt we were clean again.

'Make sure you wash yourselves well,' one of the guards urged us, through the tent wall. 'Spend as long as you like. If not, you'll get sick.'

We took our knickers with us so we could wash the blood out of them. The guard had given us some old shirts, which were so big that we could wear them like dresses over our knickers. They were the same sort of shirts that the soldiers wore, although ours were all worn out and stained. But at least they were clean.

Later, we found out why they had been so keen that we clean ourselves up. It was so that we could look more presentable. The army officer came to our tent again, this time with two Arab men. They looked around and started to pick out ten girls.

One of the first they chose was a girl called Kumal, who was a friend of mine from a neighbouring village. I had met her at the wrestling matches and invited her to my house to eat with us. I was one of the last to be chosen. I knew then that I would not be coming back. So I turned to Sharan and hugged her goodbye. She burst into tears and would not let me go.

'Look, Sharan, just like the other girls, once I go I won't be coming back,' I told her gently, taking her face in my hands and looking into her eyes. 'Even you, you won't be allowed to stay here forever in this tent. I don't know where we're all going. But try not to cry. Say goodbye to me now. And try to be brave and strong.'

We were taken to 'the office', another tent at the far end of the camp. As we waited, we could hear the camp officer in discussion with the two Arab men. Finally, all three of them came out of the tent, joking and laughing. They seemed very pleased with the outcome of their discussions. The Arabs shook hands with the officer and said, 'Shokran — thank you.' After that, they divided us into two groups of five girls. The guard said that we had to leave our army clothes behind, so the Arabs asked him to guard us for an hour while they went to buy us some clothes.

As we sat waiting in the sun for the two Arabs

to return, I thought back over what had happened. First, the raid on the village. Then, I was captured. After that, the nightmare ride through the forest to the soldiers' camp. And now, the soldiers were passing us on to the two Arabs. I couldn't believe this was happening to me. We waited for about two hours, no one saying very much, exhausted and apprehensive. Finally, the Arabs returned, carrying bundles of new clothes fresh from the shops. They told us that there was a pair of knickers and a dress for each of us.

'Look, I told you that you were going to a good place,' the friendly guard told us. 'Now, you've got beautiful new clothes to wear. So you see, I was right.'

We went to the bathroom to change, trying on different dresses until we each found one roughly our size. When we came out again, the Arab men thanked the guard and handed him a few rolled up notes. 'Here. This is for looking after them for us.' Then they turned and said, 'Follow us.'

11

To Khartoum

Outside the camp gates, there were two pick-up trucks waiting for us. One of the Arab men helped the five of us up into the back of his truck. Before we drove off, he warned us that he'd be keeping an eye on us in his driving mirror. But we didn't understand him. We didn't have any mirrors in the Nuba Mountains, so none of us knew what a driving mirror was. As we set off bumping down the track, I looked around at the other four girls. By now I knew their names: Ashcuana, Khumal, Kayko and Ammo. I was the oldest; the rest were in the year below me at school. We reached a larger track and speeded up, the wind in the back whipping our hair around our faces.

After a few minutes we came to a river, and I immediately recognised where we were. It was the same river I had slept beside over a year earlier, with my father and uncle, on our way to see my brother Babo in hospital. Then, the river had been swollen with rains and virtually impassable. I remembered it all so well — especially when we took Babo back home from the hospital on the donkey. The memories brought tears to my eyes. Where were my family now? Were any of them still alive?

But at least I knew where we were now. The army camp must have been just on the outskirts of Dilling. Now the river was dry. The Arab man drove the pick-up down across the hard-packed riverbed. Half an hour later, we were speeding down Dilling's main street. I recognised some of the buildings. The last time I had been here, I'd walked down the main street with my father and uncle, a little girl sick with worry about her brother in hospital. Now, I was being driven through town on the back of a pick-up truck by an Arab man who was treating us as if we were just five head of cattle.

Because I was the oldest, the other girls looked to me for some sort of leadership. As soon as I realised that we were in Dilling, I started to think about escaping. I told the others that I had been in this place once before. (None of them had ever left the village.) I thought I could remember the way back to our village. 'When we reach the centre of town, he'll have to slow down for other traffic,' I whispered to them. 'When he does, I'll make a signal and we jump. And then we make a run for it.'

At first, the girls were scared, but I explained that this might be our only chance. So we stood up in the back of the truck, looking out for our chance to escape. But there was very little traffic, and we were driven through the town at speed. When the Arab did have to slow down, he was careful not to stop the truck completely. And then, Ashcuana caught sight of his eyes watching us closely in his rear-view mirror.

'Mende!' she hissed. 'You've forgotten that

127

special thing he's got for watching us. He can see us back here.' Just then, he slowed down to avoid a truck coming the other way. Maybe this was our chance? But as he pulled into the side of the road, he leaned out of his window and shouted back at us, '*Salaam alaikum!* Everyone all right? What's going on back there?'

He'd clearly got wind of the fact that we were up to something. We sat back down dejectedly. We began to speed up again, and soon Dilling was lost behind us in a cloud of dust. The truck started to bounce and rattle along a dirt road leading out into a vast expanse of flat bush. With each turn of the wheels, we were moving further and further away from the Nuba Mountains.

We sat in a hot, dusty backdraught as the vehicle bucked along the road. There wasn't much we could say to each other above all the noise, so we each remained quiet, with our own, sad thoughts. After two or three hours' driving, we were hot and thirsty. There were some bottles of water in the back of the truck, but we were worried that if we drank, we'd need to relieve ourselves. After our recent experiences, we were all very reluctant to go and pee in the bush with any Arab men watching over us.

The truck had a hard wooden floor and metal sides and we were constantly being thrown around. In normal circumstances, this would have been bad enough. Now, it was much worse, because we were all still in such pain. I could see the others were in worse shape than me. As the afternoon wore on, the driver increased his speed. We tried to hold onto the sides of the pick-up as he swerved to avoid potholes, but the sun had made the metal too hot to touch. We lay down in the back and tried to wedge ourselves together so that the journey would be less agonising.

We kept driving on into darkness without stopping. The temperature plummeted in the desert night. This, coupled with the wind-chill of the speeding vehicle, made it bitterly cold. All we were wearing was a pair of knickers and a light summer dress. We huddled together and tried to keep warm. Finally, I banged on the top of the pick-up cab. I yelled to the Arab man that we were freezing, but he just pointed to a black canvas cover stuffed in one corner of the pick-up.

'If you're cold, use that,' he shouted back, without stopping. 'It's the rain sheet for the back of the truck. It should keep the wind off you.'

We all pulled at the cover, but it was heavy and stiff. Eventually, we half spread it over us and half crawled under it. Finding shelter there from the biting wind, we cuddled up together for warmth and slept. By the time the first dawn light began to paint the distant horizon, we were frozen stiff. We were also so desperate to pee that we couldn't hold it any longer. I banged a frozen fist on the pick-up roof and told the Arab man he had to stop. He had been driving now for over eighteen hours, and he looked completely exhausted. He pulled over to the roadside.

'What is it?' he asked, coming around to the back of the truck.

'We all need to pee-pee,' I said.

'Oh. You need to pee, huh? OK. You go one by

one, behind the truck right here.' He pointed to a spot next to the truck wheel. 'But no one goes off into the bush. Got it?'

We tried to jump down, but we were too frozen to move. He had to lift each of us to the ground. We stopped maybe for five minutes. It was clearly agony for the others to pee. Before we set off again, I told him that we were all starving hungry. He raised an eyebrow. 'Hmmm . . . You're hungry, eh? I suppose I should stop and get you some food.'

The sun rose to reveal a flat, featureless desert landscape. It seemed a deeply depressing place after the beautiful, sweeping grace of the Nuba Mountains. As the sun warmed us a little, we sat on the black cover to try to cushion the ride. We drove on for what seemed hours, and had almost given up hope of food, when the truck pulled over at a small hut. It was a roadside café.

Inside, there were delicious cooking smells wafting out from the kitchen at the back. The café owner brought over some loaves of bread, some meat, some lentil dhal and salad. Despite being famished, we shared the food equally between us, just as we would have done at home. The Arab man ate alone at the table next to us. When we'd finished, he looked over. 'Had enough?' he asked. 'Or do you need some more?' We told him that we were full. But we did ask for some milk. Back at home, we always washed our meals down with milk. 'There's no milk around here,' he said, laughing at us. 'It's the middle of the desert. Where d'you think they'd get it from?'

We got back into the truck. 'So. D'you know

where you're going?' he asked us, before getting back into the cab. 'To a beautiful place, a very big city. It's called Khartoum.'

★ ★ ★

None of us knew where Khartoum was, or even what a 'city' was for that matter. We drove off again. It was around midday by now, so we had been travelling for over twenty-four hours. The sun warmed us up after the freezing night and, with full tummies, we all dropped off to sleep. I must have slept for hours, although I was jolted awake by the bigger bumps, for when I awoke properly it was early evening. I looked up to see a truly magical sight. Far away in the distance was a huge expanse of beautiful lights. There were many different colours. Some of them were moving, others were flashing on and off. I had never seen anything like it before.

'Look! Look!' I shouted, shaking the others awake. 'Look! There's no moon. So where's all that light coming from?' We had no electricity in the Nuba Mountains and thought that all light must come from either the sun, the moon or from a fire.

As we got closer, we realised that the light was coming from hundreds and hundreds of buildings. Some were so tall they were like the mountains that surround our village. For a while we forgot our fear and our pain; we were overcome by this magical place. As we drove into the city we stood up in the back of the jeep, holding on for dear life as the driver fought his way through the traffic. All these shiny cars were snarled up bumper to bumper. Back in the Nuba Mountains, the most any of us had ever seen were a couple of old trucks.

'Is this city made for the people, or the cars?' Ashcuana asked. There seemed to be so many cars that none of us knew the answer.

'Where do all the cars live?' wondered one of the others.

'Maybe in those huge houses,' I suggested. 'Maybe that's why they're so big.'

'So do the big cars give birth to the small cars?' Ashcuana asked. 'Maybe that's why there's so many of them.'

Then I saw a young man on a motorbike, weaving his way through the traffic. 'Look! Look!' I shouted, pointing. 'It's so small, it must only just have been born today.'

For us, arriving in this huge city after twelve years in the Nuba Mountains was like entering another world. Even the air was different. In the Nuba Mountains, it is so fresh and clean. But here, after only a few minutes in the city traffic, we felt our eyes stinging. We held our noses and complained to each other about the bad smell. We didn't know where it came from. Was it the cars, the houses, or even the people?

'Where are all the cows?' Ammo asked. We couldn't see any fields or any animals anywhere. We wondered what on earth these people ate. 'Where are the goats? Here there are only people and cars!'

The Arab man was driving hard to fight his

way through the traffic. He leaned on his horn and stamped on the accelerator when he saw a gap in the traffic. We had to hold on for dear life. Some of the houses had many storeys, with all the windows lit up by a shining yellow light. But it was the street lamps that had us really confused. We passed these rows of black posts planted along the pavement, with round lights on top like tiny suns. We didn't know what on earth they were.

'Look! Look!' I shouted again. 'Those trees must grow light for their fruit! Let's call them the 'light-trees'.'

'Look! Look! That house is as big as the hills back at home,' Ashcuana shouted, as we passed what must have been a tower block.

'Look! Look! That man has no legs. How can he walk?' shouted one of the other girls, pointing at a man wearing Western-style trousers.

There were so many strange looking people wearing beautiful clothes. None of them looked like they could be Nuba. Some of the women had hair that was very long and beautiful. They caught sight of us staring at them and pointing. But they weren't interested in us — five little black girls wearing cheap dresses in the back of a pick-up. Eventually we came to a stop outside a beautiful house. The Arab man walked up to the door, pressed something, and we heard a ringing noise. To our surprise, the man who came to open the door looked like a Nuba. He was wearing an Arab-style *Falabia*. And I could see that his sleeves were wet through.

'*Salaam alaikum,*' the man said, which is the

traditional greeting in Arabic. '*Salaam alaikum,* master.'

'*Alaikum wasalaam,*' said the Arab man, which is the traditional response. 'Go take the bags from the front of the car.'

The Nuba man came out, leaving the door open. Behind him, there was a large pile of clothes on the ground. I could see that he had been washing them in a big tub.

'*Salaam alaikum, atfall*' — 'Hello and welcome, children' — he said quietly, as he came over to the car. He had a very kind face, I thought. But he wouldn't look at us or make eye contact. How had this Nuba man come to be here, so far away from home, I wondered? Had he come here of his own accord? Or had he also been captured in a raid? He looked about as old as my father. But before we could ask him any questions, the Arab man snapped at him, 'Go on! No time for talking! Take my bags into the house.'

Then he turned to us: 'Come on, follow me inside.'

12

Slave Traders

There were two entrances to the house, each flanked by a pair of poles with lights on top of them. We were taken into a front yard. There were two cars parked inside under a roof made of a wooden lattice, which was covered by a huge grapevine.

We followed the Arab man, looking around us in awe: at the vine-covered roof, the two shining cars and at the house towering in front of us. It was made of bricks and all the windows had glass in them. There was a beautiful yellow light shining out from the windows into the yard. It looked like a magical palace to us. This Arab man must be very rich indeed, I thought to myself. He led us down a passageway and through two doors, the first one made of metal and the next of wood. As the last of us filed in, he locked the doors behind us. We were in some sort of hallway. I could see steps going up to another floor above, and stone steps going down below. I had never even been inside a house with more than one floor. The most sophisticated building I had ever seen was the school classroom — one room with bare stone walls and no glass in the windows.

The Arab man led us down the steps into a

basement. It had tiny windows high up at the top of the walls, and one shining light-bulb hanging from the ceiling like a star in the sky. We stood huddled in one corner. I glanced around. There was a pile of mattresses and, along one wall, three big white boxes, which made a loud humming noise. I had no idea what they were. Later I discovered they were deep-freezers, of course.

'Joahir!' the man shouted upstairs. 'Joahir! Come down and help.'

'Abdul Azzim? Is that you?' a female voice shouted back. So that was his name — Abdul Azzim.

'Yes, yes. Now come down and help me with these girls.'

A few seconds later, an overweight Arabic woman bustled into the room. First, she rushed over to Abdul Azzim and gave him a big hug, so I presumed she had to be his wife. Then she turned around to us, and we looked away when she just kept staring at us. 'Excellent! It looks like it's been a great journey,' she enthused with a big grin. 'They're pretty slaves this time, eh?'

She used the Arabic word *abid* — the plural of the Arabic word *abda*, or slave. At the time, none of us knew enough Arabic to understand what she meant. Then Joahir called upstairs and another, older woman came down to join them. When I caught sight of her my heart leapt. Although she was wearing a pretty dress, this woman also looked Nuba. Joahir ordered her to take some mattresses from the corner and put them out on the floor for us.

'I've been driving all day and all night, you know,' Abdul Azzim complained to his wife. 'I can't do this alone anymore. I need someone to help me, like an assistant or something.'

Joahir nodded sympathetically. 'Where did you find these girls? Were they expensive?'

'Look, I'm tired. Let me take a shower first,' Abdul Azzim replied. 'You can leave Asha to get these girls settled. Then I'll tell you all about it.'

Asha seemed to be the name of the older, Nuba-looking woman. Abdul Azzim and his wife disappeared upstairs. Asha stayed with us to help arrange our mattresses. Once we'd finished doing this, she told us to take some rest until she came back down again. Once she'd gone, the other girls started to ask lots of questions. 'Where d'you think we are? Whose house is this? What's going to happen to us now?' I told them that we must be in Khartoum, as Abdul Azzim had said that's where we were going.

About twenty minutes later, Asha came back downstairs and set out some yoghurt and bread for us on the floor and five metal spoons. We were all starving hungry, and when Asha noticed that no one had started eating she asked why. We told her we didn't know what to do with the 'shiny metal things'. Asha burst into a deep, kindly belly laugh. She picked up one of the spoons, scooped up some of the yoghurt and popped it into her mouth. With a wide grin, she swallowed hard. 'Delicious!' she declared. 'Now, all of you try it.' She handed us each a spoon and we tried as best we could. But we ended up with more yoghurt on the floor and on our faces than

137

in our mouths. After the first few messy attempts, we gave up, ripped the bread into strips and used it to scoop up the yoghurt, just like we would at home. Asha was right. It was delicious. She'd put lots of sugar into it, and all the yoghurt disappeared in a matter of seconds.

Later, Abdul Azzim came and asked if any of us needed the toilet. All five of us needed to go. We followed him back up out of the basement, across the yard and into an outhouse. Abdul Azzim told us that inside the toilet we would find a rope hanging from the ceiling. Once we had finished, we should pull the rope. Inside it was the most beautiful toilet we'd ever seen. The floor and walls were covered with shiny white squares and there was a hole in the floor to pee into. I was the first and as I squatted down, I noticed something hanging from the ceiling. It was made of metal and it looked a bit like a snake. I smiled to myself as I remembered the snakes in our 'toilet' in the Nuba Mountains. This must be the rope Abdul Azzim mentioned — but it didn't look anything like the ropes my father used to make from baobab tree bark. After I'd finished, I gave it a pull. I shouted out in surprise as the toilet made a loud gurgling noise and a stream of water gushed down the hole. Back in the basement, as I was dropping off to sleep, I saw Asha come quietly into the room. Just as she was getting into her bed, she realised that I was still awake.

'You're still not asleep, *beti*' — 'my daughter' — she whispered, gently.

'I'm so tired and I want to sleep but I can't,

Khalti Asha' — 'Auntie Asha' — I whispered.

Asha came to sit next to me. 'If you're very quiet, we can have a little talk,' she whispered. 'But if they hear us, they'll come down and ask why we're still awake. So, quietly, quietly — all right, my daughter?'

'OK, Auntie, I'll be quiet,' I whispered back. 'My name is Mende.'

'Where are you from?'

'I'm from the Nuba Mountains.'

'I'm also from the Nuba,' she exclaimed. 'Which tribe are you from?'

'The Karko.'

'I've not heard of the Karko. But it's enough that you're Nuba, and I'm Nuba too.'

Asha hugged me tightly for a few minutes. For the first time since the raid, I felt an adult treat me with real human warmth and kindness again, and I felt so happy. 'How long have you been here for, Auntie?' I asked, looking up at her.

'For over twenty years.'

'Over twenty years! But where are your mother and father?'

'Let's not talk about that,' she said, quietly. 'Why don't you tell me your story?'

I tried to tell Asha about what had happened, but as soon as I started to think about it, I felt myself starting to cry. Asha hugged me close to her and told me to have a good weep.

'I know, I know,' she whispered, as I sobbed quietly. 'You don't know whether your mother or father are alive or dead.'

'How did you know?' I asked through my tears.

139

'It's the same with me,' she said. 'I haven't heard anything about them for twenty years, now. I don't know if my parents are still living.'

I looked up at Asha's face, and I could see tears running down her cheeks. I hugged her back as tightly as she was hugging me, and we sobbed out the pain and the loss of our families together. 'Why haven't you seen your family for so long?' I finally asked her.

'Well . . . When I was just ten years old, very small like you are, I was captured and brought here, and I've been here ever since. I don't know what else to say. All I can say is, just be patient and do whatever they tell you to do. If you don't, they'll beat you.'

'Who will beat me?'

'You know, you won't be staying here long. Soon, you'll be sent to another house.'

'Which other house?'

'This man, Abdul Azzim. He brings a lot of girls like you here. Each week, he brings more. And then other Arabs come to take these girls to their own homes.'

'What for?'

'To work for them.'

'Is that what happened to you?'

'Yes. First, I worked for Abdul Azzim's mother and father. After they died, Abdul Azzim brought me here.' Asha hugged me and kissed me on the top of my head and told me to go to sleep.

★ ★ ★

When I woke the next morning, I was still thinking about what she had said. Abdul Azzim had a big chest full of children's clothes in the basement. That morning, he told us each to choose something our own size. Then we had to go outside to wash. We were told to wash our old dresses, and put on the new clothes he had given us.

The washroom was another room with shiny white tiles, and here we had our first close-up encounter with a mirror. In the Nuba Mountains, when it rained a lot you could catch a glimpse of yourself in the surface of a pool, but it was nothing like as clear as the mirror. We stood in front of it, made faces, stuck out our tongues and rolled around in laughter. We looked at each other in the mirror and talked about who was the most beautiful. The other girls told me that I was the prettiest, because I had the longest hair and the lightest skin.

Then we looked around for some water to wash ourselves with, but all we could see was a hole in the floor and a metal tube sticking out from the wall above our heads. Back at home in the rainy season, we used to wash ourselves in the waterfalls in the mountains. We'd use the leaves of a special forest plant as soap. But in the cold, dry season, we would use a bowl of water to wash. As all the water had to be fetched from the water-hole by hand we only used to wash once a week. Even then, when my mother called me to wash, I used to shout and run away. Often when I refused to wash, my mother would rub me with sesame oil instead. I especially hated doing my hair, which would only get washed once every three months or so.

As we were wondering where the water was, Asha stuck her head around the door and pointed at a knob under the pipe. She told me to twist it and see what happened. As I did so, water came gushing out of the shower head and we shrieked and squealed as it drenched us all. After we'd finished washing, we had nothing to do. I asked Asha if she could bring us some small stones so that we could play *Kak* — the stone game. We sat down in a circle and began to play. Very quickly, there were cries of excitement and laughter in the basement as we played *Kak* over and over again. After we'd been playing for about half an hour, Joahir poked an angry head around the door.

'What's all this?' she barked at us.

'We're just playing the stone game,' I said quietly. Being the oldest, it had been left to me to reply.

'What? What d'you think you're here for? To play? There's no time for that. I've got work for you to do. Come on,' she said. 'Up we go, all of you, out into the yard.'

It was good to be outside in the sun and fresh air after the dark basement. Joahir returned a few seconds later with a big sack full of onions, a large bowl and some knives. 'After you've peeled them,' she told us, 'you must slice them very thinly. D'you understand?'

We sat in a circle around the sack. After a few minutes of slicing onions, we all had tears streaming down our faces. I called to Asha, who

I could see at a window, to come and join us. But she shouted back that she had too much work to do as there were many guests coming that morning. Soon, I could hear them arriving at the front of the house, and then laughter and loud talking in one of the rooms upstairs.

As we sat there peeling the onions, I caught sight of the old Nuba man sweeping the yard. After that, he started to clean the balcony where the guests would sit later. As I sat there I thought back over what Asha had told me the night before. 'Is this how I'm going to end up,' I thought to myself, 'working for Arabs just like Asha and the old man?' For the first time since I was captured, I started to realise just what the future held for me.

After an hour or so, two young children came running into the yard. 'Look, look!' said the girl to her brother, pointing at us. 'Don't those girls have funny hair?' She came running over and took a lock of my hair between her two fingers, holding it gingerly, as if it was a worm.

'Don't touch their hair!' her brother shouted, rushing over. 'It's nasty. It smells bad.'

Joahir must have overheard, because she leaned out the window and called down to them. 'Don't play out there. It's dirty! And the onions will smart your eyes. Go out the front if you want to play outside.'

After we had finished the first sack of onions, Joahir brought another one out for us. 'I want you to finish all these onions today,' she said.

At lunchtime, Asha brought us some salad, rice and lentils. She sat with us, and chatted all through lunch in an attempt to cheer us up. She explained that the food we were preparing was for the festival of Ramadan, which was still some months away. The onions would be put out to dry in the sun, along with chopped chilli, garlic and meat. Come Ramadan, the dried ingredients would be used to make a spicy meat stew.

'What happens in that room?' I asked her. 'The one where I can see all the people talking and drinking?'

'Oh, that's their most beautiful room,' said Asha. 'I have to keep it very clean. Abdul Azzim uses it for entertaining his guests. There's a big table and chairs, and they can sit twelve or more people around the table if they want to. It's very hard work doing all the cooking for them all.'

Just then, Joahir brought some of the party guests into the yard. They came out of the back door and stood over us watching us work — four women in their mid-thirties. I thought that they looked like princesses, their clothes were so beautiful. They had long, styled hair and they were wearing gold bracelets and necklaces. I could smell a beautiful scent coming from them, even over the onions we were chopping. At the time, I thought that they must smell like this naturally. Later I realised it was their perfume.

'What a great idea, Joahir,' said one of them, in a simpering voice. 'You can get them to do anything you want — like preparing all the things you need for Ramadan. You're so lucky! I haven't even started preparing my Ramadan dishes. You know, I can't bear the smell of the meat and the onions. I can't touch them!

Perhaps I also need some *abids* like yours to do this nasty work for me.'

As soon as I heard her talking like this, I was so angry. She was acting like Allah had made them better than us. I knew this wasn't true. When I was young, my father had told me that God created all of us equal. I wished for all the world that he could be there with me now. I knew what he'd say to these women: 'My daughter is the most precious thing in the whole world. Don't you dare talk about her like this!'

After they'd gone in again, Asha explained that whenever Abdul Azzim brought groups of girls like us back to the house, he and Joahir threw a big party. 'They invite them here so they can inspect the girls, and choose one to take away with them. This is what happened to me, many years ago. I'm telling you this because I don't want you to get into trouble later when you leave here,' Asha continued. 'You have to understand — if they order you to do something, you have to obey them.'

The next day we were given huge hunks of meat to cut into long strips, which were then hung up to dry on a rope strung out across the yard. On the third day, Joahir brought out a sack of beans to husk. After husking, we had to beat them to a pulp, using a pestle and mortar. The bean pulp was used to make jars of humus, which were put in the fridge until the time of Ramadan. By the end of the third day, my hands were red, blistered and raw. We were all exhausted. That evening, Joahir ordered us all to go and take another shower.

'But we had one this morning,' I said, without thinking. 'We're too tired to go and have another one now.'

'I told you to have a shower now!' Joahir snapped at me, her eyes flashing fire. 'Don't you dare talk back to me.'

After our shower, Asha brought us some food in the basement. Our dinner consisted of bread and jam, with some milk. When Asha sat down to eat with us, I could see that she was worried. 'Don't answer back to her like that, Mende,' she whispered. 'You must obey her. If she tells you to take a shower, you have to have one. That's the end of it. Or d'you want her to beat you?'

'No, Auntie Asha,' I said, shaking my head. 'I don't want her to beat me. But we were so tired.'

'Asha, I've never had to work like this before in my life,' Ashcuana whispered, showing her red and bleeding hands. 'Why does she make us work like this?'

'I know, I know,' said Asha. 'Trust me, if you were my children, it would be different. But that's the way these Arabs are. You're going to have to get used to it.'

After dinner, I sat down to plait Ashcuana's hair. It was very short and wiry, but I wound it into tight twists, so that it would stay like that for a few days. 'D'you remember, when we arrived here, we saw the wooden things with the lights on top and thought they were trees?' said Ashcuana. 'They weren't trees, they were lamps.'

'Yes,' I said, smiling. 'And then when we drove through the city, we thought that the big cars had given birth to the small cars!'

For a while, we carried on talking like this, and soon Asha was laughing fit to burst. Then I asked Asha a question that had been troubling me ever since we arrived. 'Why is there such a big room down here under the ground? It's like a grave, but graves are only for people who die. So why do we have to stay down here? We're not dead. Why do the Arabs build their house on top of a big grave like this?'

'When I was in Abdul Azzim's father's house, they put me in the basement just like you,' Asha answered. 'And just like you, I was scared. It was a hole in the ground like a grave and I thought it would be full of ghosts. But I had to stay down there all alone. Imagine what *that* was like! This isn't a grave — it's just the way the Arabs build their houses.'

Just then, we were interrupted by Joahir bringing a group of women and their husbands into the basement. We stopped talking and Asha got up quietly and left. They came strolling across and stopped to stare at us.

'Oh . . . So this time Abdul Azzim has brought very pretty girls,' said one of them to Joahir. 'They're much more beautiful than the last. And they look very clean too.'

'Yes,' said Joahir, smiling. 'We make sure they have one shower in the morning and another one in the evening. So that's two showers every day.'

'Oh, and they don't mind? Well, I'm thinking about taking one of them. What d'you think, Joahir?'

'Well, this one is Ashcuana and this is Ammo,' said Joahir, pointing to each of us in turn. 'They have such stupid names. This is Mende, that's not so difficult to say. But anyway, it doesn't matter. When you take one you can call her whatever you like. So, which one d'you think you'd like?'

'Oh no, not now. I can't decide right now,' said the woman, shaking her head. 'I'll phone you tomorrow and let you know.'

'Well, if you don't decide now, someone else may come in the meantime and choose the one you want,' warned Joahir.

'All right then,' said the woman, laughing. She inspected us for a moment longer and then turned to Joahir. 'Let's go upstairs, drink some coffee and discuss it.'

As they climbed the stairs out of the basement, I could hear Joahir shout up to Asha. 'Asha, hurry up and prepare some coffee for the guests.'

'Yes, master,' Asha replied. 'Of course, master. Right away.'

13

Sold

When Asha came down to sleep, I was still finishing Ashcuana's hair. 'You're still awake?' said Asha, gently. 'You've still not finished?'

'It's nearly done,' I said, glancing up at her.

'Oh, it's really lovely. I'd love you to do mine like that, but I just don't have the time to stop.' She was silent for a second, watching us. 'Mende, listen to me. I've just heard that you may be leaving tomorrow.'

'Leaving for where?' I said, dropping the last few strands of Ashcuana's hair in alarm.

'You remember the women who came down to the basement earlier? Well, I think you'll be going home with one of them.'

'How do you know?'

'When I took them coffee in the sitting room, I overheard them talking. Joahir said to one of the women, 'So, have you decided? Which one would you like?' 'What's her name?' the woman replied. 'You know, they're so difficult to remember. She's the one with the easiest name.' 'You mean Mende?' said Joahir. 'Yes. That's it. She seems a good girl, very clever,' said the lady. 'Yes. She's helped me so much, preparing all the food for Ramadan. I think she's better educated than the others, too,' said Joahir. 'When Abdul

Azzim comes back I'll let him know. Then you'll need to discuss the details with him.''

'I'm not going!' I blurted out, bursting into tears.

'I'm sorry,' said Asha, hugging me. 'I'm so sorry. But, you know, Mende, there's nothing you can do about it. I've been trying to prepare you for this, so it wouldn't be such a shock for you.'

'But Mende can't just go all on her own,' said Ashcuana, who was now crying too. 'I want to go with her.'

'I know, Ashcuana,' said Asha, wearily. 'But you can't. You will also be taken away by someone. Maybe none of you will ever see each other again.'

I could tell that Asha hated having to tell us this. 'Come on, Mende. Don't worry. It's going to be all right,' she said, taking my hand. 'Come on. Come and sleep in my bed. I'll cuddle you all night long.'

Asha wrapped me up in her big arms and rocked me to sleep. That night, I dreamed that I was sleeping with my father in our hut, but every time he tried to hug me, I kept slipping from his grasp and falling away from him. The next morning, when Asha went to get up, I tried to stop her. I felt that if only I could keep holding on to her, no one could take me away. But she gently pulled my hands from around her. She left, saying that she'd see me again later.

I lay on Asha's bed feeling lost and empty. I so desperately wanted to stay with Asha and the other girls. As I couldn't, I thought about trying to escape. But I knew that the doors were all locked. Even if I did manage to get out of the house, what would I do then? I would be a little Nuba girl lost in this huge city of the Arabs where I knew nothing and I had no friends.

I could hear a couple of the other girls waking up. 'Today, I think I'm going to be leaving,' I said in a low voice.

'What! Why? Where are you going?'

'Joahir has found a lady who wants to take me to live in her house,' I mumbled. Up until now, I had always tried to be strong in front of the younger girls. Now, I just broke down and wept in front of them. 'I don't want to go,' I wailed. 'I just want to stay here. I don't want to leave you all.'

They rushed over and sat next to me on Asha's bed. 'Don't worry, Mende. Don't cry,' they said, stroking my hair and holding my hands. 'Maybe it won't happen. How do you know you're going away? Who told you?'

'Asha did,' I sobbed. 'She overheard Joahir talking with one of the ladies.'

Just then, there was the sound of someone coming down the stairs. The girls ran over to the doorway. When they saw that it was Asha coming with our breakfast, they crowded around her asking her to explain.

'Well, yes, I think Mende is going away today,' said Asha, setting down the breakfast tray. 'Soon, all of you will be taken away. And then I'll be left here on my own again. I told you this before. I know it's difficult. I'm sorry. But there's nothing any of us can do about it.' Asha looked over at

151

me on the bed. 'Mende, d'you remember what I said to you?'

'No. I don't remember.'

'I said that if they tell you to do something, you have to do it. If you disobey them, they will beat you.'

'OK. I remember now,' I sobbed.

'Mende, we're unlikely to ever see each other again,' Asha told me, putting her arms around me. 'I'm not allowed outside this house. And you probably won't be allowed to go outside of your master's house, either.'

We were interrupted by a call from upstairs. 'Asha, where are you! Why aren't you here in the kitchen?' shouted Joahir. 'What are you doing down there?'

'Sit down now and eat your breakfast,' Asha whispered, fiercely. 'Yes, master. Sorry, master,' she shouted up to Joahir. 'I'm down here in the basement. I won't be long.'

We could hear Joahir banging about upstairs. Then we heard Abdul Azzim calling her: 'Joahir, can you come with me? I need to go shopping in town.'

'No, go on your own,' Joahir shouted back. 'I have to get these *abids* to do some more work.'

We heard the front door slam as Abdul Azzim left the house. Then Joahir shouted down the stairs again. 'Asha, hurry up! And get the girls ready too. There's lots to do.'

The rest of the morning, we spent husking chilli and crushing it with salt. Then we had to work this into the strips of meat. It soon burned its way into all the cuts and blisters on my hands.

It was agony. That evening, we were sitting in the basement when I heard the noise that I'd been dreading — a ring at the front door bell. Shortly after, I could hear the excited chatter of women coming from the living room. Then Asha came downstairs.

'Mende,' she said, 'those women who were here yesterday have come back again. I think tonight they'll be taking you with them.'

'I don't want to go.'

'Don't say that,' said Asha, softly. 'You've no choice. Mende, try not to look too upset — or they'll take it badly.'

We sat there in the basement in an awkward silence, no one really knowing what to say. These were Nuba people and they were my friends. For a short while, they had also become my surrogate family. What would I do without them? The Arab women stayed upstairs for what seemed like an age. Had they really come to take me today, I wondered? I prayed that they had just come for another social visit.

Finally, Ashcuana broke the silence. 'If they take you away, Mende, when will we see you again?' It was the question that was on all of our minds.

'You may never see Mende again,' said Asha, sadly. 'You should say your goodbyes now. Otherwise, you might not get the chance.'

I turned to the other girls. 'I may never see you again,' I said, tears streaming down my face. 'That's what Asha says. I love you all and I don't want to go.'

We were all in tears now. I hugged each of the

girls in turn, Ashcuana last of all. Just then, Joahir shouted down the stairs.

'Asha! Are you still in the basement?'

'Yes, master. I'm here,' Asha called up.

'Well, come upstairs! And bring Mende with you.'

Asha took me by the hand and led me up the stairs. I knew now that this was it, that I was being taken away.

'Asha, you're always down in the basement these days,' Joahir said accusingly, as she met us in the hall. 'Why? When other girls come, you don't spend so much time with them. Why are you always with these girls?' Asha just hung her head, hunched her shoulders and looked at the floor. 'I won't have it! You even keep stopping work to go down and see them. It's just not good enough, now is it?'

'No, master,' said Asha, quietly.

'Right. Now go to the kitchen. There's a mountain of washing up for you to do.'

Asha was at least ten years older than Joahir. In our culture you always respected your elders. I felt so sorry for her as she disappeared into the kitchen. I was left standing there alone, at the entrance to the living room. The three Arab women whom I recognised from the night before were sitting with Joahir and Abdul Azzim. They just ignored me and carried on chatting. It was the first time that I had seen the living room. The floor looked like a shiny, flat expanse of water. I could even see my reflection in it. I stepped gingerly out into the room, putting one foot carefully in front of the other.

154

A huge wooden sofa stood against each of the walls, upholstered in white. In each corner, there was a polished wooden table, holding a round mirror and a vase. Next to each of these was a tall standard lamp. The front of the room gave onto a beautiful balcony, with silver tiles and white metal railings. Two panelled doors led out onto the balcony, and these were thrown back against the wall to let the evening breeze in. Another door led into the large dining room. I peered inside and I could see the huge polished wooden table that Asha had told me about, with dining chairs arranged around it. On either side, there were glass-fronted cabinets full of silver dishes and glasses. Just then, the ladies started getting up from their seats. Abdul Azzim turned to me.

'Mende, you're leaving with this lady,' he said, gesturing to one of them. 'You must obey her, as she is now your master.'

I looked over at the woman, but she just ignored me and carried on chatting about the weather and the forthcoming Ramadan festival. As they were preparing to leave, Joahir remembered something. 'Oh, one minute,' she said, 'I almost forgot. She's got another set of clothes. Asha!' she called. 'Go down and get Mende's other dress.'

'It's all right,' I said quickly. 'I'll go down and get it.'

'No! I told Asha to go!' Joahir yelled at me.

'I thought I could go and say goodbye to my friends,' I stammered.

'You've spent every day since you arrived with

155

your friends,' Joahir snapped irritably. 'You mean to say you've not found time to say goodbye to them? Too bad. You won't be seeing them again, anyway.'

The guest looked over at me and laughed. I was about to answer back, when I caught sight of Asha in the doorway. She had her index finger held to her lips and tugged her ear, as if to say to me, 'Don't answer back! Just listen to what they tell you.' I kept silent.

Asha rushed off downstairs to get my clothes. Dejectedly, I followed Joahir, Abdul Azzim and the three women out to the front of the house. They called for their driver, and as we stood waiting in the front yard, Asha came hurrying over with my dress. She grabbed my hand and squeezed it hard. 'Bye-bye,' she said, softly. 'Bye-bye, Auntie Asha,' I mouthed back at her. The woman who was now my 'master' got into the front of the car and I got into the back, alongside the other two women. As we drove off, Abdul Azzim and Joahir shouted goodbye to the Arab ladies. But neither of them said goodbye to me.

14

Master Rahab

On the drive across Khartoum, the Arab ladies chatted amongst themselves. No one talked to me, or even acknowledged my presence. It was as if I was invisible. The two ladies congratulated my master on making a very good choice. I knew they were talking about me and the other girls and calling us *abids*, but I didn't know that this meant 'slaves'. Then they started gossiping about their friends, the clothes they were wearing for Ramadan and their new perfume.

'Oh, did you see Joahir?' one of the ladies sitting next to me said. 'That new necklace she was wearing? I pinched you on the knee so that you'd notice it. It looked so expensive.'

'Could I miss it?' said the lady sitting next to her. 'It was so beautiful. But it must have cost a small fortune. Don't you think so, Rahab?' she asked the lady in the front seat. So that was the name of my so-called master.

'Of course, we all saw it,' she replied. 'Those people have a lot of money — they can buy anything they want.'

'You know, Rahab,' one of the two ladies said, 'if Dhalia hears that you have this girl in your house, she'll be very jealous. She'll have to go and get one herself.'

'Well, she should go quickly, while Abdul Azzim has any left,' said Rahab, laughing.

After we dropped off Rahab's two friends, we drove on in silence. Eventually, we slowed down at a set of metal gates in a high brick wall. Rahab got out of the car and unlocked them. Then she turned to me: 'Come on. Out you get. Follow me.'

Rahab locked the gates behind us and I followed her down a long gravel driveway. We went through the front door of the house into a large, open-plan living room. The whole of the front of the house was one long wall of glass. I followed her into an adjacent room, which turned out to be the kitchen. Rahab pointed at a stool in one corner. 'Sit down there and wait for me,' she said curtly.

She left me alone in the kitchen. I looked around me. There was a long wooden table and some chairs — this much I was able to recognise. Up on the wall, there were rows of wooden boxes with knobs on them. These, I would learn, were built-in kitchen units, containing dishes and cooking utensils. There was a blue metal cylinder under a large, shiny metal surface covered in knobs and dials: this, I would find out, was a gas cooker. I noticed that there was a pile of dirty cups and plates in a metal bowl on legs, with metal tubes underneath it. But I didn't even know that this was a sink, or how it worked.

Rahab returned with an Arab man I guessed must be her husband. 'Here she is, Mustafa,' Rahab said, pointing at me. He just stood there for a few seconds looking at me and then he left without saying anything. Rahab had changed into some soft pyjamas, with a dressing gown thrown over the top. Her skin colour was a little lighter than mine, I noticed, and she had long glossy black hair. I thought she looked very beautiful with her lovely clothes and her wonderful hair.

'Come with me,' she said, turning to leave the kitchen. I followed her back outside and down an alleyway at the side of the house. Here, there was a small brick shed with a wooden door. Rahab fished for a key in the pocket of her gown and unlocked it. She reached inside and there was a click and as if by magic a bare bulb hanging from the ceiling lit up. 'Come inside, *yebit*,' she said. Yebit is an Arabic insult, which literally means 'girl worthy of no name'. I was shocked; it was the first time that anyone had used this word for me. I stepped inside. The floor was dirty and in one corner there was an old wooden box and a broken table. Leaning against one wall was a thin mattress.

'Put that on the floor, *yebit*,' said Rahab, pointing at the mattress. 'This is where you will sleep.' Then she turned to leave. She was about to shut the door when she stopped. 'Oh. This is a light switch,' she said, pointing to a white box on the wall. 'When I leave, you must turn the light off. You do that by pushing the switch up like this.'

She shut the door and I heard the key turn in the lock. I looked around the tiny room. It was horribly dirty, as if it hadn't been used for years. I searched for something to sleep under and found a dirty sheet rolled up in one corner. I pulled it out, shook it and put it on the mattress. Then I sat down, pulled my legs up under my chin, put my arms around my knees and tried to hug myself as tightly as I could. But I couldn't hold back any longer and I started to cry quietly into my dress.

My thoughts crowded in on me. At first, I thought about Asha. Then I thought about all the other girls, who would be curled up asleep in Abdul Azzim's basement by now. Then I started to think about my father and my mother asleep in our little, cosy mud hut. I thought about my brother Babo, about Ali, and the others asleep in the men's house. About Kunyant and her husband, sleeping nearby in their own hut. And I thought about my cat, Uran, curled up alone in the corner of the hut instead of sleeping soundly on my tummy.

I couldn't help thinking about the raid too. Were any of my family still alive? Did our village still exist? Where was poor Uran? I was overcome with grief. But, more than anything, I was filled with an intense loneliness. I had been enfolded with love and kindness all my life. Now, I was completely and utterly alone. Finally, exhaustion got the better of me and I crawled under the sheet. That night was the first of many that I cried myself to sleep.

It wasn't long before I was awake again, as the chill of the night seeped into the shed. I sat up, put my spare dress on over the one I was wearing, and curled up like a cat to try to get warm. But I was still freezing. Finally, I lay across the mattress, pulled the bottom half of it over on top of me, and curled up inside. But I was still cold and all night long I drifted in and out of a fitful sleep. Early in the morning, I was woken by Rahab unlocking the door. 'Come on. Get up, *yebit*. Go to the bathroom and clean yourself. I don't want you stinking up the house.'

At the end of the alleyway, against the high brick wall that ran around the house, there was a shower and toilet, similar to the one at Abdul Azzim's house. I tried to wash the sleep out of my eyes. Then, as I went to walk back to my room, Rahab saw me out of the kitchen window. 'You've finished washing, *yebit*?' she called over. I nodded. 'Then come inside.'

Rahab was sitting at the table in the kitchen with her husband, having tea and biscuits. 'Good morning,' her husband said as I walked in, without looking up from his paper. But Rahab tutted at him in disapproval and pointed me to my stool. 'Go and sit there,' she said. She handed me an old cup, bowl and plate. 'These are yours,' she instructed me, 'for you to eat and drink from.' She opened one of the cupboards. 'This is where you'll keep them.' Overnight, a small metal table had appeared next to my stool. 'This is where you'll sit. Do you understand?'

I nodded. 'Now, listen,' she said. 'You are going to live here and work for me. You will stay here for the rest of your life. D'you understand me? You can have some tea now. When you've finished, I'll show you exactly what work you have to do.'

As I sat with my tea, she started to instruct me

161

on what I had to do in their house. As she did so, I wanted to curl up in the corner and disappear into the floor. I felt I wanted to die.

'I have two little girls that you have to look after. You must treat them very well. You have to clean the house and keep it very, very neat and tidy. You have to clean the yard and the patio, at the front of the house.'

She told me that I had to wash their clothes and 'iron them'. I didn't even know what an iron was. But I remembered what Asha had told me. So I just nodded and said, 'Yes, master,' to everything.

When I had finished my tea, she told me to start washing up the breakfast things. She showed me how to use the taps and the detergent and how to remove the plug to drain the water away. She showed me how to rinse everything and how to stack it on the draining board. 'Once I've shown you how to do something,' she added, 'I'm not going to repeat myself. Tomorrow, you have to get up and start your work on your own.'

Then she left me at the sink. Everything was covered in slippery suds and I had to be careful not to drop anything. I was terrified that I would break something, or that she'd come in and shout at me for taking so long. I could feel myself trembling all over. Once I'd finished, she checked to make sure everything was clean.

'Yes,' she said. 'Good. Now, this is where the cups go, this is where the plates go and all the pots and pans. Here's a drying-up cloth. Dry all of these things and then put them away.'

After the drying up, I had to clean the kitchen. I was amazed at how dirty everything was. The kitchen floor was sticky with spilt food. Even the insides of the cupboards were filthy. Back in our village, my mother had taught me to be clean and neat. We may have lived in a mud hut with an earth floor, but it was swept every day.

I started cleaning the kitchen around 7.30 a.m. and wasn't finished until noon. By now I was starving hungry. Rahab came in to inspect it, with two children in tow. One looked about two years old and the other around four. As soon as they saw me the girls asked, 'Mamma, who's this?'

'She's called Mende,' Rahab replied. 'She's going to be living here with us now.'

'She'll be cleaning the house and washing our clothes? Like Sadhia? Is Sadhia not coming back again, Mamma?' asked the older girl.

'No, no. Not like Sadhia,' said Rahab. 'Sadhia's gone back to live with her parents. She's going to be married.'

'But Mamma, she's cleaning and washing our clothes, just like Sadhia did. Why is she not like Sadhia, Mamma?' the little girl persisted.

'Come on, darling, drink some milk,' said Rahab, sitting the girls down at the table. 'Once you've had breakfast, we'll go into the living room and I'll explain it to you.' Rahab sat the smaller girl on her lap and began to feed her a meal of bread and butter, and eggs, then she turned to me. 'Oh. When you've finished cleaning, you can eat these,' she said, pointing at a bowl of nuts she'd put out on my table.

Who was Sadhia, I wondered? Where had she gone to now? After they finished eating, Rahab showed me the rest of the house. It was a long, one-storey building, with the kitchen at one end. A large lounge ran almost half the length of the house. Next to the lounge was a smaller 'ladies' lounge' for Rahab to use with her friends, and a formal dining room. At the far end of the house there was a bathroom, Rahab's bedroom and the girls had their own bedroom too.

Rahab's house was smaller than Abdul Azzim's, but it was also beautifully furnished. It had heavy wooden sofas and there were fancy lamps and vases in all the rooms. In the main lounge, there was a huge TV, a video recorder and a music system, although I didn't recognise any of these things. In Rahab's bedroom there was another TV, and a third one in the ladies' lounge. Rahab told me that I had to keep all the rooms clean and tidy, including the bedrooms. I'd never seen anything like the carpets they had in the house, which at first I thought must be made from some sort of animal skins.

The house was dusty and messy, but the worst were the two bedrooms, which were in complete chaos. I started in the lounge, but I was already feeling exhausted from my cold, sleepless night. All I'd had was a cup of tea and a few nuts to keep me going. How could I possibly finish all the work that I had been told to do that day? Rahab sat around in the lounge, reading magazines. I worked in silence around her. Every now and then, she'd pick up a strange white object, hold it to her ear and start talking into it.

It had a long, curly lead attached to it, and when she put it down it made a 'ding'. But I couldn't understand who she was talking to.

Then she turned on the television. I watched transfixed from the corner of the room, as little people moved around inside this square black box with a shiny glass front. I couldn't understand how they could have got inside, but I could see them walking around and hear them talking. It was so hard to carry on cleaning and not watch. To me, it seemed completely magical. But I knew that if Rahab caught me looking, she would be angry.

Later, Rahab's children came home. The oldest one came and found me in the small lounge. 'Mende,' she said, 'come and play with us. Come on.' She was carrying a box full of toys. They sat down and started to get them out. So I put down my cleaning things and sat down beside them. I was still only a child myself, and I had never seen such beautiful toys before. I picked up the youngest girl and gave her a cuddle. But as I did so, Rahab came rushing into the room.

'*Yebit*,' she yelled at me. 'Put her down! Don't you dare touch my children! D'you hear me?'

She crouched down in front of her two little girls. 'Usra. Hanin. You don't allow her to touch you, OK? Come on. Come away. You've both had a long day. It's time to get some rest. Later on, you can watch some TV.'

Then she turned back to me. '*Yebit*, you've got work to do,' she snapped. 'So, you don't have time to play, do you?'

As Rahab led her little girls away, another bit of my spirit died. A few minutes later she came back and stood in front of me with her hands on her hips. '*Yebit*, I want you to finish all this work today, no matter how long it takes you. Do you understand?'

I nodded, and carried on cleaning. I managed to finish the two lounges and the dining room quite quickly, despite them being so dirty. After Rahab had made the family lunch, they all went to their rooms for an afternoon nap. Before going, she said to me, 'There's food in the kitchen for you, *yebit*. When you've finished, do the washing up.'

On my little table in the corner of the kitchen, I found that she had put the leftovers from their meal on my plate. I was so hungry I could have eaten anything. But I'd never eaten a meal alone before in my life. In the Nuba Mountains, no-one ever ate alone. It was against our tradition of hospitality. In our village you would give a dog what you couldn't eat in a bowl in the corner of the room. That's exactly how these people were treating me.

After I'd eaten, I started to do the washing up. By the time I'd finished, the whole house was silent; everyone was sleeping through the afternoon heat. At least now there was no one around to shout at me or check on my work. At around seven o'clock, I could hear noises from the children's room. Rahab went into the living room and turned on the TV and Hanin and Usra joined her.

I left cleaning the bathroom to last, once the whole family had gone to bed. Then I went into the kitchen and ate the leftovers from their dinner. After that, I did the washing up, dried up and put everything away. By now it was around midnight and I was practically dead on my feet. As I was finishing up, Mustafa, Rahab's husband, came in for a glass of water. As he walked back into their bedroom, I overheard him remark to Rahab, 'Hey, the house is really great, eh? The kitchen looks like new.'

'Yes. Well, she had very good instructions, didn't she?' Rahab replied, smugly. 'I think she'll turn out to be a very good *abda*, this one, don't you?'

'What's her name again?' Mustafa asked.

'Her name? Her name? I keep forgetting,' said Rahab, sleepily. 'I just call her *yebit*.'

'Well, I think after a few weeks, *Inshallah* — God willing — she'll be able to do everything, eh? Maybe you could even show her how to cook.'

'Maybe,' said Rahab. 'But you never know, she's probably got diseases. I'll make sure she has a shower every morning and every evening. Once we know she's clean and healthy, then maybe she can start cooking.'

Rahab came into the kitchen in her dressing gown. '*Yebit*, have you finished everything?'

I nodded.

'OK, it's time for you to go to bed. There's more work for you to do tomorrow. Come with me. Oh, I forgot,' she said, as she was about to shut the door to my shed. 'You have to shower before you go to bed. Go and start and I'll get something for you.'

I was so tired that I wanted to cry. The last thing I had energy for was a shower. I washed as quickly as I could. Then Rahab came back with some oil, some creamy stuff in a jar and a small white stick. 'Every morning I want you to cream your body with this, oil your hair and rub this under your arms and on your neck,' she said, pointing at the white stick. 'I don't want you smelling bad in the house.'

Then she locked me in my shed. I put my extra dress on, curled up into a ball and pulled the mattress over me. I didn't even have the energy to cry. I just went straight into an exhausted sleep. At six the next morning I was still in a deep, deep sleep when Rahab woke me. After showering, I dressed and went into the kitchen.

'*Yebit*, you can't wear that dirty dress again,' Rahab tutted, when she saw me come in wearing the same clothes. 'Why haven't you changed?'

'I've only got two dresses,' I mumbled. 'They're both dirty.'

She sighed, and disappeared into her bedroom. She came back a few moments later with three dresses and a skirt of her own. 'Here, you can have these old clothes of mine. Now go and change.'

Rahab had said they were old clothes, but I thought they were very beautiful. They weren't my size, of course, as I was only a twelve-year-old girl. But I managed to knot the skirt at the waist, so it wouldn't fall down. Rahab told me that every morning I must start by cleaning the whole house. She then showed me how to wash their clothes in the yard and where to hang them to dry. She warned me to wash my clothes separately from the family's clothes. 'We don't want to catch anything from you,' she said. I was also shown how to empty the two large barrels at the back of the house, into which all the household dirty water drained. I hated this job. Each tank contained about ten bucket-loads of stinking water, which I had to empty out.

After the family had eaten lunch, I was sent to have mine. They had left the remains of their meal on the main table, so I took their plates and sat down to eat in my corner. Just then, Rahab came in. '*Yebit*,' she screamed at me, when she saw what I was doing, 'don't you dare eat off our plates! Put the food in your own bowl! I showed you how to do this yesterday. Didn't I? Or are you stupid or something?' With a trembling hand, I tipped the food into my bowl. What was wrong with me? Why was she treating me like this?

And so it went on — day after day, the same drudgery, the same constant abuse. One day merged into the next, almost without my noticing. That first week, the children kept trying to play with me. The small one, Usra, would keep coming up to have her hair stroked. I so wanted to kiss her and hug her, like I used to do with the little children in my village, and when Rahab wasn't looking I did so. I craved human affection and warmth. But when I went to stroke

169

the hair of the older girl, Hanin, she jerked her head away.

'Don't do that,' she snapped at me. 'My mamma said I mustn't let you touch me. She said that you're sick and have diseases and that you're dirty. I'll tell on you.'

'I'm not sick,' I mumbled. 'I'm not sick.' I was so upset, I felt that my heart was breaking. I looked myself up and down. 'I'm clean,' I said to her. 'I'm not dirty.'

'Well, my mamma says you're not allowed to touch me,' said Hanin, turning her back on me.

Now even the children were treating me like an animal. Worse than an animal: even dogs were patted and stroked. I wanted to sob my heart out, but I knew that, if I did, Rahab would come storming into the room and start shouting at me. By the end of that first week I was physically and emotionally exhausted. I was trying to hide my sadness and my pain, trying not to react to the rejection. I felt hunted and watched and deeply abused.

It was hardly surprising that something went badly wrong. I was using a duster to swipe cobwebs out of a corner in the lounge, as Rahab had shown me. But the duster caught the lip of a vase and it went crashing to the floor. For one moment I just stood there, rooted to the spot, staring down at the smashed glass and the flowers strewn across the carpet in a big pool of water. I didn't know what to do. I felt myself starting to shake with fear.

'Idiot! Are you blind!' I heard Rahab scream,

as she came rushing into the lounge. 'What have you done?'

'I . . . I . . . I've . . . ' I stammered, without looking round at her. I couldn't get the words out.

'I can see what you've done!' she raged. 'Do you know how much this cost me? This one vase is worth more than your whole filthy tribe!'

My head jerked back as she grabbed me by the hair and I felt a stinging slap across my cheek.

'*Mailesh* — I'm sorry. *Mailesh*, master Rahab,' I cried. 'I'm sorry. Please don't hit me.' But she did, again and again.

'You stupid girl! Why don't you watch what you're doing? I'm warning you, if you break anything else, you'll see what happens!'

'I'm sorry. I'm sorry,' I sobbed. 'I'm sorry.'

'Stop crying and clear up the mess,' she snapped. 'I don't want to find a single piece of broken glass. If the children cut their feet, then you'll be sorry.'

I got down on my hands and knees and started to pick up the pieces of broken vase. I was in shock. This was the first time that I'd ever been beaten in my life. I thought back over how gentle and loving my parents had always been. I couldn't remember my father ever hitting any of us. When there was a problem, he would always talk it through rather than use physical punishment. I could remember my mother hitting me only once. She'd asked me to go to the market to buy some salt, and I'd refused.

'Leave me alone,' I'd said to her, cheekily. 'I'm not going.'

'Why not?' my mother had asked me, in surprise. 'I'm ordering you to go. Who d'you think you are?'

But I didn't answer because I was sulking. It was the only time that my mother lost her temper with me, and she hit me on the shoulder. I burst into tears. Then my mother took me on her lap and hugged me. 'I'm sorry I hit you,' she said, rocking me backwards and forwards. 'But if I ask you to go to the market you shouldn't refuse. Don't cry. I'll go and get the salt myself.'

After my sobbing died down, I said to my mother, '*Umi*, I'll go to the market for you.' I knew that I'd behaved badly and that my mother was right to punish me. But here, I'd broken the vase by accident. It was clear that I couldn't expect any fairness or kindness from these people.

15

No Escape

I spent hours thinking about escaping. One day, while I was emptying the wastewater out the back of the house, I spotted a broken chair lying on its side. I tried the chair to see if it would bear my weight. I was very good at climbing and if I stood on the chair, I thought I could just reach the top of the garden wall that surrounded the house. Then I might be able to haul myself up, drop down the other side and sneak out onto the road. But what would I do then? I'd be lost and alone in the middle of Khartoum, with only Arabs around. Who would help me? The more I thought about it, the more I knew that it was hopeless to try and escape alone. I would need help.

Each week, a man came to cut the grass and look after the garden and fruit trees that surrounded the house. Rahab called him their *janiney* — the gardener. When I'd first seen him, I'd greeted him politely: '*Assalam alaikum.*' '*Alaikum wassalam, biti*' — 'Hello, my daughter' — he'd replied, smiling. He was an Arab, but he looked poor and he had a kindly way about him. After two months, I plucked up the courage to try to talk to him. I went into the orchard and found him mowing the lawn.

When I tried to ask him a question, he motioned to me that he couldn't hear properly over the noise of the mower. So he bent down and turned it off. 'Do you have a daughter, Uncle?' I asked.

'Yes, *biti*, I do. She's about your age,' he said. 'Hey. Would you like me to bring her to play with you?'

'Yes! Yes, I'd love that,' I said, breaking into an uncertain smile.

'All right. Or, better still, why don't you come to our house next time you have some time off. Before you, a girl called Sadhia worked here. She used to come to our house for her holidays. Why don't you do the same?'

So that's who Sadhia was — someone who worked here like me. But she was allowed holidays and to go out of the house. I had worked every day since I'd arrived and Rahab had told me I could never go outside the house. 'But I can't leave the house, Uncle *janiney*. Can you bring your daughter here instead?'

'Why not, *biti*? Sadhia used to come to our house all the time.'

Before I could answer, I heard shouting from the house. '*Yebit!* Where are you? Come here at once!' It was Rahab.

'I'm here, *saieda* Rahab' — 'master Rahab' — I shouted back. I rushed off towards the yard without another word to the *janiney*. 'I'm just cleaning the yard.' Rahab came striding towards me. 'Were you cleaning or were you talking?' she demanded, menacingly. 'Come inside!'

I followed her into the kitchen, my head hung

low. She turned on me, her face black with fury. 'Who were you talking to? Tell me!'

'I was talking to the *janiney*, master Rahab,' I murmured.

'What were you talking about? Do you know him from somewhere?'

'No, I don't. I just met him in the garden.'

'You're lying!' she raged at me. 'You were talking for ages! I heard you. You think you can get away with lying to me?'

She grabbed one of her shoes, a wooden-soled sandal, and started to beat me around the head with it. I screamed and put my arms up to protect myself. 'Now. Are you going to tell me what you said?' she demanded, breathlessly. 'Or do I have to beat you some more?'

'I asked him if he had a daughter that I could play with,' I sobbed. 'That's all.'

'And what did he say to you?'

'He said that he'd take me to his house if I liked so I could play with his daughter.'

'Oh well, that's all right then, isn't it?' she said mockingly. 'So, he's going to take you to play with his daughter. Very nice. You really think so, do you?'

'*Mailesh* — I'm sorry,' I sobbed. '*Mailesh*, master. Maybe he can bring her here to play with me?' I murmured, staring at the floor.

'Oh yes! Let's bring her here! Who do you think you are?' she snarled 'You think you're my daughter? You think you can invite girls here to play with you? Don't you know what you are? Well then, let me tell you. You are an *abda*. *Abda*. *Abda*. *Abda*. You know what that is, don't you?

Well, don't you ever forget it.'

'No. I'm not Abda. I'm Mende,' I murmured. In the Nuba Mountains, Abda is a girl's name. I just thought that Rahab had got my name wrong.

'Yes. I know you're called Mende,' Rahab sneered at me. 'But you're an *abda*. Don't you know what that means?'

'I'm Mende,' I repeated, quietly.

'No! You are my *abda*!' she yelled. 'So don't you argue. That means you stay here in this house and you do what I say. You work. You don't play. Got it? *Abda!* Abda! One *abda*, many *abids*.'

I suddenly remembered the story my father told me about the Arabs who had raided the Shimii village. He said they had taken the girls as *abids* — as slaves. Now I finally knew what Rahab was calling me. She was calling me her slave.

'I'm sorry, master,' I whimpered. '*Mailesh*.' I was terrified she'd beat me again.

'You think it's as easy as that, do you?' she demanded, sarcastically. ''*Mailesh, mailesh*,' and then everything's OK? You think I should just forget it, do you? Well, I don't think so.'

I didn't know what to say, so I stared silently at the floor. I could feel a big bump coming up on my forehead where she'd beaten me with the shoe. 'You're not to go back outside,' she snapped. 'I have some clothes in here you can wash. And don't you ever let me find you talking to that man again.'

Then Rahab leaned out of the kitchen

window. '*Janiney! Janiney!* When you finish your work, come over here. I have something I need to discuss with you.'

After an hour or so, the gardener came and knocked at the door. Hanin went to open it. 'Mamma! Mamma!' she called. 'The *janiney*'s at the door.'

They went and sat on one of the benches in the front yard. I crept across to the kitchen window, where I could overhear what they were saying. '*Janiney*,' said Rahab. 'I'm going on holiday and I've asked a man to come here and look after the house. So, I won't be needing you again. How much money do I owe you?'

'Oh,' he said, surprised. 'You're going away very suddenly.'

'No. Not really. I just forgot to tell you, that's all.'

Rahab gave the gardener his money. As I watched him disappear up the path, I started to cry. He was the only person who had shown me the slightest bit of kindness in this house and now he was going. I couldn't hold back the tears, so I shut myself in my toilet and let myself cry properly. A little later, Rahab's husband Mustafa came home from work. He walked into the lounge with a satisfied look on his face.

'Aha! Today the *janiney* came, eh?' he announced generally. 'He's cut the trees in the orchard and mown the grass too. Good worker, that *janiney*.'

'Shut up about the bloody *janiney*!' snapped Rahab.

'What's the matter?' asked Mustafa nervously.

'I've had it up to here with the *janiney* and this *yebit*. They want to drive me crazy!'

'Come on, honey,' said Mustafa, soothingly. 'What's wrong? Who's upset you, eh?'

'I've had a nightmare day,' said Rahab. 'And I'm dying of hunger. I'll explain it all over dinner.'

I was left in the lounge doing the ironing while Rahab and Mustafa went to eat in the kitchen. Being a slave, nothing was ever explained to me. But as no one seemed to notice I was there most of the time, I could glean some information by eavesdropping on other people's conversations. As time went on, I found myself doing it on almost a daily basis: I became an expert in eavesdropping. This time, I listened in on what they were saying in the kitchen.

'Today, the *yebit* and the *janiney* were having a very nice conversation,' said Rahab.

'What about?'

'The *janiney* asked her to visit his house to play with his daughter!' said Rahab, with a snort.

'Really?'

'Yes. And then she didn't want to tell me about it. So I had to beat it out of her.'

'Well done,' replied Mustafa. 'I hope you put the *janiney* in his place, too?'

By now, I knew what Rahab's husband was like. It was clear who wore the trousers in that household. I thought to myself: 'He's just like a sheep. She is the master. A man would never allow this to happen back home in the Nuba Mountains.' Mustafa would never beat me or scold me himself. And secretly, I think he didn't

178

like Rahab doing it. But he would never have said so. He just tried to act as if I wasn't there.

'Hah!' Rahab continued. 'I kept the *janiney* in his place all right. I paid him his money and sent him packing.'

'You sacked the *janiney*? Well . . . Well done,' said Mustafa. 'It sounds like he'd have caused trouble if he'd stayed, eh?'

★ ★ ★

As the weeks passed, the incident with the *janiney* seemed to be forgotten. For the time being, I had given up any hope of escape. I had to concentrate on survival. Rahab seemed to be happy with me as long as I worked hard, did what I was told and kept a low profile. So, that's what I tried to do. I tried to be invisible. Then, one day, Rahab asked me to help her cut up some onions. They were for a stew that Rahab was cooking for dinner. For the first time ever, she was actually allowing me to touch their food. She must have decided that they wouldn't catch diseases off me after all. The next day, Rahab told me to husk some beans that she was preparing for Dahir, the second most important Muslim festival after Ramadan. We were sitting in the kitchen, when there was a ring at the doorbell. Rahab made the four visitors tea and took them into the lounge.

'So, you've found yourself a slave,' I heard one of the women say, in a hushed voice. 'We'd love to see her. Where is she? What's she like?'

'She's in the kitchen,' said Rahab, proudly. 'Come and see.'

Rahab and her three female guests appeared in the kitchen doorway. I was sitting at my small table, husking beans. I glanced up briefly to see a row of painted Arab faces staring at me, as if I was an animal or something. Then they cast admiring glances around the kitchen.

'Ooooh. Your kitchen is so clean,' one of them said. 'It's gleaming like new.'

'Yes,' said Rahab. 'I've shown her how to do everything, apart from the cooking. Every day, she cleans the house, does the washing up and washes our clothes too.'

'Hmmm . . . That's wonderful. And you don't need to pay her anything? Anytime you need her, she's here? Is that how it works? She never has days off or anything?'

'No,' said Rahab. 'No days off, no holiday, no wages. She's always here. She belongs to me.'

16

Blood Rites

After I had lived in Rahab's house about six months, I had a horrible shock. One morning I went to shower and was shocked to find that my knickers were stained with blood. I had no idea where it had come from. I didn't feel any pain down there and I couldn't have cut myself. I was worried, but I knew that I had to start work. So I put on my other clean pair of knickers and hoped that that was the end of it.

About an hour later, I started to feel pains in my tummy. I ran to the bathroom to discover that I was still bleeding. I was really worried now. What was wrong with me? I looked around the bathroom, but I couldn't find anything to stop the bleeding. I went outside and got a small stone from under the guava tree. Back in the bathroom, I tried to use it to stop the bleeding, but it was too painful. All I could do was wash my knickers out again and go back to work.

If I'd been back in my village, I would simply have shown my knickers to my mother. 'Look, Umi,' I'd have said. 'What's happening? Is there something wrong with my circumcision?' And then my mother would have sat me down and explained everything to me.

A little later, I was at the sink doing the

washing up, when Rahab came in and let out a shriek. '*Yebit!*' she cried. 'Yuk! *Yebit*, what's this?'

'What's what, master Rahab?' I said, nearly jumping out of my skin. I was terrified that I had done something wrong.

'Stop washing up,' she ordered me sternly. '*Yebit*, are you having your period?'

'My period?' I asked. 'What's my period?'

'Look at your dress. Look! There. What's all that mess?'

I looked where she was pointing and there was a big wet patch at the back of my dress. I felt so ashamed — like some animal that had gone and soiled itself in the kitchen.

'You don't know what a period is?' she demanded incredulously. 'You've never had this blood before?'

'No,' I said, in a shaky voice. 'I must have cut myself or something.'

'No. You haven't cut yourself,' she sighed. 'Wait here a minute. Don't you move and don't sit down anywhere.'

Rahab disappeared into the family bathroom and came back with some cotton wool. 'Put this inside your knickers to soak up the blood,' she said. 'And change your clothes! The ones you have on are filthy.'

'But I don't have any more,' I whispered, close to tears.

'Oh. I see. Well wait here then.' She sighed, disappearing into her bedroom. This time she came back with two pairs of her own knickers. I stood under the shower for a long time, trying to feel clean again after the shock and the humiliation of it all. I still didn't know what was wrong with me, but at least I now had something to stop the bleeding. I balled up a piece of cotton wool, and pushed it up inside me. 'There,' I said to myself, 'that should at least stop the blood.' I changed my clothes and went back into the kitchen.

'You've had a shower?' she asked me. 'Did you clean yourself properly?'

I nodded.

'Good,' she said. She handed me a little white deodorant stick that I'd now got used to using. 'Here, put this on. And then finish the washing up.'

After that, Rahab told me to slice some onions, as we were still preparing things for Dahir. After half an hour she came back into the kitchen to check on me. I'd just put the knife down and I was wiping my eyes with the back of my hands, to try to stop the onion tears.

'Look, *yebit*,' she said, 'why don't you take the onions and the knife and chopping board and go and sit in the front yard. There's a nice breeze out there, it'll be easier for you.' But as I stood up, she stared in horror at my back again.

'What on earth's going on, *yebit*?' she asked, in an angry voice. 'You're all dirty again! What did you do with the cotton wool I gave you? Eat it? How have you managed to get blood all over yourself again? Go back to the bathroom and change again.'

The first time around, Rahab had been almost kind to me; now she was shouting, and she was

183

really angry — as if she thought that I was doing this deliberately.

'*Mailesh*, master Rahab,' I whispered. 'I'm sorry.' I put the knife down and went to leave the kitchen.

'Hold on, *yebit*,' she said. 'How much cotton wool did you use? Go and find it and show me.'

I fetched the cotton wool and pulled off a little tiny ball like the one I'd used. Then I took it into the kitchen to show Rahab.

'Where's the cotton wool, *yebit*?' she demanded. 'I told you to bring it here.'

'I did, master Rahab,' I said, holding out the little white ball in my palm for her.

Rahab looked at my hand and snorted. 'You think that you're a bottle, do you? And that you can put a cork in it to stop the blood?'

She stood there laughing at me while I looked at the floor. 'But I don't know what to do,' I mumbled, close to tears.

Rahab laughed for such a long time that tears started running down her cheeks. After a while, I started to think that maybe there was a funny side to it too, really, so I laughed a little with her. It was a strange feeling. After six months of hell in her house, suddenly here we were laughing together.

'Look, you take the cotton wool, pull off a big piece like this, fold it three times and make yourself a pad,' she said. 'It has to be big enough. You put it in your knickers and change it three times each day. All right?'

I nodded at her.

'Now, go back to your bathroom and when

you've finished, wash your hands very well. I want you to come back and finish the onions.'

The next day, there was less blood and less pain in my tummy, so I thought I must be getting better. Three days later, it had stopped completely. At first, I thought the cotton wool must have magical healing properties. But a month later, I was horrified to find my period back again. Then, some time later, I overheard Rahab moaning on to her husband.

'Mustafa, I have my period today and the pain's worse than normal. Can you go to the shop and get me some cotton wool and some painkillers? I'm going to stay in bed today and try to sleep it off.'

So now I knew that it wasn't just me who had periods. Rahab had them too. She also used cotton wool, and she even took pills for the pain. I felt much better when I realised that Rahab went through this every month too. It seemed like it was normal and that I wasn't dying of a terrible illness.

17

Death Threats

That first year, I came to expect a beating from Rahab more or less every week. Often, she would beat me for no reason at all. I wouldn't know what I was even supposed to have done wrong. Sometimes she would just slap me once around the face; at other times she would use whatever came to hand. Often, she'd beat me around the head with her wooden-soled shoes. Or she might pick up the broom and hit me with that. Or she'd take a belt and whip me with it.

One day, Rahab ordered me to go and hose down the patio at the front of the house. It was early evening at the start of the hot season. At this time of year, the family and their guests would sit outside until late in the evening. I went out to the front of the house and turned on the tap. Then I followed the hosepipe into the garden and found the end of it spurting water in a big arc, where it had been left hanging in a grapefruit tree. The water sparkled in the evening sunlight. For a moment it reminded me of when the rains came in the Nuba Mountains and all the children would run out and shout and dance, singing the rain song.

Before I knew what I was doing, I had dived under the water and I was leaping about singing,

186

'*Are kukure, Are kondu dukre*' — 'The rain is coming, Too much rain!' For a few blissful moments, I was a thousand miles away from that terrible house, back in my village. I was with my friends singing the rain song and we were happy because we knew there would be a good harvest that year. I was enveloped in the love and kindness of my family again. But Rahab must have heard me singing. Suddenly, the water was turned off. I stopped dancing, the smile frozen on my face. There was a moment's deathly silence. Then Rahab stepped out from behind a tree.

'Why don't you continue?' she said, sarcastically. 'You looked like you were having such a nice time.'

I stood there in silence, my shoulders drooping. I realised that I was dripping wet and I was dreading what was coming next.

'Come here!' she barked at me. 'And give me that hosepipe. And what's that stupid song you were singing?'

I unhooked the hosepipe from the tree and squelched over to her, staring at the ground. 'D'you know what time it is?' she snapped. 'The guests are coming very soon. Give me that hosepipe.' I reached out to give it to her, thinking that maybe she was going to wash the patio down herself. But she snatched it from me and grabbed my arm. And then she started to beat me across the back and shoulders with the hosepipe. She struck me again and again and again and I was crying and pleading for her to stop.

187

'Shut up!' she screamed. 'Shut up! Shut up! Shut up!'

She carried on beating me, harder than ever. I could hear the rubber pipe hissing down through the air. My thin, wet dress was no protection at all. I tried to choke back the screams and the tears, because the more I cried, the more crazed she seemed to become. Then she hit me one last time, extra hard, across the shoulders. As she let go of my arm I collapsed to the ground. I lay there at her feet, trying not to cry. But I could feel myself heaving noiselessly into the damp grass.

'Stop your whimpering!' she sneered. 'You don't know how to behave unless you're whipped. If you ever do something like this again, I'll get a real whip and then I'll beat you just like a donkey. You hear me? You're no better than a donkey, anyway.'

I lay on the ground in agony, curled up in a ball, praying that she would go away.

'Now, go and clean the patio like I told you to,' she ordered. 'I'm coming to check in ten minutes. If it's not finished then, I'll kill you.'

Rahab turned on her heel and marched off. I stumbled to my feet, grabbed the hosepipe and rushed off to wash down the patio. At that time of year, during the hot season, the Harmattan blew every day — a hot, dry wind off the Sahara desert. It carried with it huge clouds of dust that settled over everything. There was a thick film all over the patio. Trembling so much that I could hardly hold the hosepipe, I worked feverishly. I really believed Rahab would come and kill me if

I didn't finish in time.

Later, when the guests were sitting chatting outside, I found a moment to go into the bathroom. I pulled up my damp dress and took a look in the mirror. There were raw red cuts scored across my back and shoulders where she had beaten me. That night, I lay in my shed and I couldn't sleep. I had to lie on my side all night long, because of the pain. I had got used to crying on my own by now. Somehow, it was a comfort to me.

I thought back over what had happened. For a few moments in the garden, I had felt so gloriously happy. I thought about my home, and how I danced and sang with all the other children when the rains came, and my mother and father watching me smiling from the hut doorway. Later, I would come in dripping wet and my father would tease me and my mother would find me a warm place by the fire. How I longed for home. I was more determined than ever now to escape. If I didn't, Rahab was surely going to kill me. I made a promise to myself that night: whatever it takes, I will escape and — somehow — I will return to the Nuba Mountains. I will go home.

Why did these Arabs hate us so much? I remembered my first days at school, when the Arab teachers would beat us if we tried to speak Nuba. Nothing seemed to enrage them more than when we spoke our own language. I suppose it was because they couldn't understand it, and so it threatened them. Now, it was the one part of me that Rahab couldn't control. She could shout orders at me all day long in Arabic. She could curse me in Arabic when she beat me. But she couldn't take my Nuba language away from me. It was like the one little corner of my soul that she couldn't quite kill.

One day, two of Rahab's friends came to visit with their husbands and their children. Rahab made the tea, while I put the best bone china cups on a silver tray. She wouldn't let me touch the biscuits yet, as she still feared I was unclean, so she arranged these herself on a fancy plate. 'When the tea's ready, bring the tray into the lounge, *yebit*,' she commanded.

Five minutes later, I carried the tray laden with the tea things into the lounge. But the children had been playing with a skipping rope, with one end tied around a table leg. As I walked in, one of the boys deliberately tripped me up. I felt myself falling in slow motion. I tried to save the tray of tea things, by taking the full impact of the fall on my front. But of course everything went flying — cups, sugar pot, the plate of biscuits and the milk jug. And the pot of scalding hot tea went all over me. For a split second, I just lay where I'd fallen. After the crash of the tea things, there was now a deathly silence. I was trembling, as I knew what was coming.

'Hahaha!' said one of the boys, pointing at me. 'Look! She's smashed everything.'

'Don't go any nearer!' Rahab said to them. 'Put your shoes on in case you tread on the broken glass.'

Then she turned on me. 'Are you blind, *yebit*!' she screamed. 'Are you blind!' She

190

grabbed the skipping rope and began beating me. The first few blows hit me on the head, so I threw up my hands to protect my face.

'*Mailesh, mailesh*' — 'Sorry, sorry' — I moaned.

Rahab stopped for a moment to catch her breath. But then I heard one of the female guests goading her on. 'Yes. Go on. Beat her! Beat her!' she cried. 'It's the only way! Then she'll remember not to do it again, won't she?' I hunched myself into a ball as Rahab redoubled her efforts, moving from my shoulders to my back. As she whipped me her female guests applauded and I could hear the men laughing, too.

'Stop your crying!' Rahab yelled at me, breathlessly. 'Shut up! Shut up! I don't even want to hear you breathing.'

I was terrified that she was really going to kill me with that rope. When she did finally stop beating me, one of the guests leant over, smiling at me. 'So, are you blind?' he asked.

I thought he might be trying to be kind. 'No,' I sobbed, 'I'm not blind.'

He threw his head back and burst into laughter. 'She's not blind,' he guffawed, 'so maybe she's just stupid!' All the others started laughing too.

'I didn't see the rope,' I sobbed. 'I tripped. I didn't mean to.'

'Shut up, *yebit*,' hissed Rahab. 'Shut up. And clean up all this mess you've made.'

The cups were lying broken on the floor — their precious bone china, which she only ever brought out for guests. And there was sugar and broken biscuits all over the carpet. Most of the tea had gone over me, scalding me. And the milk had spilled on the carpet too.

'Quickly! Get some soapy water,' snapped Rahab. 'I don't want the smell of rancid milk on my best carpets.'

I fetched the dustpan and brush, but I had to pick up the biggest pieces of broken china by hand and, as I fumbled around on the carpet, a thin splinter sliced deep into my little finger. I knew that I mustn't start bleeding onto the carpet, so I hurried into the kitchen, emptied the dustpan and started to fill a bowl with soapy water. At the same time, I washed my cut finger under the cold tap. Just then, Rahab came into the kitchen.

'What're you doing now?' she shouted. 'Don't wash your blood off into our sink! This is where we prepare our food! You're disgusting. Go and clean it off in your bathroom. And you'd better be quick. I don't want that milk on the carpet starting to smell.'

I rushed off to my toilet, glad to have a few moments alone. First, I washed my finger under the tap. Then I ripped off a long strip of cotton wool to make a bandage for my finger. As I was doing this, I had a flashback to a day in the Nuba Mountains that now seemed like a lifetime ago. I must have been about nine years old and I'd been getting ready to go to bed. 'Mende,' my mother had said. 'Do you want a drink of hot milk?'

'I'd love some, *Umi*,' I replied. But while my

mother was making it, I dropped off to sleep.

'Come on, Mende, the milk's ready,' my mother said, waking me up. Seeing how sleepy I was, she carried me over to the fire and sat me on a stool, picked up the steaming gourd full of milk, and put it to my lips.

'Come on, sleepy head,' she said, smiling at me, 'drink the milk that I made for you.' Then she handed me the gourd. The milk was delicious. When I'd drunk as much as I could, I went to put the gourd down. But it slipped and the hot milk went all over my legs. I yelled out in surprise and my mother and father both jumped up.

'Did it scald you, Mende?' my mother asked anxiously. 'Where? On your leg?'

My father was also worried. 'Was it hot?' he asked me. 'Did it hurt you?'

'No, *Ba*. It wasn't really that hot. I'm fine, *Umi*,' I said. My father picked me up and cuddled me until I went back to sleep.

I glanced up from my cut finger and caught sight of my face in the toilet mirror. I could see the tracks of my tears glistening in the light of the bare bulb. What a different life I now led. I'd just spilled scalding tea all over myself and no one had cared. I'd cut my finger and no one had helped me. Instead, I had been beaten and cursed and abused. And they had all cheered at my pain and laughed at my fear and my embarrassment. I felt like I just wanted to die. But I went back into the kitchen, took the bowl of hot, soapy water and started to wash down the carpet.

18

Faith, Hope and Identity

Sometimes, Rahab would catch me daydreaming. I might be hiding in the bushes, staring at the gate leading out onto the street. She would watch me for a long time before I finally noticed her. Then she'd start accusing me.

'So, what're you thinking about, *yebit*? Oh, don't tell me, you're thinking about escaping. Well, let me tell you what will happen to you if you try to escape. I'll get Abdul Azzim to take the raiders to find and kill all your family. Once you've been brought back here, I'll shave your head and I'll circumcise you. Everyone knows that all the Nuba are *khulluf* — that they're unclean. And that they're infidels.'

There was no point reminding Rahab that I was already circumcised and that I was a Muslim. Rahab and Mustafa believed they were very good Muslims. Every Muslim has a prayer mat, a *Muslaiyah*. Rahab and Mustafa had the most beautiful *Muslaiyahs* — soft and silky and decorated with intricate Islamic patterns. Rahab told me proudly that their *Muslaiyahs* came all the way from Saudi Arabia, the most holy country in Islam. At least once in their life, every Muslim is supposed to make a pilgrimage to Mecca, in Saudi Arabia, the birthplace of the

194

Prophet Mohammed. I knew that Rahab and Mustafa were planning to go one day soon. Before each of their five daily prayers, they would go through ritual cleansing by washing their arms, face and feet. Then they would face towards the east, and recite their prayers quietly and devoutly.

From the very first day I spent in Rahab's house, I knew that I needed to continue my daily prayers, just like I did at home. There was nothing to use as a *Muslaiyah* in my room, so I used the sheet off my bed. It was the best I could do. Whenever I managed to find time I would disappear into my shed and pray. My prayers were a source of great strength to me. During the first weeks in her house I managed to pray without Rahab realising. She would abuse me for disappearing, but I never told her what I was up to. One afternoon, I went to pray without checking where Rahab was. I knelt down and held my hands out, palm upwards. I asked Allah to help me escape and take me back to my family. Suddenly, I heard Rahab calling: '*Yebit*, where are you?' I tried to finish my prayers quickly, but the door burst open and Hanin came running into my shed. When she caught sight of me, she turned and shouted, 'Mamma! Mamma! She's in here and she's praying!'

Then Rahab appeared in the doorway. 'Hmmm . . . ' she said, with a scornful expression on her face. 'So — now you're trying to copy us, are you? Do you really think prayers are for people like you? Black people like you? Do you?'

I hung my head in silence. But deep in my mind I said to her: 'D'you think I started to pray today? I've been doing this ever since I was born. You can take me away from my mother and father and my home, but you cannot take me away from my faith. You'll have to kill me first.'

After that, Rahab was always trying to stop me. 'You're not going off to pray, are you?' she would demand. 'You don't have time for prayers. And anyway, what do you think you're doing? Don't you know? Islam isn't for black people like you.'

Each time that I defied her by saying my prayers, I felt the spirit of resistance growing in my heart. I believed that Allah was helping me by giving me the strength to stand up to this cruel woman. I am a Muslim and she is a Muslim, I used to think to myself. We are both of the same God. So why does she try to stop me? But the more I thought about it, the more I realised that all my oppressors had been Muslims. The raiders had all shouted '*Allahu Akhbar*' when they had attacked our village. The slave trader Abdul Azzim had also been a Muslim. And now Rahab and her family. All these people believed themselves to be good Muslims. Yet they had killed and raped and tortured and enslaved the Nuba people from my tribe, who were all Muslims too.

I remembered my Koran lessons from school. I remembered that it said that all Muslims must respect each other. It said that there is no difference between white people and black people — that all people are equal. It said that

196

the only differences between people lie in how they act: whether they are good and devout, and whether they respect God. One day, I managed to sneak an old sugar sack out into my shed, and this became my *Muslaiyah*. It was brown hessian and it had SUGAR written on it in English. Every day I asked God to help me be free and take me back to my family. And sometimes, I prayed for revenge. 'Please Allah, let me escape. Please Allah, let me go home. Please Allah, let me find my family. Please Allah, make Rahab die. But please God, first make her suffer like she's made me suffer.'

One morning, after I had been in the house about a year, I was tidying up the girls' room. As usual, their things were strewn all around the floor. I was becoming more and more attached to the girls, despite their untidy ways. They especially loved me telling them stories. Their favourite was a story that I remembered from my own school days about the tiger who had to tell the truth. My Arabic teacher Fatimah had told it to us. The first time I told it to the girls they were scared, because it was about a fierce tiger. But when I'd finished the story, Hanin came and gave me a big hug. 'That's a great story, Mende,' she said. 'The tiger's nice really, isn't he? Because we all should tell the truth, shouldn't we?'

As I picked up Hanin's things off the bedroom floor, I stopped and flicked through one of her schoolbooks. It brought back all the memories of my earliest days at school. I remembered how I had been top of the class, along with my best friend Kehko. I had studied so hard, because I dreamed of becoming a doctor. Now, the closest I could get to school was looking at the books that Rahab's six-year-old daughter had left lying around her room. These people had stolen my childhood and my dreams.

I knew that I had to be careful. I mustn't let my tears stain the books. If I did, Hanin would tell Rahab. As I continued tidying, I spotted a tiny little teddy bear under the bed. To me, it looked just like my cat Uran. Without thinking, I scooped it up and hid it under my skirt. Every night after that, I would cuddle up to this stuffed toy and talk to it as if it were Uran. Silly, really, because cats can't talk. But in my mind Uran could, and she became my only friend.

'D'you remember, Uran, when you were pregnant that first time?' I'd whisper to her, in the dark. 'And I thought you'd eaten too many mice. But really you were about to have kittens.'

'Yes, I remember, Mende,' Uran would answer. 'How could I forget? It's not so easy carrying four kittens around in your tummy.'

'And then when you had the babies, you were so proud. And you let me pick them up and cuddle them.'

'They're kittens, Mende, not babies. Yes, I'd spent all night licking them clean, just so you could see how beautiful they were when you woke up in the morning.'

If I could have risked it, I would have taken another of the children's teddies to be my father and one to be my mother too. Soon, I'd have had the whole of our family in there with me. I was living increasingly in my memories and my daydreams. Life at Rahab's was too harsh to contemplate. I had retreated into some happier, alternative reality.

★ ★ ★

As time went on, I developed a set of rules to live by. If I stuck to them, I was less likely to get beaten. Firstly, if Rahab told me to do something, I had to make sure I'd understood exactly what she wanted. I would listen very carefully and then repeat it back to her. Secondly, when I was told to do something, I had to do it as quickly as I could. I wouldn't stop to talk or play with the children or do anything that would delay me. Thirdly, I had to try to minimise any chance of having an accident. It didn't matter whether it was my fault or not, I would always get a beating. Fourthly, whatever she might say to me, I must never answer her back.

Finally, I learned to hide anything that might remind her of my Nuba identity. I never spoke my Nuba language. I never sang any Nuba songs. And I never, ever mentioned my past life. After the raid, I managed to keep one set of my beads, which I wore around my neck. It was a single string of beautiful white beads, each of which was tipped with black on either end. I had been given them by my mother and I never took them off. But one day, in the kitchen, Rahab caught sight of them under my dress.

'What are those, *yebit*?' she asked. 'Beads?

199

They're only worn by savages. Get them off.'

'I'll take them off,' I said, 'but please let me keep them.'

Just then, Rahab took a step towards me, grabbed the beads and tried to yank them off. But she couldn't break the string. Then she seized one of the kitchen knives and sliced through it. 'Look,' she sneered, holding them out, 'look how dirty they are.' Then she held the beads up, sniffed and screwed up her face. 'They stink,' she said. 'They stink like black people. Like savages.' With that she turned to the waste bin.

'Please don't throw them away,' I pleaded with her. 'Please. Just let me keep them. Please.'

'No, *yebit*, you can't keep them.' But just as she was about to throw them away, she changed her mind. She took a plastic bag out of a drawer, threw the beads inside and put them in her pocket. Maybe she knew that I would try to rescue them if she put them in the rubbish bin. All that week I kept checking the bin, but I never found them. The last, tangible reminder of my family had been stolen from me.

As time went by, I started getting closer to Rahab's children. I was doing all the cooking and feeding them by now and they were spending more time with me than with their mother. If I wasn't there, they would cry for me. If they were in their room playing, they would call, 'Come on, Mende, come and play! Come and read to us.' At first, I feared that Rahab might resent this closeness. When I'd first arrived in her house, she'd told them that I was 'dirty' and 'diseased'. But she soon realised that I could be both a domestic slave and a nursery maid to her children. It meant she could spend even more time out shopping, lazing around at home watching TV, or entertaining her friends. As the children started to show me real affection, I reciprocated, and I gradually started to feel a little bit more human again.

I had lived there for about two years without ever leaving the house when, one morning, Rahab casually told me that she was taking me to the park. 'Change out of your dirty clothes,' she said. Rahab was pregnant with her third child, and I think she needed me to help her as she was always tired. When I'd finished changing, I found Rahab combing the children's hair. They were wearing pretty party frocks and shiny shoes. We went out to the car. 'Open the gate, *yebit*,' Rahab told me.

As she drove past me, she told me to shut the gate after them and get into the back of the car next to Usra. We drove out into a small street lined on either side by fine houses. I was glued to the window, fascinated to see what lay outside the four walls of the house that had been my prison for the last two years. People were walking around freely on the streets. The sun was shining and they looked happy. I envied them their freedom, but at least I was finally out of the house.

We drove for ten minutes or so and then came to a huge expanse of water. I had never seen anything like it before: I couldn't see from one side to the other. To my horror, the car turned off the main road and headed straight towards the water. Suddenly, we were driving high above it, up into the sky. I thought that at any moment the car must come crashing down into the river. I stared out of the window with a morbid fascination at the water down below us. But when I looked around at the others, they all appeared completely unconcerned.

Then I caught sight of these things plunging in and out of the water and making big splashes as they did so. From that distance, they looked to me like some sort of giant water animals. Of course, this was the River Nile and they were boats — but I didn't know that at the time. I thought to myself, 'Here in Khartoum, the water is as big as the sky! And the frogs that live in it are giant monsters. If we do fall in, they're bound to eat us.' Finally, we made it across the river safely. Half an hour or so later we arrived in the park, where one of Rahab's friends was waiting for us.

'*Yebit*, take the children off to play,' she told me. 'But remember, I'll be keeping an eye on you.'

Rahab and her friend settled down in the shade of a tree, while I went off with the children to play hide and seek. I kicked off my sandals and walked through the grass, amongst the trees. It reminded me of walking in the forests in the Nuba Mountains. Of course, there were no big hills here, and the trees were smaller, but it reminded me so much of home that I felt happier than I had done for a very long time. After this, we started going to the park every month. I looked forward to these family outings with all my heart. But of course, I was kidding myself if I thought I was really becoming accepted as part of their family. I was still their slave.

During the wet season, swarms of mosquitoes invaded the house. I was ordered to spray mosquito killer in the bedrooms every night, but out in my shed, I had nothing to protect myself at all. One night, I woke up in the early hours and started vomiting. Soon, I was shivering uncontrollably and I felt freezing cold. I began drifting in and out of consciousness and I was having terrible nightmares. I relived the raid on our village and my poor father trying to save me — all in delirious, psychedelic detail. I dreamed that Rahab was beating me to death and I couldn't escape. I dreamed that the bed was rolling over and over with me trapped in it. Eventually, I tried to get up but I was far too weak. When Rahab came to wake me in the morning, even she could see that something was badly wrong.

'*Yebit*, what's the matter?'

'I'm sick,' I whispered. 'I have a fever and vomiting.'

'You're vomiting? Is it bitter?'

'Yes. It's bitter and it's yellow.'

'Ohhh . . . You've just got malaria, that's all. I'll bring you some pills.'

Rahab came back five minutes later. 'Here, take these,' she said. 'You can sleep for an hour and then you'll feel better and you can start work.'

I took the pills, but they were very, very bitter and as soon as I swallowed them I vomited them up again. I piled my sheet and my blanket and my mattress all on top of me, as I was so cold. Half an hour later, I was burning hot. The fever raged on and on like this, and I stayed in my shed for three days. Each day, Rahab would ask me if I was better and ready to start work. She would call me to come in to the kitchen, saying there was food for me on my table.

'Look. There's no point in taking you to a doctor,' Rahab said, when I was too ill to get up on the second day. 'He'll only give you the same medicine as I'm giving you.'

The children came in my room often. 'Come and play with us, Mende,' they said, tugging at my hair.

'I can't. I'm sick,' I'd say. 'But please, bring me some water.'

As I lay in my shed, I thought back to the time when I was sick at home in my village. My mother had warmed oil over the fire to make an infusion with tea and aromatic spices. She had rubbed the mixture all over my body. She had made me some soup out of special forest seeds and flowers. It was thin and easy to drink, but it was also very nutritious. 'You must eat, otherwise you won't get better,' she'd told me. Although there was no doctor in our village, my mother did everything she could to make me well.

By contrast, Rahab did almost nothing for me this first time that I had malaria — and I now know malaria is a killer disease. Later, I would have a second, even more serious bout of malaria. I also started having splitting headaches as a result of Rahab beating me around the head. But she never once took me to a doctor, or showed any real concern for my well-being. Yet if I thought that her treatment of me couldn't get any worse, I was very wrong.

19

Murderous Intent

One day, Rahab and Mustafa were having yet another dinner party. A dozen or so families were coming. After cleaning the whole house, I spent the day in the kitchen with Rahab. We cooked beef and chicken curry with rice and lots of salads. I also made fresh juice by squeezing oranges, grapefruits and guavas. At around seven, a stream of people started arriving. First, the guests had drinks out on the patio. Dinner was to be served later in the formal dining room. Once they had sat down to eat, I stayed in the kitchen to clean up the mess, but I kept getting interrupted by the guests' children.

'Give me more juice! I want another coke! Give me some more crisps!' they demanded.

Soon there were at least a dozen children climbing all over the furniture and trying to grab things off the kitchen surfaces. I couldn't clean up and control them all at the same time. Their parents seemed to make no effort to control them at all. 'It's great,' I heard one of them say, 'Rahab's house is so large, there's lots of room for the children to play.' As far as they were concerned, it meant they could have a nice peaceful evening without their children pestering them.

206

By the time I'd started to serve tea to the guests, the kitchen had become the focus of the children's activities. They were climbing all over the chairs, opening cupboards and pulling out their contents. It was dangerous and I wanted to make them stop. But I knew that I wasn't allowed to discipline the children. Once, when I had found Hanin jumping off her bed, I had told her off. Rahab had overheard me and came storming into the room. 'Don't you dare scold my children,' she'd yelled at me. 'If you see Hanin doing something naughty, you come and tell me.' So I just took Hanin to one side and spoke to her quietly.

'Please, Hanin, calm down,' I said. 'Take the children into the lounge to play.'

'I'm not going! I'm not going!' she yelled at me. 'I want my cup.'

'I'll get your cup for you.'

'No! I want to get it myself.'

'But if you all keep climbing over the chairs and tables you'll fall and hurt yourself,' I reasoned with her.

'I won't fall over. I won't.'

There was nothing more I could do, so I turned back to the sink. Suddenly there was a crash and a scream. I spun around, only to see that Rahab's youngest, Usra, had fallen off the table and hit her head on the floor. She'd been following Hanin's lead, reaching for her cup. I ran to pick her up and I could see that she had cut her lip. It wasn't serious, but there was a lot of blood and Usra was wailing loudly. The children gathered round as I held her and tried to comfort her.

'What's happened! What's happened?' Rahab asked, rushing in from the patio. Then she saw Usra. 'What's happened to my baby?' she cried, taking Usra in her arms.

'She was climbing on the table . . . ' I began, but Rahab interrupted.

'Why didn't you tell her to stop?'

'I tried to. But she wouldn't listen,' I said. 'I was busy washing-up . . . ' But before I could finish my sentence, Rahab had exploded into a wild fury. She started screaming at me, punctuating each sentence with a hard shove in my chest.

'You think that's important, *yebit*! The bloody washing up! You think that's more important than my little baby? Are you completely stupid? You should have been looking after them, not doing the bloody dishes.'

I had never seen Rahab so angry. I tried to back away, but I was cornered. And then she punched me so hard that I fell backwards and crashed into my little table in the corner. The table was made of metal. As I keeled over, one of the sharp edges ripped deep into my leg. I felt a stabbing, searing pain. And then I was lying on the floor, staring down in shock. My right leg had been sliced open from below the knee right up to my inner thigh. For a split second, I saw two flaps of pale flesh hanging down, and then the blood began spurting out of the wound.

I could hear myself screaming out in shock and in pain. I felt Rahab grab my arm and I heard her shout, 'Mende! Mende! Oh my God!

Mende! Speak to me.' But already, I felt like I was falling down a long dark tunnel. The last thing I remember was the look of terror on Rahab's face as she turned to her friends and said, 'Oh my God. If she dies, I'm in big trouble.'

I must have been unconscious for some time. When I finally came to, it felt like I was in a dream. My eyes flickered open and I found myself lying in a bed in a strange room. I saw Rahab pacing up and down, up and down, and then I fell back into unconsciousness. A little later I came around again. I looked about me groggily. I saw Rahab, Mustafa and one of the female guests standing by my bed, looking anxious. A nurse sat next to me. I saw her turn to them. 'She's coming round,' she said. 'She's going to be OK.'

Rahab came rushing over and grabbed my arm. 'Mende? Mende? Oh, *Alhamdallilah* — praise be to God,' I heard her say. I smiled weakly at her. Everything was still very fuzzy. I was trying to remember what had happened. I remembered falling and hurting myself. But I couldn't understand how I'd ended up in a bed in what looked like a hospital. It was all very confusing. And I was so used to Rahab being cruel to me, never showing a shred of remorse or concern, why did she now seem so happy that I was alive? I was hurt and she seemed concerned for me. Somehow in my groggy mind, just for a few moments, Rahab reminded me of my mother.

My mind drifted back to a time in the Nuba Mountains when I was still very young. I had gone to fetch firewood from the forest with my best friend Kehko and two other girls. We were walking back to the village with big bundles of dry branches balanced on our heads. But as we set off through the forest, I felt a searing pain in my foot. I screamed and fell and the bundle of wood went tumbling down on top of me.

My friends ran over to help. They feared I might have been bitten by a snake. So did I, as the pain was unbearable. But when we took a look, there was a big thorn sticking out of the top of my foot. It had gone right through, but there was hardly any blood as it was jammed so tight into the wound. With each arm around a shoulder of my friends, I hopped along the path until we reached the river. There was no way I could cross, so Kehko stayed with me while the other two rushed on ahead to get help.

I remembered lying on the riverbank as dusk began to fall and the night sounds of animals started up in the forest behind us. I was very glad that Kehko was with me. I was so relieved when I caught sight of my father hurrying along the path, leading my mother on the donkey. They decided to try to remove the thorn back in the village. As my father readied a makeshift stretcher, my mother cradled my head in her lap. I remembered how concerned she looked. She stroked my hair and kissed me and kept repeating softly: 'Mende, my little girl, you're going to be all right. Don't worry. Don't worry. I'm here.'

Was Rahab now showing me the sort of love that my mother had done, I wondered? I didn't have to wait long for an answer. That illusion of motherly concern didn't last. As soon as there was a moment when there were no hospital staff around, Rahab sat down next to me to have a word in my ear.

'Now listen, *yebit*,' she whispered. 'I'm warning you, if anybody asks you what happened, you tell them you were standing on a chair to reach something in the kitchen and you fell over. If they ask you who I am, you tell them that I pay you to work for me as a servant. And if they ask about your parents, you say that they live in the Nuba Mountains and that you came to Khartoum to find work. D'you understand?'

Then Rahab and the others left and I was on my own again. I was still only a child and I craved the love and affection of a family. Rahab was a poor substitute for a mother — the worst, in fact, that any little girl could wish for. But I had no one else. And somewhere, deep in my heart, I guess I still nurtured a hope that she would change — that she would love me and look after me.

In reality, Rahab didn't want it to be known publicly that she had a slave, and if I had died she would have been guilty of my murder. I stayed in the hospital for three days, on a drip, being looked after by a lovely nurse. She was from South Sudan and her name was Nungha. She was black like me, and she had strong Negro features. Rahab came to the hospital to visit me every day and on her third visit, she had her first run-in with Nungha.

'I want to take Mende home with me today,'

211

Rahab told Nungha. 'I can look after her there and she can take the medicines at home too.'

'Not a good idea, I'm afraid,' Nungha replied. 'She has a very deep wound. She has to stay on this drip, as she's lost too much blood. And we have to change the bandage three times a day.'

'Well, we can do all that at home,' Rahab insisted.

'I'm sure the doctor won't allow you to take her home,' replied Nungha, firmly.

I could see that Rahab was irritated — I was getting to really like Nungha. As Rahab continued to argue, Nungha was losing patience with her. 'Who is this girl, anyway?' she finally demanded of Rahab. 'Is she your daughter? She can't be. She doesn't look anything like you.'

'No. She's my servant,' Rahab snapped. 'What business is it of yours, anyway? She works in my house.'

'Oh! So that's the reason you want to take her home,' said Nungha, flying into a rage. 'Because she's your servant! How you think you can possibly give her a drip at home I don't know. If she was your daughter, would you be taking her home? I don't think so!'

'I'm only asking because I'm worried about her,' said Rahab, trying to calm Nungha down. 'I'm just worried about her and I can't sleep at night when she's not at home.'

'Well, if you want to argue, you can do so with the doctor. As far as I'm concerned, she's not leaving this hospital until the doctor decides she is well enough to go. And that's the end of it.'

Shortly after that Rahab left. But Nungha

stayed behind to have a little chat with me.

'Mende, my dear, tell me, where is your mother?' she asked, settling down on the edge of my bed.

'My mother's in the Nuba Mountains, Auntie. That's where I'm from. I came here on my own to work for that lady,' I added, remembering Rahab's instructions to me.

I had been amazed to see Nungha standing up to Rahab: a black woman like me facing down an Arab. All the black people that I'd seen since the day of the raid seemed to live in total fear of the Arabs. In fact, apart from Nungha, they had all been slaves.

'Where are you from, Auntie?' I asked her.

'I'm from the south of the country, from the Shuluk tribe. D'you know the Shuluk?'

'No, Auntie, I don't.'

'Well, we're the same as you, really. You're Nuba, we're Shuluk, and then there's Dinka and Nuer and many other black tribes in the south. See, my name even sounds like your tribe. I'm called Nungha and you're a Nuba,' she said, laughing.

When Nungha laughed, it was a big, hearty belly laugh. It was very infectious. I laughed with her. It was such a good feeling to laugh happily with someone again.

'I have a little girl of five and a boy of twelve,' she told me. 'Do you have any relatives here in Khartoum?'

'No. They're all in the Nuba Mountains.'

'No cousins at all?' she said, with a sad smile. 'Well then, I will be like a cousin to you. When do you have your day off? On Fridays?'

I remembered Rahab's warning to me. I nodded.

'OK. On Thursdays, when you finish work, come to the hospital and we'll go to my house. You can stay until Saturday morning and then I'll take you back home.'

I loved Nungha and her bravery in standing up to Rahab. I loved her warmth and the fact she was protecting me. But I had to tell her lies and I hated doing it. This was the first time that I had left Rahab's house for three years, apart from a few visits to the park. I wanted to tell Nungha the truth about everything. But I was afraid that if I did, Rahab would take me away from the hospital and kill me. I had spent three long years completely under Rahab's control. She had beaten me, abused me and killed any sense I once had of my own worth. I believed that I was her slave and that she was my master. I believed that she was in absolute control and that she held the power of life or death over me.

After her argument with Nungha, Rahab couldn't keep away from the hospital. But whenever Nungha saw Rahab arrive, she would bustle over with her starched uniform crackling and her hands on her hips and stare Rahab down. The two would lock eyes for a few seconds and the sparks would fly. Nungha always won these battles, forcing Rahab to look away. Then she would lean over me and stroke my hair.

'My lovely girl. How are you today?' she'd say. 'What would you like me to get you? Some juice? Some sweets?'

'I'd like some juice, please, Auntie,' I'd reply. I was laughing inside, as I could see that Rahab was steaming with suppressed rage.

'OK, Mende, I'll go and get you some,' Nungha would say, with a deliberate glare over her shoulder at Rahab. 'Don't worry. I'm coming back soon.'

As soon as Nungha bustled off, Rahab would move in. She would lean over me and hiss in my ear: 'Has that black woman been asking you any questions? What have you told her?'

'Nothing,' I'd say. 'She hasn't talked to me. She just gives me my medicine and looks after me.'

I didn't want to get better. I loved it in that hospital and prayed that I'd never have to leave. I would have been so happy if only I could have stayed there and never gone back to Rahab's. But Rahab had realised that there was trouble afoot. So she dreamed up a cruel trick to play on me. One morning, after I'd been at the hospital for two weeks, Nungha came and gently removed my stitches. Once she'd finished, she helped me hobble up and down the ward a few times.

'You must be tired, my lovely,' she said to me, finally. 'Come and lie with your head in my lap and have a sleep. Now we've got your stitches out,' she continued, smiling down at me, 'I think you may be able to go home soon. We'll have to see what the doctor says first. OK?'

Just then Rahab arrived. She had seen me lying with my head in Nungha's lap, talking and laughing. Once Nungha had gone, Rahab looked down at me with a sneer on her face.

'Oh . . . So you've found someone to stroke your hair and cuddle you, have you? You really think she likes you, don't you? Well, let me tell you something. You're so stupid. Haven't you realised? Think about it. Are all the nurses like this? No. Just this one. She treats you very nicely, doesn't she? Haven't you wondered why? Well, once you really trust her, she'll give you a secret injection and that's the last you'll know about anything. Once she's put you to sleep, she'll take all your blood, and sell it to the other patients. And then she'll make a cut here,' she added, marking a line with her finger across my abdomen, 'and she'll cut out all your organs and sell those too.'

'No!' I said to myself. This couldn't be true. I didn't believe it of Nungha. But Rahab had been so convincing that I didn't know what to think. Either way, I was devastated by what she'd said.

'I could see you getting too friendly with her and starting to trust her,' she added. 'So I thought I'd better warn you. And that's why I've been trying to take you home.'

After Rahab left, I was quiet and withdrawn. I just couldn't believe what she had told me was true. But Rahab had been so convincing. I didn't know who to trust anymore. Later, Nungha told me that the doctor had said that I could go home — but only if I was ready to go. I didn't know what to do. Rahab had said that Nungha might kill me and sell my body parts, but the alternative was to go back to my prison again. I started to cry — and despite what Rahab had told me, I clung on to Nungha for dear life.

'Don't cry, my lovely,' she said, stroking my hair. 'I'll see you again after two weeks, and then we'll go to my house and have a big party.'

At that moment, my instinct told me that Nungha was a kind, honest, caring person. I was tempted to tell her the whole truth — to let it all spill out in a big, breathless, tearful rush. But the terror of Rahab held me back. I just wasn't able to conquer that fear. The next morning I was discharged from the hospital and I never saw Nungha again. The doctor had told Rahab that I must rest up for at least two weeks. But as soon as we got back to her house, she ordered me to start work again.

'You've been in that hospital far too long,' she snapped. 'Anyway, the doctor said you were better. The house is now very dirty. So, you can start in the kitchen.'

★ ★ ★

One night, a few weeks later, Rahab forgot to lock the door to my shed. It was the first time this had ever happened. When I woke up in the morning, everyone in the house was still fast asleep — so I went to empty the wastewater barrels at the back. When Rahab came to unlock my door, she found it open and my room empty. She went into a complete panic, thinking that I must have run away. Then she realised that I had simply got myself up and started work. I think this convinced her that I had given up all hopes of escape.

From this moment on, she started to take me out with her more often. She even started to call me 'Mende' when we were out, although her favourite name for me at home was still *yebit*. I was no longer verbally abused as much and the beatings became rarer. By now, Rahab had a third daughter, called Tuta, and a fourth called Abir. Both had been born after my arrival in their home, so they grew up to see me as a permanent fixture in their lives. Abir especially really attached herself to me.

And I, for my part, began to forget my own family. I'm ashamed to say this now, but after I had been with Rahab four years or so, my memories just began to fade. Rahab had told me when I first arrived that I would stay with her for the rest of my life. I'd started to really believe her. And if I did ever think about my wonderful, loving family, it just caused me grief and pain. For all I knew, they had all died in the raid. It was too horrible to think about. So I just blanked it out completely.

I had started to tell myself that my future, such as it was, now lay here, in Khartoum. I had a new family now, albeit that I was their slave and they were my masters. There was no one that I could turn to to talk about the past — to remember the laughter and the love, to reaffirm my true identity. I had nothing tangible to remind me of my life as a Nuba, as not one single thing had survived the raid. I had started to believe that these Arabs were all-powerful, that they had some God-given right to rule over us. I saw this evidence in my day-to-day

218

life in Khartoum. I'd started to believe that this was how the world was: the Arabs enslaved the blacks. I had become convinced that they were invincible. But all of that was about to change.

20

Revenge

Every day, I would hear the thump of soldiers' boots, as they ran past the house. I think there must have been a military training camp nearby. One morning I peered out through the gate and saw lines of young recruits stomping past. They had shaven heads and they were wearing baggy white trousers and tops. They were singing as they ran. They reminded me of the men who had raided my village:

'*Allahu Akhbar, yahoude — God is Great!*
   He is with us.
Allahu Akhbar, yahoude — God is Great!
   He is with us.
We make our devout prayers! He is with us.
We make our devout prayers! He is with us.'

I didn't know where these men came from, but they looked like they were training for war. As time went on, I heard more about the war. Friday is the Muslim holy day, and there would be a special programme on television: *Sahad El Fidah* — 'Redemption'. If Rahab was out of the room and had left the TV on, I used to sneak in and watch this programme. It held a weird fascination for me.

220

The programme showed pictures of the Sudanese army and the Mujahidin fighting alongside each other and being victorious in the war against the rebel army from South Sudan. There were lots of graphic images of dead black people, with patriotic music playing in the background. The highlight of the programme was a segment called *Shuhada* — 'The Martyrs'. This showed all the young men that had died that week, supposedly fighting Jihad, or Holy War, against the 'infidels' of South Sudan. Mothers would hold up family photographs and talk about how happy they were that their sons were martyrs and had gone straight to join Allah in paradise.

Watching this programme and seeing all these dead black people reinforced in my mind the impression that the Arabs were invincible. But, one night, all that changed. I was jerked awake in the very early hours of the morning by the very air reverberating with a series of massive whooshing sounds, right above my shed. These were followed a few seconds later by a number of enormous explosions. Shortly after, I could hear the sirens of emergency vehicles racing across the city. I wanted to go and see what had happened. But I was locked in. In the morning, I listened to Rahab and Mustafa talking excitedly over breakfast. They had also been woken by all the noise. They had gone outside to see a huge orange glow on the horizon. Clearly something was on fire, but that was as much as they knew.

Years later, I learned the truth about the attack. The whooshing noise we had all heard

221

was later revealed to be the sound of six cruise missiles passing low over our quarter of Khartoum. One week before, the American embassies in Kenya and Tanzania had been blown up by terrorists, killing hundreds of Africans and Americans. Sudan was one of the two countries accused of backing Osama Bin Laden, the terrorist who was suspected of being behind the embassy bombings. The explosions I had heard were the missiles blowing up a factory in Khartoum that was supposedly making deadly weapons for the terrorists. The attack had been timed for the early hours of the morning, before the workers arrived, and fewer than a dozen people had been killed. Of course, I knew nothing about any of this at the time.

That evening, a constant stream of visitors came to Rahab and Mustafa's house to discuss the events of the previous night. I was kept busy serving tea to all the guests. As I went in and out of the lounge, I overheard them talking and they were looking angry and worried.

'These Americans are evil!' a male guest shouted. 'They want to kill us all.'

'These stupid Americans,' said another. 'They sit out there safe in their warships and fire their missiles at us. It could have been our families and our children that had been killed.'

'How many people died?' asked someone else.

'Hundreds. And there are many more in the hospitals, wounded.'

'This is very bad news, very bad news,' Mustafa kept repeating, over and over again, shaking his head. They broke off to watch the television as scenes of a large factory on fire flashed across the screen. On the ground there were bottles of medicine and they kept exploding with the heat of the flames.

'These Americans are infidels,' Rahab said contemptuously. 'You know why they do this? They do this because they don't know Allah. They don't know God and they think they can just go around killing Islamic people.'

Later, alone in the kitchen, I pondered on what I had heard. 'Somewhere in the world, there are people who are stronger than the Arabs,' I said to myself, with grim satisfaction. I couldn't stop myself breaking into a big grin. For the first time in my life, I was seeing the Arabs on the receiving end of trouble. They were no longer all-powerful. They were no longer invincible. I sat there and prayed silently to Allah that the Americans would fire enough missiles to burn Khartoum to the ground. I didn't care if I was killed alongside everyone else. 'I pray these bombs come right here, into your house, Rahab, and that they kill you, too.'

All that night, I lay awake in my little shed, waiting for the American missiles to come raining down on Khartoum. But no more came. The next day, there were pictures on the TV of crowds of angry people on the streets, burning American flags and shouting 'Death to America' and 'Death to Britain'. They were throwing stones at the British and American embassies and smashing all the windows. All that month, Rahab's house was full of angry visitors cursing the American and British people.

21

Rescue Me

Rahab would often go to visit her mother in a distant town called Kassala, leaving me to look after the children. One day, when I had been with her for almost four years, she decided to take me with her. I was so excited: it would be my first chance to leave Khartoum. Mustafa drove us to the bus station and we set off for Kassala. It was a six- or seven-hour drive, through a flat, arid landscape. It brought back memories of the drive from the Nuba Mountains to Khartoum, in the back of the truck of Abdul Azzim, the slave trader.

Rahab's parents had a huge house. They were clearly very rich. Rahab's mother had three servants. When we arrived, I was sent out to stay with them in their quarters behind the main house. There was a cleaning girl, a washing girl and a girl to do the cooking. They all came from Eritrea, one of Sudan's neighbours. But Rahab's mother saw my arrival as a good opportunity to give her servants their time off. So I ended up having to do all their work as well as my own.

After a week off, the serving girls returned. Their work was easy compared to what I had to do every day, and yet I knew they were paid wages. They could take time off to visit family and friends. And they were never beaten or abused. I wondered why. I concluded that I must be different from them in some way. But how? Was it because I was black and they were Arab-looking? Was it because I was a Nuba? Who had decided that they would be servants and I would be a slave? Who? Was it Rahab? Was it fate? Was it God?

As the days wore on, I grew more and more aware of the difference between us and I became more and more depressed. They had new clothes; mine were old rags. They were treated well; I was cursed and beaten. Early one morning, I was out in the yard laughing and chatting with the servant girls. We were making so much noise, that I didn't hear Rahab calling. 'Why didn't you answer, *yebit*? Where are the children?' She shouted at me as she appeared in the doorway. 'Why aren't you looking after them like I told you to?'

Without waiting for me to answer, she grabbed her wooden-soled shoe and hit me around the head. For a second there was a deathly silence as I cowered down on the ground. Then, as Rahab went to hit me again, one of the girls jumped up to stop her. Jaimaea was a very beautiful Eritrean girl. She had already been really kind to me.

'What d'you think you're doing!' said Jaimaea, her eyes flashing angrily. 'Why are you hitting her? Your children are in the front room, playing with your sister's kids. I've just seen them. What are you hitting her for?'

'This is none of your business,' Rahab retorted, 'so don't interfere.'

'Oh no? Well, I'm making it my business,' Jaimaea replied, defiantly. 'If she's your servant, then she works for you. But that's all. It doesn't give you the right to hit her.'

Rahab looked around her. All the serving girls were now on their feet. She realised she was outnumbered. 'Come on, *yebit*,' she snapped at me, as she turned on her heel, 'follow me.'

Rahab took me out the front of the house. She was seething with rage, but now it wasn't against me, it was against Jaimaea.

'Listen to me carefully,' she hissed in my ear, grabbing my arm. 'If those girls ask you, you tell them you work for me. And that I pay you a lot more money than they ever get paid. You'd better watch out. If you tell them anything else, I'll kill you.'

That evening, I went to eat with the serving girls as usual. 'Are you OK, Mende?' Jaimaea immediately asked me. 'Why did that bitch hit you?'

'She hit me because I had forgotten to keep an eye on the children,' I said, quietly.

'That's no reason to hit you. Why d'you let her do it?'

'I work for her,' I murmured, remembering Rahab's threats. 'She pays me a lot of money, more money than you girls get.'

'Oh, so that's a good reason to let her hit you, is it?' said Jaimaea, scornfully. 'Mende, she calls you *yebit*. You know that *yebit* is a real insult, don't you? Doesn't she know your real name?'

'She does know my name,' I whispered. 'But she's always called me *yebit*.'

'Well, she's a stupid bitch,' said Jaimaea. 'She pays you a lot of money so she can beat you and insult you. Listen. When you go back to Khartoum, promise me you'll leave that woman's place, OK? Go and find another Arab family to work for. There's lots that need servants. Even if they pay you less.'

Just then, Althoma, Rahab's sister, walked into the room. She looked over at Jaimaea. For a few seconds, there was a tense silence. 'Why are you causing trouble, Jaimaea?' she said, angrily. 'I overheard you just now. Why are you lying to Mende? Why are you making trouble?'

'I am not lying and I'm not making trouble,' Jaimaea replied. 'I'm just telling Mende the truth. Mende is a servant. If she doesn't want to stay with Rahab, she can leave her.'

At this, Althoma flew into a temper. 'This is none of your business,' she shouted, 'so stop interfering! Rahab told me what happened earlier. It's nothing to do with you.'

'Yes it is. Mende is only small,' said Jaimaea, protectively. 'She's not old enough to stand up to Rahab. That's why Rahab treats her like this and it's got to stop.'

A bitter shouting match ensued between Althoma and Jaimaea. I sat next to Jaimaea, cringing and trying to hide. I just knew this would end up being very bad for me. Then Rahab came in and joined in the argument. I was terrified and stared at the floor, sobbing. No one had ever talked to Rahab like this before, openly trying to defend me.

'I told you to keep your nose out of this!'

Rahab screamed at Jaimaea.

'So what? You are a cruel, wicked woman,' Jaimaea retorted. 'Why should I take any notice of you? You treat Mende badly just because she's little. I wouldn't stay for one hour in your house.'

'I don't need to listen to these sort of things from a mere servant,' Rahab snapped. 'We don't need people like you working here for our mother either. There's a lot of servants needing work around here. In fact, it's time you were leaving.'

'Good. Because I'm not staying in a place like this. Pay me my money now. I'm going.'

'You can come tomorrow to get your money. It's the middle of the night now.'

'No. I'm not coming back tomorrow. And I'm not leaving this place until I'm paid.'

Rahab disappeared for a few minutes and returned with a wad of bank notes. She paid Jaimaea her outstanding wages and told her to go. She didn't even have time to say a proper goodbye to any of us, least of all me. After she'd gone, Rahab told me that I was not allowed back in the servants' quarters and I wasn't even to speak to the servants. We left two days later and I never saw Jaimaea again.

Why didn't I tell the truth to Jaimaea when I had the chance? Why did I lie to her on Rahab's instructions? Why did I lie to the very people who tried to help me? After all those years, Rahab had completely destroyed my sense of my own identity and my own self-worth. I believed that I was no longer valuable as a human being. I lived in a state of complete terror of her. And I was still only a child.

To rebel against all that, to rebel against the woman whom I called 'master' and who called me 'slave', had become unthinkable. It lay outside the range of possibilities that I could contemplate. I now know that I should have trusted Jaimaea, and I believe she would really have tried to rescue me. Perhaps she would even have helped me return to the Nuba Mountains to try to find my family. But instead, I returned to Khartoum with Rahab. And I was about to discover just why it was that she believed that she actually owned me.

22

Of Slavery and Chastity

One evening, shortly after we returned to Khartoum, three of Rahab's friends came to visit. As usual, I served them tea and cake in the lounge. Two of the guests had never been to Rahab's house before, so she gave them a quick tour. When they settled down in the lounge again, I think Rahab was under the impression that I was in the children's bedroom and couldn't overhear what she was saying, but actually I was in the kitchen.

'You know, your house is so nice and airy,' said one of the women. 'And it's so clean. Even your yard is clean. How d'you find time to keep it like this?'

'Oh, I don't do it,' said Rahab, laughing. 'It's the girl who served you the tea.'

'What?' said this woman, in surprise. 'That little girl does all this? She keeps your house spotless and tidy like this all by herself?'

'Yes,' said Rahab, proudly. 'And guess what? She looks after the children too. And she does most of the cooking.'

'What? That's amazing!' said the woman. 'Where did you find her? I'd love to have a girl like her in my house.'

'Sure,' said the other woman. 'We'd all love to

find a girl like this. But how much do you have to pay her? And where d'you find them these days?'

'Oh no,' said Rahab, lowering her voice conspiratorially. 'You've missed the best bit. You see, I don't pay her any wages. Not a thing. But I did have to pay a lot of money for her in the first place.'

'Sorry,' said the other woman. 'What did you say? Did you say you have to pay her a lot of money? Or that you had to pay a lot of money *for* her?'

'I said I had to pay a lot of money *for* her,' said Rahab. 'You know, to buy her. She's mine.'

'Ohhhhh . . . ' said the other woman, 'now I get it. You bought her. She's an *abda*. Isn't she? Well, all I can say is, tell us where we can go and get one like her!'

'So . . . You want me to tell you, do you?' Rahab teased. 'Well, how much do you really want me to tell you?'

'Come on, Rahab,' the women implored. 'We're dying to know. You know how useless normal servant girls are.'

'Yes. Completely useless. Well then, you mean to say you don't know Abdul Azzim?'

'No. Who's Abdul Azzim?'

'He's the man who brings the *abids* here to Khartoum. You can go to his house and buy one too, if you really want one. But, bear in mind, you have to pay a lot of money. D'you really think you can afford it?'

'Oh! So how much is it? Take your *abda*, for instance. How much did she cost you?'

231

'Hmmmm . . . Let me see if I can remember. I know I thought it was a lot at the time,' said Rahab. 'No. I can't remember exactly. It was a few years ago now. But she's certainly been more than worth it. The price will have gone up by now, anyway. The best thing to do is go and see Abdul Azzim and ask him.'

'Well, it's got to be worth it, hasn't it? You make the initial investment, then it doesn't cost you anything after that, does it? I mean these servants, all the time they want to take days off and go and see their family and everything. But an *abda* stays with you all the time, doesn't she?'

'Yes,' Rahab agreed, enthusiastically. 'Let me tell you, if you have an *abda* in your home, like her, it's like a blessing. Your life's just never the same again.'

'But does she ever make trouble? I mean, does she just do whatever you tell her to do?'

'You know,' said Rahab, in a hushed voice, 'that's the most amazing thing. She never causes any trouble. I think these blacks are just sort of made for it. I suppose their people have been slaves for generations. They never complain. They just get on with it.'

Then they all started discussing how nice it was not to have any housework to do. I stopped listening. A final piece of the jigsaw puzzle had just fallen into place for me. From what Rahab had told her friends, it seemed Abdul Azzim made a living out of selling girls like me to Arab families. Abdul Azzim had sold me to Rahab, and that was why Rahab believed that she 'owned' me.

When I was locked in my shed that night, I was unable to sleep for hours. I couldn't believe that this was my fate — that I had been sold as a slave and would remain a slave for the rest of my life. It all seemed so final. That night, I prayed to God: 'Oh Allah, please help me. Please find a way for me to escape Rahab and the raiders and Abdul Azzim — those who have enslaved me. Allah, only you can help me.'

By this time, I had a few more freedoms as Rahab believed that I'd given up all thoughts of escape. But I still wasn't immune to her moods, which could turn violent without warning. During the school holidays, she would give me a key to the door of my shed. As all the family would sleep late, I was supposed to get up early and start cleaning the front yard. One morning, around breakfast time, she came out of the house. '*Yebit!* Go to the shops with this money and buy me some eggs.'

I had been allowed out to the shops a few times before, but always with one of the older children as a chaperone. Each time I had returned obediently with her shopping, Rahab had become a little more confident that I wouldn't try to escape. In fact, I treasured these little moments of freedom so much that I didn't want to jeopardise them. Just to leave the house and walk down the street was a joy in itself.

This was the first time that I was allowed out on my own. On my way, I met some children playing in the road. I hurried along, got the eggs and rushed back again. The children were still there, playing tag back and forth across the street. I was sixteen years old, but I had been stopped from playing when I was twelve. For a few minutes, I just watched them running and laughing together. Then I heard Rahab shouting for me.

'*Yebit*, I sent you to buy eggs! I didn't send you out to play. Come here!'

'I wasn't playing,' I said to her, as I went inside the gate. 'I just wanted to watch the children, that's all.'

Rahab's reaction was to rap me three times across the head with her knuckles. 'I saw you playing,' she snapped. 'Now, Hanin is waiting for her breakfast and she's hungry. Go and make her some fried eggs. After you've done that, slice some onions.' I could tell that Rahab was in a very bad mood. I went into the kitchen and fried the eggs. Then I sliced the onions and started deep frying them, as instructed, using a metal ladle to stir them.

'Have you made the eggs?' Rahab asked as she came into the kitchen.

'Yes, master.'

'Hanin,' she called through to the lounge. 'Hanin. Come and eat breakfast.' Hanin came running in and sat at the table, and Rahab went to pick up the plate of eggs. 'What do you call this!' she yelled, staring down at the plate, her bad mood boiling over into a fury. 'I told you to make poached eggs, not fried ones.'

Before I could react, she grabbed my arm. With her other hand, she seized the ladle out of the frying pan, and thrust the burning hot metal against my forearm. I cried out in agony, as she

234

ground it, sizzling, into my skin. Boiling oil spattered down my arm.

'You stupid girl!' she yelled above my screams. 'You've made one mistake too many today! First, I catch you playing, when I sent you to buy eggs. Then you make fried eggs instead of poached eggs. This'll teach you a lesson you won't forget.'

With that, she yanked the ladle away, ripping off a layer of burned skin as she did so. I clutched the inside of my forearm, feeling I was going to faint with the pain.

'Now, *yebit*, make poached eggs, like I told you,' she snapped, turning her back to me. 'And when you've done that, go and get me the key to your shed. I want it back. You're obviously getting stupid ideas into your head. You're not allowed out on your own any more.'

Carrying my burned arm like a broken wing tucked in at my side, I forced myself to pick up the remaining eggs. But I couldn't fill the pan with water and break the eggs into it all with my one good hand. I started to sob.

'What are you crying for?' Rahab asked harshly.

'Look. You burned my arm,' I sobbed. 'I can't do the eggs. It hurts too much.'

'Look at what! At what, *yebit*! You make a mistake, you do something stupid, and you get punished. What d'you expect?'

* * *

But it wasn't just Rahab's violent moods that were a problem for me. By now I was around sixteen, and I had grown into a young woman. Of course, I wasn't ignorant of my charms. I knew that I was slim, dark and attractive. None of the men would openly look at a black girl like me, especially if they had their wives with them. But when they were alone in the house, it was a completely different story.

One day, Mustafa had some visitors, a male friend and his new wife. They had only just got married and the woman still had intricate patterns painted all over her feet and hands in black henna from the marriage ceremony. Rahab was away for a few days. As I made the visitors breakfast, I could hear them telling Mustafa all about their wedding. They were just about to leave on their honeymoon and would only be staying a couple of days. I was unusually relaxed and happy, because Rahab was away.

Later, as I was serving them tea, I noticed that this man was staring at me, but I just thought he was being arrogant and insulting. His wife took her tea into the front yard, where she went to burn some incense. She sat over a ceramic incense burner, lit the sandalwood, wrapped a blanket around her body and enveloped herself in the sweet-smelling smoke. The incense is supposed to prepare the new wife for her husband by making her smell beautiful and alluring.

I went over to help her, as the blanket kept falling down. She smiled up at me and I stood there breathing in the lovely smoke. Just then, Mustafa called me into the house to make more tea. As I'd only just made some, I was a bit

236

surprised. I went in and saw Mustafa taking Hanin outside to show her the incense burning. I was now alone in the house with the visitor. I was in the kitchen, bending over to light the gas stove, when suddenly I jumped out of my skin with fright. I could hear heavy breathing and someone was standing close behind me. The Arab man had sneaked into the kitchen.

I tried to spin around and confront him, but I was grabbed from behind. He started to thrust his body against me. Then, he slipped one arm around my stomach and started to grope me. I could feel him trying to press himself against me. For a few seconds, I was frozen in fear, remembering the Arab raider who had assaulted me in the forest. But by now, this man was trying to slip his hand under my dress. I came to my senses, twisted around and shoved him violently away. But he just came back at me, trying to clamp his mouth over my mouth and force me into his sweaty embrace again.

'Come on! You know you like it!' he whispered, menacingly.

'Are you crazy!' I hissed at him, in desperation. 'What're you doing! What do you want? You want me to scream so loud your wife can hear?'

'No! No. Shhhsh,' he said, putting his finger to his lips. 'Don't shout, or there'll be trouble. Come on. Don't tell me you aren't enjoying this.'

'Get off me,' I hissed, pushing him away, 'unless you want your wife to hear me screaming! If you've come in here wanting tea then ask me, and wait in the lounge and I'll bring it in for you.'

He stood there grinning at me. I noticed he had some spittle in the corner of his mouth. I was angry and I was scared. I knew he hadn't come into the kitchen for tea. I knew very well what he'd come for. I knew that the only defence I had against him was to shout loud enough so that his wife would hear. But if Rahab heard about it later, I was bound to get the blame.

'Come on,' he wheedled. 'I know you'd like to. You know you'd like to. So what's the problem?'

'The problem is, if you don't leave now I'm going to scream for your wife,' I retorted icily. 'Remember, she's the woman you just married.'

This seemed to cool his passion. He backed away from me and turned to leave. But as he walked out, I saw him make the thumbs down sign to someone sitting in the lounge. And then I heard Mustafa burst into laughter, and the visitor joined in. Five minutes later, I took in their tea. I banged it down on the table. I was still shaking with fear and anger. Later, I got Hanin to tell Mustafa that the children wanted me to sleep in their room that night as Rahab was away. I knew that I would be safe in there.

The following day Rahab returned, and that put an end to it all. Mustafa had never tried to molest me. Rahab ruled the household with an iron fist and Mustafa was scared of her, but this wasn't the last of such trouble from men who visited the house. After this, there were other encounters. But I had learned how to defend myself by now. The one advantage of having

Rahab as my master was that she was the most fearsome woman. No man wanted to cross her, or face her wrath — or have her telling his wife that he'd been caught in the process of molesting her Nuba slave.

23

London Bound?

One day, after I'd been with Rahab for six years or so, she called me into the lounge. She had just finished a long telephone call. '*Yebit*, make me some tea,' she ordered. 'Then I want to talk to you.' When I came back in, she asked me to sit down. It was so unusual for Rahab to ask this of me that I didn't know what to do. So I sat on the carpet in front of her.

'Don't sit there,' she said with a smile. She patted a seat next to her. 'Come and sit here, next to me. So, *yebit*, by now you know exactly what you do in this house, don't you?'

'Yes, master,' I answered.

'Good,' she said. 'So, tell me what you do here.'

'I clean the house. I wash the clothes. I cook the food,' I told her, quietly. 'I make the tea. I iron the clothes. I look after the children. I clean the patio and the yard.'

'Good. So now, I want to send you to London. D'you know where that is?'

'What?'

'I said that I want to send you to London. In England. I want to send you to my sister's house. You remember her, don't you? You met her once when she came to visit with her husband.'

I was taken so completely by surprise that I didn't know what to say. Rahab stared at me as I looked at the floor, trying to comprehend what she meant.

'Did you hear what I said?' asked Rahab, finally.

'Yes, master.'

'Good. Well, I want to send you to London so you can do exactly the same in my sister's house as you do here. You will obey my sister, just like you obey me. You'll do everything she tells you to. Is that understood?'

'Yes, I understand,' I mumbled.

'Good,' she said again, clearly pleased with herself. 'So, now we'll make all the arrangements and then we'll send you to London. You understand?'

'Yes,' I murmured. 'But who will then clean the house? I'll have to leave Hanin and Usra, Tuta and Abir. Who will look after them?'

'I want to go to London with Mende!' shouted Hanin, who'd come over to listen. 'I want to go with Mende and stay with our auntie.'

'I know you'll miss the children,' said Rahab, smiling. 'And they'll miss you,' she added, stroking Hanin's head. 'But Hanan has just had twins. She's so tired and she needs help. That's why I want to send you to London. D'you understand?'

I nodded.

'Good. Now go back to work,' she said. 'Take the tray out with you when you go.'

★ ★ ★

Back in the kitchen, I started to wash up the tea things, but my mind was in complete turmoil and I didn't know what to think. I needed some time on my own so I could work this through. I concentrated on finishing all my work. I cooked dinner for the family, an egg salad with nuts. I served them dinner and then cleared the mess away. I sat down at my little table in the corner and ate up the leftovers. I washed up all the dirty dishes and cleaned up the kitchen. Then it was time to go to sleep in my shed.

'Where is 'London'?' I wondered, as I lay on my thin mattress? 'How will I get there? Why does she want to send me away? How will I be treated there?' I couldn't ask Rahab any of these questions. I knew that she'd just treat me as if I was ignorant and stupid. I'd learned the hard way that it was best simply to agree with whatever she said. But I was very worried. Over the last six years, I'd learned how to survive as a slave in Rahab's house in Khartoum. I'd learned how to behave to avoid getting beaten. I'd learned how to stop the worst verbal abuse. I'd learned how to evade sexual assaults. I'd learned how to safeguard my few joys in life. In short, I knew the rules. Now, all that was about to change.

But more than anything, I was also very close to Rahab's daughters. They had become my family and my friends and I didn't want to lose them. Then, just as I was thinking these thoughts, I realised the sad absurdity of what was going through my mind. 'What on earth am I thinking?' I asked myself. 'I'm sad because I'm going to leave behind the children. Hanin, Usra, Tuta and Abir. Rahab's children. Rahab's family. But what about my own family? What about *Ba, Umi*, Babo, Kunyant, Shokan and Kwandsharan, and everyone back at home in the Nuba Mountains?'

I sat there in the darkness and realised that I had actually given up my real family for dead. I had become used to not thinking about them — it was too painful. This realisation rocked me to the core. I lay down and cried and cried into the night. Later, in the early hours of the morning, I thought over everything that had happened to me. The raiders had taken me away from my village to Dilling. Then Abdul Azzim had taken me to Khartoum. Then Rahab had taken me to this house. Each time, I was taken further away from my family and my home. And now I was to be moved even further, right out of Sudan and right out of Africa too. 'Has Rahab sold me to her sister?' I wondered, angrily. 'Or has she just given me to her, like a useful gift?'

The news that I was being sent abroad reawakened my love for my family. I had been sleepwalking through a nightmare. I had been clutching onto a false hope — that here in Khartoum was my new home. But now I was simply to be passed on, like a useful household appliance. The only place where I had ever found real love and loyalty was with my real family. Somehow, I had to find them. So much time had already gone by. I didn't even know if they had survived the raid. The last thoughts coursing through my mind in the early hours were of anger and escape — and the hope of being reunited with my family. As I drifted off to sleep, I prayed to Allah to bring me news of my family. Little did I know that my prayers were going to be answered so quickly.

24

They're Alive!

A few weeks later, Rahab was preparing to go to a wedding. She was wearing her most expensive shoes, a beautiful dress and lots of gold jewellery. I was reading the children an Aesop's fable in the bedroom. It was the one where the little boy cries wolf three times. The first two times he does so, his father comes running to save him, only to discover that the little boy was just pretending the wolf was there to get his attention. So, the third time he hears the boy crying wolf, he thinks he is messing around and ignores him. Only this time, the wolf really does come and carry the boy off into the forest.

We had just reached the moral of the story when there was a ring on the doorbell. I went and opened the door. It was a woman who was going to the wedding with Rahab. I glanced over her shoulder and saw a car full of children. And then I almost jumped out of my skin. Sitting in the back of the car was a Nuba girl who I immediately recognised. It was Kumal — my friend from a neighbouring village who'd been seized in the same raid as me. Just at that moment, she caught sight of me. I could see the shock of recognition written all over her face.

245

For a few seconds, our eyes locked across the space between us.

'*Yebit! Yebit!*' I came to my senses with Rahab's friend shaking me by the shoulder. '*Yebit!* Are you asleep or something? I asked you where Rahab was? Is she ready?'

Rahab? I didn't know. I ran back into the house. She was not quite ready, so she asked me to bring her friend into the lounge to wait. As the lady stepped into the house I pretended to close the door behind her. But instead, I slipped out and ran across the gravel drive to the car. Kumal was staring right at me, as I bent down to the window.

'Is it Kumal?' I said. 'Kumal! Is it really you?'

I saw her mouth a reply to me, but I couldn't hear, so I motioned to her to roll down the window.

'Kumal! Is that Kumal?' I repeated, breathlessly.

'Mende!' she cried. 'Mende! It can't be you.'

Then she jumped out of the car and we were in each other's arms. I could feel her shaking as she sobbed into my shoulder.

'I can't believe it's you,' I said through my tears.

'Oh Allah! It's so good to see you. So good to see you,' she cried.

'Who is that woman you're with?' I asked her, once I'd recovered a little. 'Is she a friend of Rahab's? I've never seen her before.'

'Yes, yes, she's Rahab's friend,' Kumal replied. 'But I don't want to talk about her. Listen. Tell

246

me. Have you heard any news about your family?'

'No. Why? D'you know something? Oh, please tell me! Please!'

'Then I've got good news for you. Listen . . . '

'But how?' I said, grabbing hold of her arm and interrupting her. 'How did you hear? What d'you know!'

'Mende, calm down. We must be careful they don't see us. One day Hallah, that's that woman, sent me out to the shop. When I got there, I saw a man who looked Nuba and I couldn't help staring at him. At first, I didn't recognise him, but he came over and asked me where I was from. I told him I was Nuba, from the Karko. Then he grabbed me by the shoulder. 'Is it Kumal?' he said. 'Yes. Who're you?' I said. 'You don't recognise me?' he asked. 'I'm Shadal. We've met at the wrestling matches. After the raid, all the people from the village thought you were dead! I'm from Mende's area. You do know Mende, don't you? She disappeared in the same raid as you.'

'Then he told me all about my family. He asked me about you and I told him that the last I saw of you was in the army camp at Dilling. Then he told me that he had news of your family too. They're all alive, Mende. They survived the raid. He told me this, just in case I ever saw you. He said your mother and father and everyone are all fine.'

Oh my God! My family were alive! Oh my God! Oh Allah, thank you! Oh thank you, thank you, thank you! I felt I was going to collapse,

247

there and then. I didn't know whether to laugh or cry. But Kumal held me up and carried on talking.

'Then Shadal asked me where I lived. He said he would walk back with me, so he could take a look at the house and try to find a way to help me escape. So we walked back together, trying to keep near to the hedge. But suddenly I spotted Hallah's car driving down the road towards us. I knew that Hallah had come looking for me because I'd been away such a long time. I shouted at Shadal to hide in the bushes. Then I just rushed off up the road towards the car.

'When I reached it, I could tell that Hallah was beside herself with rage. She threw open the door, dragged me inside and started to beat me. 'Where've you been?' she kept screaming at me. 'Where've you been! You stupid, lazy black bitch. You've been over an hour!' That was the last time I went to the shops,' Kumal added, quietly. 'She never allowed me to go again. And that's the last I ever saw of Shadal.'

Just as Kumal finished her story, I heard Rahab open the door. 'Mende? Mende! Where are you?' she shouted.

'Quickly!' said Kumal. 'Go on! She's calling you!'

'No,' I said. 'I'm not going. I'm staying here to talk to you.'

'But won't she beat you?' Kumal asked.

'Of course she will,' I said. 'But I'm staying here to talk to you.'

The knowledge that my family were still alive had given me a new strength. It meant more to me than anything — more even than if I had just been told that I was being set free. Without my family to go back to, what point was there in being free? Where would I go? Who would love and care for me? Where would I make my home? And now I also knew that somewhere out there in Khartoum, people from our tribe were looking for us. This man Shadal, could he be the same Shadal that Babo had fought and beaten all those years ago in the wrestling match and who had then become his friend?

'Oh, there you are,' said Rahab, finally catching sight of me. 'D'you know this girl then?'

I was about to answer when Rahab turned to her friend again and continued gossiping. 'Darling, it's such a long, long time since you've been to Khartoum. When did I see you last?'

'Ohhh, it must have been the last wedding, d'you remember? It was Fatima's, over a year ago now.'

For the time being at least, they didn't seem interested in us. So Kumal and I carried on whispering together in Nuba. 'Do you think you'll see Shadal again?' I asked Kumal. 'Could he get a message to my family? To tell them that I'm alive? Could he get them to come to Khartoum, to help me escape?'

'I can try. But Hallah doesn't allow me to go to the shops any more now. I hate her.'

'Do you think we can manage to see each other again?'

'I don't know. If Rahab comes to visit my master, do you think she'll bring you along?'

'Maybe. But anyway, I might not be around

for much longer. Rahab's told me that she's sending me to England, to London.'

'To England! Why?'

'I don't really know. Rahab just said that she's sending me to her sister's place in London.'

'OK. Listen,' said Kumal, pulling me around to the opposite side of the car from where Rahab and Hallah were standing. 'I've got a telephone number for you. It's my cousin and I know he's in *bilabarra*. When you get there, he'll help you.' (*Bilabarra* literally means 'far away in a foreign country').

Kumal scrabbled in the small bag she was carrying and found the stub of a pencil, but I could see that she didn't have any paper.

'You're thirsty,' I said to Kumal loudly, in Arabic. 'I'll just go and get you some water.'

I rushed into the house, grabbed a glass, splashed some water into it and pulled a scrap of paper out of the bin. I ran out again, but by now they'd all got into the car. I passed the glass of water in to Kumal, and thrust the scrap of paper into her hand at the same time. Kumal gulped some water and quickly scribbled the number down. She sneaked it back to me with the empty glass, just as Hallah started the car engine. I shouted goodbye to Kumal as the car moved off. The last I saw of her was a little face, peering back at me as they drove out through the front gates.

25

New Millennium, New Slave

As the year rolled to a close, there was no more talk of my going to London. I was happy that the idea just seemed to have been forgotten. Seeing Kumal had changed everything for me. In the weeks after we met, I was filled with hope. 'Maybe Kumal has made contact with Shadal again,' I would think to myself. 'Maybe he's gone back to the Nuba Mountains to tell my family that I'm alive. Maybe they are already in Khartoum, looking for Kumal and me. Maybe, even now, they're planning how best to rescue me.' Several months would pass before I would hear mention of the move to London again.

The year was 1999, and at the approach of the New Year everyone around me was preparing to welcome in the New Millennium. Everyone, that is, except me. Whilst Rahab and Mustafa went out partying, I spent the last night of the twentieth century in the house, working as usual. I wasn't even aware that one century was ending and another was beginning. The next day, I had to get up especially early to prepare for a big outing to the park. I filled a picnic hamper with food and flasks of fresh fruit juice, which Mustafa loaded into the back of their estate car. At the park, we joined a group of Rahab and

Mustafa's friends and set out our picnic in the shade of a big tree.

The children in our party went and joined a big group of boys and girls playing hide-and-seek together. Watching over them were a dozen or so black girls, some of whom looked quite young. I was reminded of myself, when I was first brought to Khartoum. We smiled nervously at each other.

I looked around the park, hoping to spot Kumal somewhere, or even Asha, the Nuba lady from Abdul Azzim's house. Then I looked to see if Nungha was there, the kind nurse at the hospital. But I couldn't see any of them. I finally plucked up courage to talk to one of the black girls standing next to me who looked about twelve years old or so.

'Hello, little sister,' I said, in Arabic.

'Hello,' she replied, shyly.

'Where are you from?'

'I'm from the Nuba.'

'From the Nuba! Which tribe are you from?'

'The Nunghi.'

'The Nunghi!' I was overjoyed. 'I'm from the Karko. Your tribe is next to mine.'

The Nunghi used to come to our wrestling matches. They were our allies and our friends. But, of all our neighbours, they were the one tribe who didn't speak the same language as us. So we carried on talking in simple Arabic — hers was very basic.

'My name's Mende. What's yours, little sister?'

'It's Katuna.'

'Katuna. What a lovely name. Where are your family, Katuna?'

'I don't know,' she whispered. 'There was fire in our house and then the raiders came inside and captured me.'

She was just like I had been when I was first captured. 'Don't cry,' I said, holding her tight. 'Don't cry.'

'I miss my mummy,' she sobbed. 'I miss her so much.'

As I stroked her hair gently, I could see that she had a beautiful string of bright red beads around her neck.

'Oh! Your beads are beautiful,' I said, trying to cheer her up. 'But Katuna, don't wear them round your neck like that. Take them off and hide them. If you don't, they'll take them from you to stop you wearing them.'

Katuna nodded. I carried on stroking her lovely hair. If the children carried on playing together for long enough, I thought, I might have time to plait it for her. But then I felt a huge lump on the back of her head. I parted her hair carefully, and found an angry, scabbed-up wound.

'What happened here, Katuna?' I asked her gently.

'She pushed me and I fell down and hit the back of my head on a wall,' she said quietly. 'There was lots of blood.'

'Did she take you to hospital?'

'No,' she whispered. 'She just gave me some soft, white stuff and told me to hold it on the back of my head.'

'Is that all?'

Katuna nodded. 'Now, when I oil my hair I

put some there to try to make it better. But it still hurts.'

I told Katuna that we should walk around together as we talked, in case Rahab or her master came and overheard us. I then found myself giving her the same advice that Asha had given me at Abdul Azzim's house when I had first arrived in Khartoum.

'Listen to me, Katuna,' I said. 'If she tells you to do something, you have to obey her. If she calls you, you have to go to her. When she gives you an order, listen carefully so you can do it properly. And whatever you do, never answer her back.'

How many other slave girls like us were there today, in that park, I wondered? Hundreds probably. How many would have stories just like ours — of being beaten, abused, exploited and lonely? So many broken hearts, stolen child-hoods and wrecked lives. There wasn't much more time to talk to Katuna. I had to take the children back and serve dinner. But what more was there to say to her, anyway? I was powerless to help her. That evening, we stayed late. Candles were lit to symbolise hope at the start of the New Millennium, but what hope did the New Millennium hold in store for slaves like Katuna and me?

* * *

Just after New Year, Rahab decided to visit her sister Hanan in London. '*Yebit*, I'm going to London, in about a week's time. You're going to stay here with the children. My sister Althoma will come and stay here with you. D'you understand?'

'Yes, master Rahab.'

'You're to be on your best behaviour, you hear? Anything she tells you to do, you do. And you're to look after the children too.'

'Yes, master Rahab.'

Rahab spent about a month away. Althoma was much nicer than her, never shouting or hitting me. With Rahab away, there were few visitors so I didn't have to spend all my time cooking. And the children asked me to sleep with them in their room. I was happy that month: I wasn't abused, I could sleep in the house, and there was a lot less work to do. For me, it was almost like a holiday. When Rahab returned, she brought bags of presents with her. Mustafa had a very beautiful blue tie, with a matching pinstripe suit. The children had heaps and heaps of colourful toys. And she even brought a present for me — a three-pack of knickers. One pair was red, one was purple and one was blue. I thought they were beautiful. This was the first time anyone had ever given me a real present. I wondered why. A few days later, I found out.

'Remember I told you that you were going to London?' Rahab said, coming to find me in the kitchen.

'Yes, master Rahab.'

'Well. Now you'll be going very soon. I had a talk to my sister Hanan about it. She's very keen to have you there.'

'Yes, master Rahab.'

255

I hadn't even had time to start trying to digest this news when there was a ring at the door. I went to open it and found Abdul Azzim and his wife Joahir standing there. I hadn't seen them since that first week I arrived in Khartoum, all those years ago.

'Hello,' said Abdul Azzim with a grin. 'How are you? Look,' he said, turning to Joahir and pointing at me. 'Look how big she's grown. Do you remember her name, darling?'

'Her name?' said Joahir. 'No, I can't. Hang on, let me think.'

'My name's Mende,' I said, quietly.

'Oh yes, that's right. Mende,' said Joahir. 'Mende. I do remember now, dear.'

As I was showing them into the lounge, I asked after Asha.

'Ohhh . . . You remember Asha, do you?' said Joahir. 'Well, she's fine.'

'Yes. I remember that she was very nice to me.'

'Yes,' said Joahir, smiling patronisingly. 'That's why we like her to stay with the girls when they first arrive in Khartoum. Makes it easier for everyone.'

Abdul Azzim looked exactly the same as when I'd first seen him in the soldiers' camp at Dilling, dressed in a simple *Jalabia* and sandals. But Joahir was looking more glamorous than ever. She was wearing a fine long dress and she was literally dripping in gold. I served them tea in the lounge, and then retreated into the kitchen.

'So, how is she then?' I overheard Joahir ask Rahab.

'Oh, she's great,' Rahab said, laughing. 'She's

very clean and she works very hard. I never have to beat her these days, either.'

'Well, that's just perfect,' said Joahir, laughing with her. 'We only provide the best, after all, don't we, darling?'

'But seriously, Abdul Azzim, I'm going to send her to London soon,' continued Rahab, 'to stay with my sister, Hanan. That's what I wanted to talk to you about.'

'She's very clean and she's a very good worker. But you're still sending her to London?' said Abdul Azzim. 'That's very kind of you. What a nice sister you are.'

'Well, it's easy for us to get you another *abda*, so don't worry,' said Joahir, laughing again. 'Whereas I understand it's impossible for people to find one in London, isn't it?'

'Completely impossible. Anyway, let's talk business,' said Rahab. 'Now, Abdul Azzim. If you get me another one, how do I know she'll be as good as this one?'

'Well . . . You want me to test them all out and then keep the best one for you?' said Abdul Azzim. Now they all started laughing. 'They don't come with a guarantee, you know. But I'll do my best to find you one just like her, *Inshallah* — God willing.'

'All right. But when?'

'Well, let me think about it. When do I next go down to Dilling? Hmmm . . . Probably in about a month's time. I can't guarantee there'll be any *abids* there, but I can try some other places I know too. So, how does that sound — in a month's time or so?'

'All right. But please, be as quick as you can. I've promised to send her to London in about a month. And I can't survive without help.'

'Don't you worry, Rahab,' said Abdul Azzim. 'You just leave it to me.' So, it seemed I would be going to London after all — albeit still as Rahab's slave — and Abdul Azzim was going to bring another girl here to take my place. I thought back over all that I had suffered at Rahab's hands. I knew that she would behave the same towards this next girl. All I could do, if I got the chance, was try to teach this new girl how best to handle our master. And after seven or eight years, I'd got it down to a fine art. It looked like I'd have a lot of teaching to do.

Part Three

Journey to Freedom

26

Telling Lies

Why did Rahab decide to send me to London? This was a question that I spent a long time thinking over. When I had arrived at Rahab's house I was just twelve years old. I was small, scared and easy to control. Now, I was nineteen years old and I had grown into a young woman. The time when Rahab could dominate me physically was coming to an end. I also knew that I was catching the attention of many of the men who came to visit the house. Rahab was aware of their interest, and the more she noticed it, the angrier it made her. I had grown into the old clothes that Rahab had given me, so they fitted me perfectly now. The more attractive I looked, the more jealous Rahab became. Things came to a head when even Mustafa started paying more attention to me.

'Don't wear that dress!' she'd snap at me. 'Go and put on your old work clothes.' If I oiled my hair and plaited it into braids, she'd get annoyed. '*Yebit!* Cover your hair up!' she'd yell at me. 'Put on your *hijab*' (the Muslim headscarf). 'Do you want all the men who come to visit to see your hair? Well do you?'

These men would never pay me compliments directly. They'd never say, 'Oh Mende, you look pretty today.' They couldn't admit that they found me, a black Nuba slave, attractive. But I caught them staring at me and trying to corner me in the house. Eventually, I actually wanted Rahab to lock me in my shed at night. I was worried that one of them might try something on. Strangely, Rahab's jealousy and her urge to control me probably saved me from the worst abuses. Even her own husband, Mustafa, was terrified of her. She had a similar effect on the other male visitors.

Yet, as I matured, I'm sure Rahab felt more threatened by me, and that's partly why she decided to ship me off abroad. A week after she returned from London, I had a photo taken in a studio near the house. I thought I looked very sad and ugly staring out from the little piece of paper. A few days later and that photograph had been mounted in a little book and I had my first ever passport. After that, we went to get me a British visa. Rahab had told me that she had 'connections in the right places', who would ensure that we got the visa without any problems. But it was actually to prove rather difficult. Before our first visit to the British Embassy in Khartoum, Rahab gave me strict instructions on what I was to say.

'Listen carefully, *yebit*,' she said. 'The embassy people are going to ask you a lot of questions and you must answer them exactly as I tell you to. If you don't, there'll be trouble. Do you understand?'

I nodded. 'Yes, master Rahab.'

'Good. So, if they ask you how I treat you,

262

you're to say I treat you very well. If they ask you what happens when you're sick, you tell them that you are taken to see a doctor. If they ask you about holidays, you tell them that you go to stay with your mother and father. You understand?'

I nodded. I was being told to tell lies, but I didn't have any choice in the matter.

'If they ask you who you are going to work for in London, you tell them it's a Mr Ali Bashir Gadalla, OK? Don't say you are going to work for Hanan or Al Koronky. Do you understand?'

'Yes, master,' I said quietly. Yet I was suspicious. I didn't know who Mr Gadalla was, whether he knew about me, if he was involved, or even whether he knew his name was going to be used. 'But who am I really going to work for, master? If it's Hanan and Al Koronky, why am I to say it's Ali Bashir Gadalla?'

'It's none of your business,' she said, irritably. 'Just tell them what I'm telling you to. You'll be working for my sister Hanan, of course, like I told you. But, if you tell them this, they won't give you a visa. So, you have to say it's Ali Bashir Gadalla.'

'Yes, master. But why won't they let me go if I say it's Hanan?' I persisted.

'Stop asking questions, *yebit*! Do you understand what you have to say, or don't you?'

'I have to say I'm staying with Ali Bashir Gadalla.'

'Good. Now, I'm going to make you a very special promise. If you work well for Hanan in London and do what you're told, then we will bring you back here to Sudan when the family

263

visit next. And then we'll take you to see your family. So you see, going to London is the best way for you to get to see your family again.'

I didn't believe Rahab. Even Abdul Azzim, the slave trader, didn't know where my family were, so how could Rahab take me to see them? I knew she was lying. I didn't want to go to London. Meeting Kumal had changed everything for me. I now knew that my family were still alive and that people from my tribe were trying to rescue us. Maybe my family were even looking for me right now. If I stayed in Khartoum, there was at least a glimmer of hope. I wondered what would happen if I simply refused to go to London, but I remained deeply afraid of Rahab. She still held ultimate power over me. I was so used to submitting to her will: if she said I had to go, then I had to go.

* * *

When we arrived at the British Embassy in downtown Khartoum, Rahab was told to wait in reception. In the next room, I was pointed to a glass window with a *Hawaja* — a white man — behind it. I pushed the visa money and the form towards him and he looked over it briefly. This was only the second time in my life that I had seen a *Hawaja* close up. The last time had been when the two *Hawajas* delivered aid to our village in the Nuba Mountains. He scribbled something on a piece of paper and handed it back to me. Then he started to speak to me in English, but I motioned to him that I couldn't understand. So he called over an Arab man to translate.

'First of all,' he asked, 'who are you going to stay with, what does he do and how long do you intend to stay in the UK?'

'He's called Ali Bashir Gadalla,' I said. 'But I don't know what his job is, or how long I'll be staying.'

'You don't know?'

'No. I don't know.' I saw the *Hawaja* shake his head and then say something back to the Arabic translator.

'What did he say?' I asked the translator, anxiously.

'He says he's surprised. He's surprised that you don't know what this man does for a job or how long you'll be staying there.'

I was then told to go and wait in a corner of the room. Perhaps twenty minutes later, the translator came over to me. 'Here's a letter for you,' he said. 'You must send this to your employer in the UK and get him to answer these questions for us. Once you've got a reply, come back and see us again.'

'What happened, *yebit?*' Rahab asked, as soon as I came out.

'They gave me this letter.'

As we got into the car, Rahab started to read it. 'OK,' she said, as we drove off, 'I'll have to send this over to London.

'Now, listen to me,' she said, after driving along for a few minutes in silence. 'There are some things I forgot to tell you. If they ask you what sort of work you'll be doing in London, tell them it's the same sort of work as you've been doing here. It's cleaning, cooking and washing. Don't tell them you'll be looking after the children as well.'

'All right,' I said.

'If they ask you how long you'll be staying in London, tell them you'll be staying there for six months.'

'Yes. For six months.'

Two days later, Rahab came into the kitchen to show me a fax she'd received from London, giving the details that the embassy man had requested. We drove back to the embassy, and I handed the letter to a different *Hawaja* man to read. When he finished it, he began to ask me more questions, again using an Arab man to translate. It all went fine until he began to ask me about my work in London.

'Now, your employer, Mr Ali Bashir Gadalla, how much will he pay you per week?' I didn't know what to say. Rahab hadn't briefed me on this question. 'I don't know,' I answered.

'Sorry. Did you say you don't know?'

'Yes. I don't know.'

'You're going to London to work for this man for six months, yet you don't know how much you're going to be paid?'

'No. I don't know.'

I could see the *Hawaja* was shaking his head, and staring at me. 'I see,' he said. 'So, how many days off will you have per week?'

'I don't know.'

'I don't suppose you know how many hours you'll work each day then, either?'

'No. I don't know.'

'You mean to tell me that you don't know how much you'll be paid, you don't know how many days off you'll have, and you don't know how many hours you'll work each day?' He was laughing at me now, but not in an unkind way.

'Yes. I don't know,' I said, smiling shyly at him. He was very tall, with a long nose and sandy coloured hair. He had amazing eyes of a bright blue colour, the likes of which I'd never seen before. They reminded me of the sky and they sparkled when he smiled. I was surprised at how nice and friendly he was. Then I saw the *Hawaja* say something to the translator and they both burst out laughing.

'The English man says he doesn't want to ask any more questions,' the Arab man translated. 'He says if he asks you any more you're just going to answer, 'I don't know. I don't know. I don't know.'

I was told to wait for five minutes. Then the English man handed me a letter. 'Take this away with you,' he said, with a smile. 'We're going to need some more answers. And then I'm afraid you're going to have to come back again.'

'This is my permission to travel?' I asked.

'No, I'm afraid it isn't. Not yet,' the Arab man said. 'The English man says he's never heard anyone say 'I don't know' so many time before!'

I joined in their laughter, as it was very infectious. I wondered if the English man maybe thought I was a very lovely girl. He certainly seemed to be looking at me in that way. By now, I had been with them so long that a worried

Rahab was peering around the door.

'What took so long?' she asked when I came back into reception. She started to read the letter. 'Ohhh . . . ' she said, shaking her head. 'Ohhh Allah . . . This English man is very nasty. Where did he dream up all these questions? Well, we'll just have to prepare some more answers, then. I suppose you didn't know what on earth to say to him?'

'No. All I could say was 'I don't know.''

'How many times did you say that?' she exclaimed.

'I lost count. Maybe five or six times.'

Rahab was trying to be angry with me but she couldn't help laughing. 'You said 'I don't know' five or six times? What did the English man do?'

'He was laughing,' I said.

When we got back to the house, Rahab faxed off the second letter to London and the next day we got a reply. So we went back to the embassy for a third time. When the English man caught sight of me he broke into a big grin.

'Hello there,' he said, grinning. 'Hello, 'I don't know'. How are you, 'I don't know'?'

I smiled back at him shyly and handed him the new letter. 'Aha! So, you've brought a new letter, have you? Splendid. Let's take a look.' Then the English man said something to the translator, with a big smile at me. 'He said, 'Well done, I don't know.' You won't have to say 'I don't know' any more. He doesn't have to ask you any more questions — because it's all here in the letter.'

Then the translator handed me a slip of paper that the Englishman had prepared. 'He says,

'Congratulations. You're going to England.' Now, take this number and wait over there. In an hour or so, you'll get your passport back with your visa.'

I was given my visa on 18 May 2000. About three weeks later, Rahab told me that I would be leaving for London the following week. So began my last days in Rahab's household. I had to work extra hard, doing all the laundry and ironing, and giving the house a thorough clean from top to bottom. I had to wash the walls and clean all the windows, which was a major job considering the whole of the front of the house was one long wall of glass. I polished the furniture, scrubbed the kitchen and the bathroom, tidied up the bedrooms and turned out all the cupboards.

The day before my departure, Rahab gave me an old travel bag of hers. It was made of cheap, imitation animal skin, but I thought it was very lovely. I packed my few possessions: four old dresses, two skirts, three blouses, three pairs of knickers and my orange flip-flops. And 'Uran' of course. That was all I had in the world. Then Rahab and I packed two big bags for me to take to London for Hanan: we filled them with spices, bags of nuts and an array of Sudanese sausages. Finally, I was ready to go to England.

27

Nanu's Story

That evening, I was in the kitchen when there was a knock at the door. I went to open it and there were Abdul Azzim and his wife Joahir again.

'Hello. Are you all ready to go to England then?' said Abdul Azzim, with a grin.

'Yes,' I said, showing them into the lounge. I felt sure that they hadn't come here to wish me good luck in my travels.

As they stepped into the house, I caught sight of a little black girl standing nervously behind them. She looked about the same age as I had been when I first arrived at Rahab's house. Our eyes locked across the few feet between us. She looked so young and scared and confused. I will never forget that moment. Here was my replacement slave.

'Come on, follow me,' said Abdul Azzim over his shoulder to the girl.

As she walked past me into the lounge, I tried to work out where she was from. I was sure she was Nuba, but I couldn't tell if she was from my tribe or not. As I shut the door, Rahab called, '*Yebit*, go and get your stool from the kitchen and bring it in here for this girl.'

'Sit down here, little sister,' I said in Arabic,

270

handing her the stool.

'Thank you,' she replied.

Rahab then sent me to make some tea. 'Come on, little sister,' I said. 'Come into the kitchen and help me make tea.'

'No,' Rahab snapped. 'Not her. She's staying here. I need to talk to her.'

While I was in the kitchen, Abdul Azzim, Joahir and Rahab made small talk. Then, Rahab turned to the new girl.

'Now, you are going to stay here and work for me,' she said slowly, using simple Arabic to make sure she understood. 'I hope you are going to be as good as that big girl making the tea. She has stayed with me for over seven years. She works very hard and she always obeys me. She's so well behaved that I never have to punish her.'

I came back into the room with the tea tray. The little girl was staring at the floor, unable to look up at Rahab or anyone else in the room. 'You will clean the house and wash the dishes,' Rahab continued, 'and sweep the yard and the patio too. You can leave that here,' she said to me, nodding at the tea tray. 'Go and have a shower. You won't have time for one in the morning before leaving for the airport.'

'Yes, master Rahab,' I said and turned to leave. As I did so, I was aware of the little girl looking up at me. I could see the confusion and helplessness in her eyes. I felt like she was calling out to me: 'Please help me. Please don't leave me.'

After I'd finished my shower, I caught sight of Abdul Azzim and Joahir saying their goodbyes to

271

Rahab at the front door. I thought this might be a good time to catch the little girl on her own. I went into the lounge to tidy up the tea things. Then I turned to the little girl.

'My name's Mende,' I said to her, gently, in Arabic. 'What's your name, little sister?'

'My name is Nanu,' she whispered.

'Come into the kitchen, Nanu,' I said, 'and eat some dinner.'

'I need to use the toilet. And I'm thirsty. Can I have some water?'

I took Nanu to the bathroom. As soon as the door was shut behind us, I started to talk to her in a hushed whisper.

'Nanu, where are you from?'

'I'm from Gwali, big sister.'

Gwali is far away from my tribal area, but the Gwali tribe speak a similar language to our own. So, we were able to continue talking, slowly, in Nuba, and make ourselves understood. That way, if Rahab did overhear us, she wouldn't be able to understand.

'Can you get me some hot water?' Nanu asked me.

'Why d'you need it, Nanu?'

'Because it's very painful down here,' she whispered, pointing down between her legs. As soon as she said this, I felt physically sick. I immediately knew what must have happened to her.

'Did somebody try to hurt you, Nanu?' I asked, as I crouched down and put my arms around her. As I did so, the tears began to stream down her face.

'Yes,' she whispered. 'And all this week, I've been in so much pain and it won't stop bleeding.'

'Wait here, Nanu,' I said, hugging her tight. 'I'll go and get you something to make you feel better.'

As I went into the kitchen, I tried to hide my own tears by wiping them away with the back of my hand. I knew there would be trouble if Rahab realised Nanu and I had been crying. While I was making tea, all my memories of the raid began to flood in on me. I remembered the hot, stinking breath of the Arab man on top of me. The stabbing pain and the agony I was in for days and days afterwards. When I went back to the bathroom, Nanu was sitting on the toilet waiting for me. And she was still weeping.

'Don't cry, Nanu,' I said, gently stroking her hair. I passed her a glass of squash. 'Here, drink this.'

When she'd finished it I gave her a bowl of warm tea. 'Wash yourself down there with this. It will help stop the pain. Now, you must wash yourself like this every day. Tomorrow, I have to leave and so I won't be able to help you.'

'Yes, big sister. I know you're leaving. The master told me.'

Then I took Nanu into my shed, taking care that Rahab didn't see us. I sat her down on my mattress and told her to wait for me there. 'This has been my room for the past few years,' I told her, 'but I think you'll be staying here now.'

I went to the kitchen and heated some sesame oil on the stove. When it was warm to the touch,

I went back into the shed.

'Nanu, I'm going to rub some warm oil on you,' I said, fetching my cotton wool. 'It might hurt a bit at first, but it will make you better. It's what my mother did to me, after I was circumcised.'

Nanu nodded. I sat down with her on the mattress and went to rub the oil between her legs. I was sickened by what I saw. She must have been circumcised like me when she was young, and she had been literally ripped open. I took some cotton wool and dipped it into the oil. Then I began to rub it into the wounds, trying not to hurt her as I did so. Nanu held onto me so tightly and began to cry again. But I knew it wasn't just from the pain. It was from the terrible memories of it all.

'Nanu, tell me what happened,' I asked her, gently.

'My father died about six months ago,' she said, sobbing quietly. 'He was in a fever for a long time. So I was living alone with my mother and my little brother. She was about to give birth and I was very excited, wondering if it would be a boy or a girl.

'Then, one night, we were asleep in our hut and my mother was woken by a scratching at the door. She thought it was our dog, who used to sleep outside. She went over to look, but she caught sight of a man outside trying to get in. She put her finger to her lips so I would keep quiet, and backed away from the door. Then she picked up my little brother who was still asleep and took us both to the back of our hut.

'We crouched down in the shadows behind the sorghum store to hide. Then we heard the door creak open and the man started creeping around the hut towards us. Quietly as she could, my mother picked up my little brother and put him inside the grain store. Then she put me in there beside him. But she was too big to get in with us because she was seven or eight months pregnant by now. So she just crouched down and tried to hide. Then, from down inside the grain store, I heard my mother screaming as the man grabbed her.

'I heard the man shouting at her in Arabic: 'Where is your husband? Where are your children?' 'My husband is dead. I don't have any children,' my mother said, in a terrified voice. 'I'm pregnant now with my first child.' I knew she was trying to protect us,' Nanu sobbed. 'I hugged my little brother close as we crouched down in the darkness. I was trying not to cry or make any noise, but the tears were streaming down my face. I heard the noise of a struggle and my mother screaming, 'Please don't kill me! Don't kill me! Please!' Then it all went quiet.

'The next thing I knew, the man was setting fire to the hut. I could hear the roaring of the flames and there was smoke everywhere. I poked my head out of the grain store and I could see that everything was on fire. I jumped down and turned to help my brother out,' Nanu whispered. 'But as I did so, I saw my mother slumped against the base of the grain store. The firelight was flickering in a huge pool of blood. The man had slit my mother's throat.

"'Mummy! Mummy!' I shouted. I knelt down and I shook her by the shoulders, but her eyes were open and glazed and I knew that she was dead. Then I saw that her tummy had been cut open and that her baby was lying there in a pool of blood on the floor. I didn't know what to do. I didn't know if the baby was alive or dead. I had to save my little brother. The fire was all around me. I grabbed a stool and tried to reach up into the grain store to pull my little brother out, but I just couldn't get to him.'

'I'm sorry,' I whispered to Nanu, hugging her tight and rocking her backwards and forwards. 'I'm sorry. Don't cry. The same thing happened to me. You're not alone.'

'The fire was all around me now,' Nanu shuddered into my dress, 'so I just had to run. When I reached the doorway, it was a wall of flames, so I just ran screaming through it. That's how I burned myself,' she sobbed, running one hand up her left arm and over her left cheek. I could see that her skin was scorched red and blistered.

'I ran and ran as fast as I could, but I was in such pain,' Nanu whispered. 'When I couldn't go any further, I collapsed under a big tree. People were running in all directions. I didn't know what to do. Then I caught sight of an Arab coming towards me. I jumped up and tried to run but he was too quick. He grabbed me and forced me to the ground.'

From then on, Nanu's story was pretty much a repeat of my own. She was taken away from the village by the Arab raider, along with lots of

276

other boys and girls. He put her on his horse and then raped her repeatedly when they were in the forest. After that, the raiders took Nanu and the rest of the children to an army camp, which sounded like the same one that I'd been taken to.

Just then, I heard Rahab shouting for me. '*Yebit!* Mende! Come in. It's late. Tomorrow you have to go to the airport. It's time to sleep.'

I pleaded with Rahab to let me stay with Nanu for the night, but she wouldn't let me. She told me to go and sleep in the children's room. 'And before you go to bed, I want to talk to you,' she added.

When I went back to my shed to get my sleeping things, Nanu was curled up in a ball on the mattress. 'Where are you going?' she whispered, reaching up to me. 'Stay here and sleep with me.'

'I can't stay with you, Nanu, my darling. I'm sorry,' I said gently. 'Master Rahab has told me to sleep in the house.'

I stroked Nanu's hair and held her close to me for as long as I could. 'Bye-bye,' I said to her, 'try to sleep now, Nanu. And remember, if Rahab tells you to do anything, you have to obey her. Otherwise she'll beat you. You don't want that, do you, Nanu, my darling?'

I'd just had time to put my mattress down in the children's room when Rahab came in. 'Now. You remember what I told you, *yebit*?' she said. 'That you'll be doing the same work in London as you've been doing here for me? You remember, don't you?'

I nodded.

'Good. Whatever Hanan tells you to do, you will obey her,' she added. 'Is that clear?'

I nodded again. 'Yes, master Rahab.'

That night, sleep wouldn't come. I was haunted by what Nanu had told me. I knew all too well what now lay ahead of her: years and years of beatings and drudgery. I thought about my family, too. I knew that they were still alive, but now I was going to disappear in a country far, far away. How would I ever get back home? I had barely dropped off to sleep when Rahab came in and woke me. As I went to my outside toilet, I found her unlocking the door to the shed.

'*Yebit*,' Rahab called to Nanu, 'it's time to get up. Once you've had a wash, come into the kitchen and sit at your table in the corner and wait for me.'

'Go and get your bag,' she then said, turning to me. 'Hurry now, as we have to leave soon.'

I went into my shed. Nanu was curled up in a ball on the mattress. I barely had time to give her one last hug before Rahab called me into the house. She told me I had time for one cup of tea before leaving. A few minutes later, Rahab came back in with Nanu.

'*Yebit*, start by cleaning the sink and washing all the dirty dishes,' Rahab told Nanu, as she marched her over to the sink. 'If I'm still out by the time you finish, then you can start cleaning the rest of the house. Do you understand?'

'Yes, master Rahab,' said Nanu, just like I'd told her to.

'Are you ready?' Rahab said, turning to me. 'Let's go. Bring your bags out to the car.'

'Can I just say goodbye to the children?' I asked her.

'Yes, but be quick. We have to go.'

Rahab's four children and I had become very close. A few days before, I'd told them that I was going away. They were all very upset that I was leaving. Hanin had even told her mother that she wanted to go with Mende and stay with her auntie in London. The previous evening, as they were going to bed, I'd said my last goodbyes to them. 'You'll all have to come and visit me in London,' I'd told them. Now, as I went into their room, I could see that they were all still fast asleep. So I just kissed each of them gently on the cheek and left. On the way back, I caught sight of Nanu's little hunched figure at the sink. I hugged her one last time, looking deep into her eyes and willing her to be strong.

★   ★   ★

When we arrived at the airport, it just looked to me like a bigger version of the bus station in downtown Khartoum — the one we'd left from to visit Rahab's mother in Kassala. There were thousands of people milling around, and it was chaotic, dusty and noisy. Rahab showed my ticket at the entrance, and a man in airport uniform put my bags onto a conveyor belt and they disappeared. Then Rahab handed my passport and ticket to a man behind a long row of desks. It was the first time that I'd seen my flight tickets. He looked over the passport, and then glanced up at us both.

'Which one of you is travelling?' he asked

'She is,' said Rahab, pointing to me.

The man looked at me, glanced back at my passport and then at me again. He was obviously checking that I was really the person on the passport photo. Once he'd satisfied himself that I was, he handed me a form.

'Here, fill this out,' he said, with a smile. 'You're free to proceed.'

Rahab immediately took the form from me and filled it out. Then we made our way to the departure gate, where we joined a long queue of people. As we waited, Rahab started to repeat her instructions to me all over again.

'Now, when you get to London, remember you must do exactly what Hanan tells you to . . . ' She went on and on like this, but I wasn't listening anymore. Finally, I reached the front of the queue and a man asked me for my passport and ticket. Rahab was not allowed to come any further. I stepped through the door into the departure gate. I turned and waved to her and she waved back at me. Then I walked out the entrance, down some steps and onto a wide expanse of tarmac — and Rahab was gone.

28

Fear of Flying

I looked around me. I had expected to see people getting on board an aeroplane, but they were all getting on a bus instead. I was confused. I had thought this was an airport, not a bus station. But clearly it must be both. As I stood there waiting for the plane to arrive, I watched three bus-loads of people drive off into the distance. When the bus driver came back for the last of the passengers, he shouted over at me.

'Hey! Are you travelling, or not?'

'I'm not here to catch a bus,' I said firmly. 'I'm here to catch a plane.'

At that, the man burst out laughing. He walked over and put his arm around me. 'Come on, little sister, get on the bus or you'll miss your flight. I guess you've never flown before, eh? The bus takes the passengers to the place where the plane takes off.'

As I climbed up the bus steps, I was so embarrassed I could have died. But an Arabic lady took hold of my hand and sat me down next to her. 'You look like you're travelling alone,' she said kindly.

'Yes I am,' I nodded.

'Come and sit by me then. I'll look after you.'

She told me her name was Fatima. She was

travelling with her little boy to London. 'Let me have a look at your ticket,' she said. 'Good. It's free seating. You can sit anywhere you like on the plane. Why don't you sit with us.'

The bus stopped and we climbed up some steps into the aeroplane. As we settled into our seats, a man in a smart uniform stood up in front and started to give us a talk. He began by explaining what we should do if the plane crashed in the sea. Then he showed us how to put on a yellow jacket, with a whistle and a tube attached to it. It would inflate with air, he explained, so that we could float if we fell into the sea. Then he talked about the masks that we should put over our faces to breathe. I was starting to panic. The way the man was talking, it seemed they expected the plane to crash.

'I'm scared, Auntie Fatima. What happens if we crash? I can't swim.'

'Don't worry. I can't either,' she replied, smiling. 'We just have to pray that all will be fine, and that, *Inshallah* — God willing — we'll all arrive safely.'

'But if we do crash, can you help me?'

'I can't even help myself,' said Fatima, laughing. 'I've flown so many times, but I've never managed to work out what I'm supposed to do with all those masks or those yellow vest thingies. But we've never crashed yet, so don't worry.'

Fatima leant across and helped me fasten a strap across my lap. Then I felt the plane jolt forward and begin to move slowly across the tarmac. After it turned a corner, it suddenly started to accelerate and I was forced back in my seat. As it roared off down the runway, I clutched my armrests in terror.

'Don't worry,' Fatima shouted, above the engine noise. 'Once we're up in the air it will be nice and quiet.'

As the plane climbed smoothly into the air I started to relax a little. But then I was horrified to notice that I seemed to have gone deaf. 'What's gone wrong with my ears?' I yelled at Fatima. 'I can't hear.'

'It's OK,' she laughed. 'It's normal. Just keep swallowing hard and your hearing will come back.'

We hadn't been in the air for long when another man in uniform came along the aisle and passed me a tray of food. When he saw that I had put it in my lap, he pulled a table down from the back of the seat in front of me. 'Put your tray on here,' he said, smiling at me.

'What's all this, Auntie Fatima?' I couldn't tell what anything was, as it was all wrapped up in plastic and foil.

'That's jam, that's butter, there's eggs and salad in there and that's your bread,' she said.

One sachet had a picture of a lemon on it, so I thought that I'd squeeze it on my salad. But when I opened it, there was a wet tissue inside. I ended up putting salt in my tea, thinking it was sugar. So I made do with orange juice. Then, after I'd finished the meal, I realised that I needed to go to the lavatory. I held it for as long as I could, but finally I had to wake Fatima who had dozed off next to me.

'Sorry. I need to go to the bathroom,' I said, shyly.

Fatima told me to go to the back of the aircraft, where I'd find the toilet. But I was too scared to get up and walk around the plane.

'It's OK. I'll stay here until he stops at the next station. Then I'll go to the bathroom,' I said. I thought the aeroplane must be like the bus I'd taken to visit Rahab's mother in Kassala, which had made lots of stops along the way.

'I'm afraid the plane doesn't make any stops,' Fatima replied, unable to contain her amusement. 'In fact, the next stop's London, in four or five hours' time. There's nothing to be scared of. Look at all those people,' she continued, pointing to a small queue at the back of the aircraft. 'They're all going to the toilet and they're fine. Just follow one of them.'

'But what happens if I'm on the loo and the plane suddenly changes direction? Won't I fall out of the plane?' I imagined that the toilet must be just a hole in the aircraft floor with all the waste going straight out into the air.

'You're far too big to fit through the toilet,' Fatima replied, with a reassuring smile.

Eventually, I couldn't hold on any more. So I walked slowly up the aisle holding on to the seat backs as I did so and joined the toilet queue. When my turn came, I opened the door and poked my head around to take a look inside. Then I put one leg inside and gingerly tested the floor.

'Hey, do you need the toilet or not?' I heard a male voice behind me say, impatiently.

'Yes, I do,' I retorted.

Once I was inside, I was surprised to see that it was more or less like a normal toilet. I sat down to my great relief and then tried to work out how to flush it. I could see a handle, but I was afraid to pull it, in case I was then ejected into thin air. So I just washed my hands in the little sink and left. By the time I'd finished, the little man outside had become even more irritable. So I was glad I hadn't flushed for him.

By mid-afternoon, the plane had started its descent. I felt it land with a big bump. We had arrived at London's Heathrow Airport. When I looked out of the window, I could see lots and lots of planes and miles and miles of tarmac. We trundled across to a long, low building.

'This is London,' said Fatima, sleepily. 'Do you have any family here to meet you? Or d'you want me to find you a taxi?'

'Someone should be here for me.'

'Well, come with me anyway and I'll help you through the airport,' Fatima suggested.

Rahab had told me that arriving in London would be easy, as Hanan would be there to meet me. I had expected to find her waiting for me as I got off the plane. But all I could see was a sea of strangers. Heathrow Airport was very scary. It was huge and there were crowds and crowds of people milling about. Many of them were *Hawajas* — white people — or other strange-looking foreigners. If Fatima hadn't been there, I'm sure I would have got completely lost. As we walked down a maze of passages, I had a thousand questions running through my mind.

How would Hanan find me? What would I do if she didn't? If anything went wrong, I had no money, I spoke no English and I knew absolutely no one.

I was frightened and I kept close to Fatima so as not to lose her. Soon, I found myself inside a huge building that just went on and on forever. I looked around me, half in fear and half in wonder: there were moving floors and staircases with people standing on them; the roof was a wall of glass; there were shiny, mirrored surfaces everywhere. I felt like I was inside a spaceship like the ones I'd seen on Rahab's TV when the children were watching. Khartoum airport had been like a tiny, dusty shed in comparison. There were even shops, cafés, telephones and restaurants — all inside under this huge glass roof. After a while, I wondered whether all London was like this — one huge covered building, where even the cars drove on covered roads.

Finally, we reached a large hall and joined a queue. I looked around me and saw that everyone was holding their passport in their hand. So I got mine out too. The queue crawled forward and I could see that there was a line of *Hawaja* men and women ahead of us looking at each passport and asking the owner some questions.

'What happens now?' I asked Fatima, in a nervous voice.

'Don't worry. Just hand them your passport and the form. All they want to do is check that the photograph really is you.'

When we came to the front of our queue,

Fatima stepped forward and I went to follow her. But the *Hawaja* lady behind the desk waved me back, indicating that I should wait in line. 'Stay there,' said Fatima, over her shoulder, 'I'll wait for you to join me on the other side of the desk.'

I nodded at Fatima. But I was very worried. I watched as the *Hawaja* woman leafed through Fatima's passport, and started asking her some questions. I could hear Fatima answering in English, but I couldn't understand a word. I started to panic. How would I answer the *Hawaja* woman's questions? Maybe she wouldn't let me through. What would I do then? Where would I go? Then I found myself stepping up to the counter. I handed her my passport and as I did so, I noticed that my hand was shaking.

'Thank you,' she said, with a smile. I remembered that much English from my lessons at school in the Nuba Mountains. She looked over my passport, glancing up at me as she did so. Then she started asking me questions in English. To each, I just shook my head at her. I didn't know what else to do. Finally, she motioned me to wait on one side. Then she went across to a *Hawaja* man on the desk opposite and started talking to him. I saw him nodding his head and looking over at me. My heart was in my mouth. What were they discussing? I looked past the counter at Fatima. I shook my head at her — as if to say, 'I don't know what's happening.' Just as I was really starting to panic, the *Hawaja* woman turned back to me. She wrote something in my passport, stamped it and handed it to me with a smile. I stood there waiting to see what would happen next.

'Go on,' she said, waving me on with her hand. 'Go on. You can go through now.'

I didn't understand what she said, but I did understand the gesture. '*Allhamdallilah*' — 'Praise be to God' — I said to myself, breathing a huge sigh of relief. I ran through to join Fatima on the other side.

'There! You're through,' she said, putting an arm around my shoulders. 'That wasn't so bad, was it? Come on. Let's go and get the luggage.' After descending some steps, we stopped by a large belt that kept turning with suitcases and bags magically appearing on it.

'How many bags do you have?' Fatima asked me.

'Three,' I replied.

'Well, when they come along you have to grab them, OK? Will you be able to recognise them?'

'I think so,' I replied nervously.

Fatima left her little boy with me and went to fetch two trolleys. I watched closely as the other people grabbed their bags as they trundled past. When mine came around I rushed forward and seized them. We pushed the trolleys out into yet another huge hall where we were greeted by a long line of expectant faces waiting behind a barrier. I guessed that they must be there to meet people off the plane. Was this where Hanan would meet me? Before leaving Khartoum, Fatima had shown me a recent photograph of Hanan, so that I would be able to recognise her. But I couldn't see her anywhere. Then I saw an Arabic man throw his arms around Fatima and give her a big hug. This must be Fatima's husband, I thought. He had just started to lead them out of the airport when she remembered me.

'Oh, hold on, let me just check if this girl is OK,' said Fatima. 'She's never been on an aeroplane before. I'm going to be leaving now,' she said, turning to me. 'Any sign of the person who's coming to meet you yet?'

'No,' I replied. I didn't want Fatima to leave me. I was terrified about being abandoned all alone in the airport.

'Look, I have to go now, but I don't like leaving you alone here like this. Do you have the phone number of the person who's meeting you? My husband can ring them on his mobile and find out where they've got to.'

'No. I don't.'

'Then what will you do if no one comes?'

'I don't know,' I said, now close to tears.

'Listen, don't worry. They must know which plane you're on and the time of your arrival. So you should be fine. I'm sure they'll be here soon.'

Despite what Fatima said, I felt far from all right. She found me a chair where I could sit down with my bags and wait. 'Bye-bye,' said Fatima, looking back at me with a guilty smile as she disappeared into the crowded airport.

I was really, really scared now. I was surrounded by thousands of people, but I had never felt so alone in all my life. I waited and waited, and after what seemed like an age I saw a woman coming towards me wearing a *hijab* — a

289

Muslim head-scarf. I tried to work out if it was Hanan or not. She looked like she might be, and I was just about to jump up and greet her when I saw her embrace an old Arabic lady sitting a few seats away. It wasn't Hanan after all. I was becoming increasingly convinced that I'd been abandoned. I started to wonder what would happen when it got really late. Did the airport close? If so, would I be thrown out onto the streets? Was I lost in this strange place where I didn't speak the language? Close to despair, I buried my head in my hands and started to cry. I longed for the security of someone claiming me — even as their slave.

'What's the matter?' I heard a voice say in Arabic. I looked up to see a woman sitting opposite me. 'Why are you crying?'

'I'm waiting for someone. But they haven't come.'

'Don't worry,' she said, gently. 'We're all waiting for someone. They'll come eventually. They always do.'

I told myself to stop crying and be brave. Just as I was drying my eyes on the back of my sleeve, I heard a voice behind me saying, 'Excuse me, are you Mende?' I spun around and there was a tall black man standing there. 'Mende Nazer?' he asked again. 'Are you Mende?'

'Yes,' I said, nervous and relieved all at the same time. 'But who are you?'

'My name's Peter. I've been sent here to get you by Hanan. Come on. Come with me. We've got to find two other Sudanese people that I'm collecting too.'

As I got up to leave, the Arabic lady opposite gave me a smile. 'See, I told you they'd come for you. I was right.'

'You're not Sudanese, are you?' Peter then asked her, catching the accent of her Arabic. It turned out that this woman and her husband were the two other people that Peter had been sent to collect. So, we were all travelling together. As soon as we hit the outside air, I realised with a shock that it was freezing cold. Or at least that's how it felt to me. As I walked out of the airport building, I shivered and looked up at the sky. I'd never seen anything like it before; it was flat, dull and grey. I stole a look at Peter's watch. It was five o'clock. As there didn't seem to be any clouds as such, I wondered where the sun could be.

In Sudan at this time of year, the sun would be shining brightly all day long, and I wondered if I had arrived in England in the middle of an eclipse of the sun or something. There had been an eclipse in Khartoum a few months ago, casting the day into a dull grey light rather similar to that which now enveloped the airport. Everyone had stood outside and banged pots and pans together. The noise had been deafening. It was supposed to make the sun wake up and to frighten the eclipse away. I looked around me, but no one seemed at all worried about stopping an eclipse of the sun here at Heathrow Airport.

I now know that I had arrived in London on what was just a fairly normal dreary day. Everywhere I looked, there was concrete and tarmac. We went up in a lift and out into a huge building full of cars. This just reinforced my impression that here, in this strange country, everything was kept inside buildings: the people, the shops, the restaurants and the cars. Even the sun seemed to be kept under cover.

Peter led us over to a big, shiny car. I got into the back with the Sudanese woman beside me. As we drove out of the car park, I was just overjoyed that someone had come to find me at last. I was happy to settle down into the warmth and security of the comfy seats. Although it was June, it was still really cold compared to the temperature back in Sudan. Peter put the heater on and the two men chatted away in the front. As the car warmed up, the woman next to me dozed off. But I was too excited and nervous to sleep — I just stared out of the window at this amazing new country.

We joined a queue of others cars edging away from the airport. The traffic speeded up, and we came to a huge road with three or four lanes of cars all moving along in the same direction. It was the biggest road I'd ever seen — and there were so many shiny new cars. So here I was, at last, in the land of the *Hawajas*. From the inside of the car I could stare at the other people we were passing. Their pale skins reminded me of when the men painted their bodies ghostly white at the wrestling time in the Nuba Mountains. And their long noses looked just like the beaks of the *Shengokor* — the forest chickens that used to dig up the seeds in my father's fields.

I remembered what my father had once told me about the *Hawajas* that had lived in the Nuba Mountains long, long ago. 'Your grandfather told me all about the *Hawajas* that used to live here back then,' he had said. 'They were always serious and dignified. You couldn't joke around with them — as they didn't seem to have a sense of humour.' I wondered what it was going to be like living here in the land of the *Hawajas*.

I glanced out of the car window on the other side, and noticed how green everything was. There were green trees and hedges and green fields all around us. It was so different from Sudan, where everything looked brown, dusty and dry. It must rain all the time in this country to be so green, I thought. As we drove into the city, I marvelled at the tall buildings, going up, up into the sky. I craned my head out of the window to try to get a look at the top of them. Then we started driving past long rows of identical little houses, all joined together with neat yards full of pretty flowers out in front.

Before I left Khartoum, Rahab had told me that England was very beautiful and that the people were always smiling. Well, I hadn't seen a lot of people smiling yet. But I did think that this must be the most beautiful city in the world. I felt like I was in a dream, gliding through this amazing place in this silent, smooth car. We'd been driving for what seemed like ages when we came to an area where the houses were bigger, each with their own large garden. They were very grand looking, with neat lawns and hedges and surrounded by trees. Finally, we slowed down and turned into a driveway.

29

False Hopes

I followed Peter down the big, tree-lined drive, clutching my bags and feeling very apprehensive. I had this horrible sense of starting again with a new set of masters. I remembered the time when I arrived at Rahab's house and how cruelly she'd treated me. Would these people treat me badly too? I reminded myself of all the lessons that I had learned with Rahab to avoid being beaten or abused. Never answer back. Never break anything. Always say 'yes master' to everything. As we waited for someone to answer the door, I found myself saying under my breath, 'Mende, be on your guard. Maybe she is better than her sister. Maybe she is worse. You just don't know.'

'Hi!' shouted a young boy as he opened the door. 'Who are you?' Behind him, I caught sight of Hanan.

'Hello,' she exclaimed. 'How are you all? Come in, come in.' She hugged the two Arab guests and then, to my surprise, she turned and hugged me too. I was so shocked. Why had she hugged me? For a moment, I was full of hope. Was I going to be treated well here? Is she a kind person, I wondered? Behind Hanan, her husband, Al Koronky, appeared.

'Welcome, welcome,' he said, ushering the

male guest into the house. 'How're you? How was the journey? The flight?'

I followed them down a hallway into a large living room at the far end. I could see that Hanan's house was bigger than Rahab's. Then I had my second surprise. As the others flopped down into comfy armchairs, Hanan motioned for me to sit down with them. I perched on the edge of the sofa with my hands clasped in my lap, feeling very uncomfortable. It was the first time that I'd ever actually been invited to sit with everyone like this. I just didn't know what to do. I was even more surprised when Hanan went off to the kitchen to make drinks without ordering me to go and help her. In the Nuba Mountains, if someone was very uncomfortable, we used to say that they looked like 'a soaked chicken': a chicken caught out in the rain hunches up and fluffs out all its feathers, looking very sorry for itself. That's just how I was feeling.

Hanan came back with a tray of drinks. I was amazed when she handed me some juice in a glass that was identical to those that the other guests were drinking from. In Rahab's house, I'd always been given my own plate, bowl and cup to drink and eat from. I was never allowed to use any of their things. For the first time since I'd been captured, I was sitting in a lounge being treated like everyone else. The strange thing was that I didn't really like it. I'd spent so many years being treated like a slave, that's what I'd become used to.

'How are Rahab and the children, Mende?' Hanan asked me.

'Mende.' She'd called me by my real name. Not *yebit*, or *abda*, or another such term of abuse. What would happen if I called her by her real name, rather than 'master', I wondered?

'They are all fine ... Hanan,' I replied, nervously. I was so surprised when she didn't react by abusing me, but just carried on talking.

'So you travelled together with our guests all the way from Khartoum, I take it?'

'No, I didn't,' I said.

'You didn't? Why not? I told Rahab that they'd be on the same flight as you, so they could look after you. Didn't she arrange for you to travel with them?'

'I don't know. I just met them here in London when I met Peter.'

'So how did you manage to get through passport control and customs on your own?'

'A woman on the plane helped me. She was very kind and she showed me what to do.'

'Well, praise be to Allah, you're here. That's the most important thing.'

Hanan, her husband and their guests now fell into an easy conversation about the flight, life in Khartoum and London. I was happy to fade into the background. After a few minutes, Hanan's children came rushing into the room, making lots of noise. They'd been upstairs playing. There were twin boys who looked around about two years old, and three older boys, aged around five to nine.

'This is Mende,' said Hanan, introducing me. 'Remember? The girl I told you would be coming here to work for us.'

'Come on, say 'Hello',' I said to the children.

'This is Mohamed,' Hanan continued. 'This is Ibrahim. This is Assi. And the two twins are Rami and Omar.'

Five boys! The little twins looked sweet and I was trying to get them to smile. At the same time I was remembering what Rahab had told me — that I would have to look after all Hanan's children. She'd also told me that I would have to clean and cook for the whole family. And from what I'd seen so far, the house looked much bigger and plusher than Rahab's — which would mean that I'd have more to do. Finally, after what seemed like an age, Hanan turned to me. 'Come on. You must be tired,' she said. 'Bring your bag and I'll show you your room.'

She led me off to a little room at the back of the house. It was about the same size as my shed back at Rahab's house, with no outside windows. But it was a palace in comparison to where I had slept in Khartoum. There was a dark blue carpet on the floor. There was a mirror on the wall and a desk beneath it. There was even a proper bed for me to sleep in, with a mattress, proper sheets and some sort of enormous fluffy blanket.

'Here you are,' Hanan said. 'You can sleep now. You must be very tired. Then tomorrow, you can start your work.'

Hanan was right. I was exhausted and I was still feeling cold. I crawled under the bed covers fully clothed. It was the first time in my life that I'd ever been in a proper bed. It felt wonderful. As I was drifting off to sleep, strange new hopes were running through my mind. I couldn't believe how nicely Hanan was treating me. I'd been hugged when I arrived. People were talking to me kindly. I had been given my juice in the same glass as the others. I had a room with a carpet and a real bed. I hadn't been treated so kindly since my childhood in the Nuba Mountains. Might I dare to dream that this family were actually going to treat me like one of them?

The next thing I knew, I was back on the big aeroplane, but it had crashed into the sea. All the people were putting on yellow life vests and blowing them up and swimming away but I couldn't swim and no one was helping me and I was sinking and drowning. I went down, down, down into a cold black sea. I looked up and I could see the sky as a tiny speck above me. I knew that I was drowning but I was too numb to do anything about it. And then I woke up. I sat bolt upright in bed, panicking in the darkness and catching my breath. I didn't know where I was but I realised that I was freezing cold.

My room was actually a converted storeroom, built onto the back of the house. It still had an old bicycle and some cardboard boxes piled up in one corner. But the main problem was that it was so cold. There was an electric heater that I managed to work out how to turn on. I hung my bedclothes over the heater, so that the warm air would rise up into the bed with me. I practically took the heater to bed with me that first night and for many nights following.

★ ★ ★

'Time to get up,' Hanan called early the next morning, as she opened my door. 'Come on. I want to show you how you make the kids' school lunch boxes. Hurry now. Come and join me in the kitchen.'

The kitchen was bigger than Rahab's, and there were so many shiny white machines standing on the floor and the worktops. I had no idea what any of these things were, as I'd never seen them before. My heart sank. 'I'm going to have to learn to use all these complicated new things,' I thought to myself. They looked so expensive and like they'd be so difficult to use. I was scared of getting something wrong and maybe breaking them. And I was scared of being punished for doing so.

'Rahab did tell you what you were coming here to do, didn't she?' Hanan asked me.

'Yes.'

'The same things as you did in her house. The cleaning, cooking and the washing, but it's much easier here. We have machines for a lot of this stuff. This is a washing machine for the clothes. So, you don't have to wash them by hand. I'll show you how to use it later. I also want you to iron and fold the clothes and put them away. And we have a dishwasher, for the dirty dishes, but we only use that when there's a lot of washing up. Normally, you'll just wash up by hand, all right?'

I nodded. 'Yes, Hanan.'

'I also want you to look after the children when they come back from school.'

I nodded. 'Yes, Hanan.'

'So, come and see how I make the children's school lunches. Then you'll be able to do this every morning, before they leave for school.'

Hanan showed me how to make the children's favourite sandwiches. She pointed out which cupboards had the packets of crisps in them. I had to memorise which flavours each of the children liked by the colour of the packets: green for salt and vinegar, yellow for cheese and onion and so on. After her husband had taken the older kids off to school in the car, Hanan and I sat down to have a cup of tea in the kitchen together.

'So now, I want you to start cleaning the kitchen — all the cupboards, both inside and out.'

I nodded. 'Yes, Hanan.'

'If you're hungry, there's cornflakes here and milk in the fridge. You know what cornflakes are, don't you? Breakfast cereal. You eat them with milk and sugar in a bowl, like this. You did make the tea in Rahab's house, didn't you? If you want tea, you can help yourself. Which mug would you like?'

'I don't know,' I answered, in confusion, never having been treated like this before. 'Any one of them is fine.'

'Now, let me show you how to use the washing machine,' Hanan added, opening the door. 'You put the dirty clothes in here. But you must separate the coloured clothes from the whites. You have to wash them separately, or the colours will run.'

I nodded, but I didn't understand what she

meant. I just knew from my time with Rahab that it was always best to agree to anything they said. Hanan showed me where to put the washing powder. Then she showed me a bewildering row of dials and knobs that I'd have to push to select the right washing programme. By now, I was completely lost. I was worried that I'd get into more trouble if I ruined all their clothes, than by admitting that I didn't understand anything.

'Hanan, I'm sorry,' I eventually said, 'but I'm confused about all those letters and numbers and things. And you haven't shown me how I change the water when it's dirty?'

'You don't need to change the water,' she said, laughing. 'The machine does it all for you. Look, the first few times you do the washing, call me and I'll set the machine going. But you must watch carefully and learn how to do it yourself.'

'OK, I'll try,' I said uncertainly.

'If you don't understand something or if you need anything, just come and ask.'

'Well, there is one thing,' I said, hesitantly.

'What's that?'

'I was cold last night,' I murmured. 'I couldn't sleep properly.'

Hanan told me that that had reminded her — the heating wasn't working properly in my room. She promised to ask her husband to call the man to come and have it fixed, although it never was.

As Hanan disappeared into the lounge and settled down in front of the TV, I was feeling hopeful. She was so much nicer than her sister.

She was telling me what work I had to do for her, but at least she was doing it with a friendly smile. Perhaps life in London was going to be happier for me. I spent most of the day cleaning and scrubbing the kitchen, just like I had that first day at Rahab's house many years before. I could see Hanan dozing with her feet up on the sofa. The twins were playing on the carpet at her feet. As I was still finding it cold, I worked really hard — dusting and scrubbing and cleaning — in an effort to warm myself up. Once I'd finished what I was doing, Hanan came in and pulled a new machine out of one of the cupboards.

'This is a hoover — it's for cleaning the carpets. Did you have one of these back in Khartoum?'

'No,' I said. 'I used to do the carpets with a brush.'

'Well this is much better. Watch carefully and I'll show you how to use it.'

The hoover was a cylinder on wheels, with a long flexible plastic tube attached to it. I thought it looked very ugly — just like a snake with that long black neck and a pointy snout. Hanan flicked a switch and a loud whining noise made me jump. Once she started to suck up the dirt from the carpets, the noise changed to a frightening hissing sound. It not only looked like a snake, it sounded like one too. I was terrified of it.

'You don't have a brush?' I asked her. 'I don't like this thing. Can't I do the carpets with a brush?'

'No. You can't. The brush doesn't get inside the carpets to clean them properly like this machine does. You'll get used to it. I want you to hoover every day. Here, try it.'

I held the tube gingerly, and cried out when it grabbed hold of a corner of my dress and proceeded to suck it in with a high-pitched whine. It was like it was trying to eat me. As it just wouldn't let go, I dropped the hoover and tried to run and escape. But Hanan laughed, switched the strange machine off, and told me not to be so silly.

The house was L-shaped, with the huge downstairs lounge at one end. A dining room opened off the lounge, with a polished wooden table and chairs. Upstairs, there were four bedrooms, a second lounge and two bathrooms. Out the back of the house there was a wide expanse of lawn ringed with trees and there was a smaller front garden surrounded by tall hedges. The drive ran down to the front of the house between two rows of trees. I thought that Mr Al Koronky must be a very important person, to have such a large house in London.

That first day, it was around nine in the evening by the time I'd finished all the cleaning. I was so tired, all I wanted to do was to sleep. But when I went into the kitchen, I couldn't believe my eyes. There was a new mountain of washing up in the sink and dirty plates on the table. There was even some leftover food on the floor. It turned out that Hanan's twin boys were very messy eaters. By the time I'd finished cleaning up again, the family had gone to bed. I was just about to retreat into my own little room when Hanan came down to make some hot milk for the twins.

'Ooohhh,' she said, cheerfully, 'the house is so clean. Rahab told me that you'd do a very good job. How right she was.'

It was past midnight before I finally collapsed, fully clothed, into my own little bed. I pulled the heater under my duvet and soon I was fast asleep. That first day set my routine for the next, and for so many days after that. I would get up around 6.30 a.m. and put out the breakfast things. Then I'd make tea and prepare the three older children's lunch boxes. Then I'd tidy up the breakfast mess and start to clean the house. Around lunchtime, I'd prepare a meal for Hanan and the twins, who were too young to go to school. Then I'd continue working until last thing at night. Soon, Hanan had me changing the twin's nappies too. At the weekends, I'd keep the children quiet while Mr Al Koronky rested, and do as much cleaning and washing as I could without disturbing him.

Whenever I had finished all my work, I was allowed to go and pray in my little room. I had found a *Muslaiyah* — an Islamic prayer mat — folded up in one corner. It was a little cheap raffia thing. But to me, it was very special. Here at least I didn't have to hide my praying. The one thing Hanan and her husband both seemed to pride themselves on was their devotion to Islam. Hanan always wore long, loose clothes covering her body and a headscarf when she went outside. They believed they were very good, devout Muslims.

From the very start, I was far more scared of Al Koronky that I was of Hanan. He looked strict and behaved in a very superior way. He would order me around: 'Mende, make me tea,' he'd say, or 'Mende, make me some coffee.' I started to really dislike him when he told me to clean his shoes and leave them out for him each morning. But the worst thing was the day he ordered me to clean the cars. There were two big, shiny cars out on the drive and I went out with one bucket of soapy water and one bucket of clean water to wash them. They were gleaming and looked to be very new and I was scared I might scratch the paintwork or something. I had to be so careful, it took me ages to finish the washing — by which time my hands were swollen and freezing cold. I wondered who Al Koronky thought he was that he could order me to do such horrible jobs?

A few days after being sent out to clean the cars, the boys came back from school without their father, who normally fetched them home.

'Where's your father?' I asked them, after they came charging into the kitchen.

'Oh, he had to stay at work late,' said Mohamed, helping himself to a coke out of the fridge.

'So who drove you back from school?'

'The embassy driver. We came in the embassy car, too,' he added, proudly.

'Which embassy? Why were you in their car?'

'My father works for the Sudanese Embassy. Didn't you know?'

'No,' I said. 'What does he do there?'

'He's the acting ambassador,' said Mohamed, grandly. 'D'you know what that is?'

'No.'

'Well, at the moment he's the most important man at the embassy. The man who's sort of the president of the embassy, the ambassador, he's gone back to Sudan for a while, so my father's taken his place.'

I didn't really understand. But it seemed clear to me now that Al Koronky must be someone very important. It made me feel even more scared of him, knowing that he was so powerful.

All in all, it was a confusing time for me. I wasn't being beaten or verbally abused any more and Hanan, at least, was treating me quite kindly. But I was having to work just as hard as I had done in Khartoum, if not harder. Part of me felt like I was still being treated like a slave. But another part of me felt like I was being taken in as a part of the Al Koronky family. After all, I had been sent to London under Rahab's orders, not Hanan's, and I still felt that Rahab was really my 'master'. It was her instructions that I was still following here in London, not Hanan's. She'd told me how to work, how to behave and how to treat her sister. Although I'd left Rahab behind at Khartoum airport, I still felt as if I was labouring under her shadow. Although I was in London, I was Rahab's slave, not Hanan's. And after all, Rahab was the person who'd said she'd paid for me, purchasing me like an object, and presumably it was she who still believed she 'owned' me. I just didn't know what to think any more.

Hanan would spend most afternoons sleeping. The rest of the time she'd usually be watching TV or reading magazines. She rarely seemed to have any friends come to visit her. She was very different from Rahab, whose life was a social whirl. As the weeks passed, the days all seemed to blend into one. Maybe I was being treated better than before, but my life had become a daily grind again, a soul-destroying life of drudgery once more. And I felt so very, very lonely.

It couldn't go on like this forever. Something in me had changed, maybe because I was so far away from Sudan. Three weeks or so after I arrived in London, I decided to take some action. I still had the phone number with me that Kumal had given me in Khartoum. She had told me that her cousin was in *bilabarra* — far away in a foreign country. I hoped that he was in England. If so, I wondered whether Hanan might let him come and visit me. She was treating me so differently from Rahab, I thought it had to be worth asking. In any case, what did I have to lose? I went and found her preparing to have an afternoon nap in the lounge.

'Hanan, can I talk to you for a second?' I asked her nervously.

'Yes. What is it?' she replied sleepily.

'Oh, nothing,' I mumbled, turning back to the kitchen. I couldn't pluck up the courage to ask her that day, or the next, or the next. In fact it was almost a week before I went into the lounge again to try for a second time.

'Hanan,' I said. 'Can I ask you something?'

'Yes.' She smiled at me. 'What?'

I held out the piece of paper with the number on it in a shaky hand. 'I have this telephone number that my friend in Khartoum gave me. Can you tell if it's in England? And if it's possible for me to telephone them?'

'Let me see it!' she said sharply, jumping up from the sofa. Immediately, her whole demeanour had changed. She snatched the piece of paper, took one look at it and then started firing questions at me.

'Who wrote this number down for you? Tell me! Who was it?'

'I wrote it down,' I whispered.

'No you didn't! Tell me the truth! Who wrote it down for you?'

'I wrote it down. Really. I did,' I mumbled. 'But the number was given me by Kumal.'

'Who's this Kumal then? Come on. Out with it! There's no one in our family called Kumal, is there?'

'No. She's not from your family. She's just my friend.'

'Your friend! Your friend from where, exactly?'

'My friend from Khartoum.'

'How do you know her?' she asked, suspiciously. 'I thought you didn't have any friends in Khartoum.'

With a shaky voice, I told Hanan the whole story of how I'd met Kumal at Rahab's house and how she was an old friend from my tribe. Kumal had given me the number in case I wanted to make a Nuba friend abroad. She'd told me that he was her cousin and that he was in *bilabarra* — so I didn't even know if he was in England or not.

'I'm sorry,' I whispered. 'If you don't want me to speak to him, I won't.'

'No!' she snapped. 'I certainly don't. I don't want you contacting anyone. You hear me? No one.' She looked down at the paper. 'Anyway, this is a very old number. It won't work any more. All the telephone numbers here in London have changed.'

With that, she ripped up the number, dropping the scraps of paper on the floor. 'Do you have other numbers with you? Give me your bag.' Hanan snatched it off me, but there wasn't anything else inside, apart from my passport. 'Aha! Your passport! I think I'll keep this safe with me from now on. I don't trust you with it any more.'

After this, my relationship with Hanan started to go downhill fast. She was no longer the kind woman who had hugged me when I first arrived in her house. She began to shout at me, for no reason at all. She began calling me names. And she began watching me very closely — checking on me wherever I was in the house. Ever since I'd arrived, the only time that I was allowed outside on my own was when I took the rubbish to the bins on the driveway. Now, I noticed that Hanan was keeping an eye on me from an upstairs window. I realised that the incident with the phone number must have made her worried that I would try to escape.

As time went on I started to wonder whether

life hadn't been better in Khartoum. At least in Rahab's house there were always people around. It was noisy and full of life. I could spend time in the sun, cleaning the yard next to the orchard or in the garden. I might be sent to the corner shop for some groceries, and I could watch the kids playing on the streets. But more than anything, I missed Rahab's children. The youngest ones especially had grown up with me and treated me like a big sister. I was missing the basic human warmth and affection they had given me. Hanan's boys were noisy, but well-behaved enough. I just wasn't close to them in any way.

A few days later, I was to realise just how suspicious Hanan was becoming. I was preparing some rice and chicken curry for Sunday lunch. I noticed that the bin bag was full, so I tied it up and took it out to the front of the house. As I threw it into the bin, I glanced up the driveway. There was a big crowd out on the street. I could hear them chatting merrily and singing. They sounded like they were having such fun and I had a sudden urge to take a closer look. I glanced over my shoulder to check if anyone was watching me, then slipped into the trees and crept up to the top of the drive. From there, I could see a crowd of people dressed in the most beautiful clothes. The women were wearing brightly-coloured, flowing robes. They had long, glossy black hair, which was plaited all down their backs. The men were dressed in smart suits.

They were standing outside a colourful building, which looked a bit like a mosque. It must be a wedding, I thought. People began dancing and singing along to the music, which was coming from loudspeakers on top of some parked cars. The men were knocking together a couple of sticks, to beat out a rhythm. I was suddenly reminded of the wrestling time back in the Nuba Mountains. It sounded just like the noise the Nuba men would make by hitting two hollow sticks together, as the wrestlers ran around in a big circle, chanting 'Eeh-ha! Eeh-ha! Eeh-ha!' I stayed there for about five minutes, smiling away to myself. I longed to go and join them — to play and sing and dance. But suddenly, there was a shout behind me.

'*Yebit* Mende! *Yebit* Mende! Where are you!' It was Hanan.

At the sound of that one word, *yebit*, all the worst memories of my time in Khartoum came flooding back to me. I turned and ran back down the drive as fast as I could. I hoped Hanan had not seen me — that I could get back to the house before she realised where I'd been. But as I came racing out of the trees, I caught sight of her standing outside the front door.

'What on earth do you think you were doing, *yebit*!' she cried, as I stopped in front of her.

'I was putting out the rubbish, Hanan, just doing the rubbish,' I stammered.

'Well, the bins aren't at the top of the drive! Are they? Are they, *yebit*!' she yelled. 'They're here, right in front of your eyes. Don't think I didn't see you! Don't think I'm that stupid! What were you doing up there? Answer me! What were you up to?'

'I just went to watch the wedding, that's all.

Just for a few minutes. I'm sorry.'

'Well, don't you ever do that again, do you hear me?' she snapped.

'Yes, Hanan. I'm sorry. I'm sorry,' I said, choking back my tears.

'Don't you understand? London is a very bad place. It's full of murderers and dangerous, evil people. Anything can happen to you out there! Anything! Come back inside at once.'

As I went into the house, she shut the door behind me, did something with the key and put it in her pocket as she marched off towards the kitchen. 'Follow me, *yebit*,' she snapped over her shoulder.

Ever since I'd arrived there, the front door had always been kept closed and it had a strange latch and lock, unlike anything I'd seen in Sudan. It seemed that if you were inside you could try to open it, but if you were outside you couldn't. If I opened the door, say to put the rubbish out, I'd be scared that it would close behind me and lock me outside. Sometimes, I'd jam a shoe in the door to stop it closing. But this was the first time that I'd seen Hanan remove the key, and I presumed it meant that she must have locked the door from the inside and that I wouldn't be able to open it any more. It was also the first time that she had called me *yebit* — that same cruel name that Rahab had used for me. I followed her into the kitchen with a sinking feeling in my heart.

'I've told you, *yebit*! I've told you!' she shouted, rounding on me in the kitchen. 'You are not allowed to go outside. It's dangerous out

313

there. Don't you listen to what I say?' She reminded me of Rahab now. This was much more like the behaviour I was used to in Khartoum. I felt like I was being treated like a slave again and I was very scared.

'If you don't believe me, just let me tell you something,' Hanan continued. 'This is what happened to the last girl that was here, before you. She was called Khayria and she was a very bad girl. One day, she went outside and she never came back. She just disappeared. Either someone murdered her or she was lost in this huge, dangerous city. Or maybe she just died of the cold. We don't know. We never found her. If you go outside, the same will happen to you. That's how dangerous it is. D'you understand me now?'

'Yes, Hanan,' I whispered.

'Whatever happened to her, she'll never go back to Sudan now. So she'll never see her family. Not ever again. Is that what you want? Is that what you want to happen to you?'

'No, Hanan.'

'So, you must never go outside again. Do you hear me? It's forbidden. If you do, you'll find out what will happen to you. There are so many bad people in London. They'll find you and they'll kill you. And then you'll never get to see your family again. That's not what you want, is it?' Then she came over and put an arm around me. Her anger was subsiding and she was trying to be friendly again. 'If you stay inside and work well and behave, then when we go back to the Sudan, we'll take you with us to see your family.

We plan to go back in about a month's time, for a holiday. You'd like that, wouldn't you?'

I nodded. 'Yes, Hanan,' I said.

But I didn't believe her promises. How on earth could Hanan find my family, even if she wanted to? It was just a trick to make me behave. Hanan had never shown the slightest interest in my family before now. She had never asked me about them and I had never mentioned them, but somehow she knew that I was desperate to see them again. The only thing I could think of was that Rahab had told her this. It was all so cruel, these games they were playing with me.

Later, in my room, I thought back over what Hanan had said about the girl who had been here before me. Poor Khayria. Where was she from, I wondered? Did she escape? If so, where had she escaped to? And how? Surely, she had no family here in London, so who could have helped her? Maybe she really had been murdered, just like Hanan said. I imagined her lost and alone on the streets of London. It didn't bear thinking about.

★　★　★

After learning about Khayria's fate, I became more and more depressed. There just seemed to be no way out of my present situation. I was feeling so down that I stopped eating properly. I had no appetite at all. I started living in the happiness of my past, trying to recapture the closeness and affection of my family and home. Most of all I remembered the love of my parents and how proud they were of their little girl. I thought back over the day that I won one of the races at the school sports day. The school had opened early, and we had greeted all the visitors with a special parade. After marching in formation across the schoolyard, we bowed to the headmaster and then bowed to the audience. I could see my mother and father's excited faces in the crowd. There were six different races, including sprinting, long-distance, the sack race and our own version of the egg-and-spoon race.

In place of the egg-and-spoon we played the lemon-and-spoon race. We had lots of chickens in the Nuba Mountains. But no one ever ate the eggs as that would have been seen as such a waste. We made sure that the eggs were always hatched into chicks, as we all loved eating chicken. Eggs were far too precious to waste on a real egg-and-spoon race. Instead, we started by kneeling down with our hands tied behind our backs, and with a lemon balanced on top of a mound of earth in front of us. We all held the spoon in our mouths by the handle. When the race started, we had to bend down, pick up the lemon with the spoon, and start running. The first person across the finishing line with the lemon still on their spoon was the winner.

That first year at school, I was the winner of the lemon-and-spoon race. I was so proud — I even managed to beat all the boys in my class, including Mohamed, the class swot. At the end of the day, I went up to collect my prize from the school headmaster. It was a bag of sweets, a pencil and an exercise book. I was so happy, because I knew my parents were there watching me.

When we got home, my mother gave me a big hug. 'I was so worried,' she said, 'especially when I saw how fast you were running. But you won!' My father re-enacted the sack race for me, jumping around the yard in an old sorghum sack. Soon, we were all rolling around with laughter at his antics. Then I got my bag of sweets out. They were already half finished, but I shared the rest around my family. They were a once-in-a-lifetime treat for us, as we could never afford to buy such things.

I cast my mind back to my earliest ambitions in life, my dream to become a doctor after we had taken my brother, Babo, to hospital with dysentery and he had almost died on the donkey journey to Dilling. This had convinced me that we needed a doctor in our village, and that I should try my hardest at school. I remembered talking to my father about my dream of becoming a doctor, and the way he had promised to support me in any way he could. The very thought of those happy, happy times brought tears to my eyes.

As the weeks passed, I became more and more depressed. In Khartoum, at least Rahab's children had treated me with love and affection. But here, I was a stranger to the children: I was completely isolated and alone. I stayed in the house and worked from early morning to late at night — unloved and uncared for. I was trapped in the middle of this strange city that I had been told was dark and dangerous. All I did was work,

317

work, work. The only thing I looked forward to was sleeping in my cold little room.

I felt as if I would be trapped in this house in London for ever more. I thought about Asha, the old Nuba woman at the slave trader Abdul Azzim's house in Khartoum. Just like me, she had been captured when she was just a little girl. But when I met her, she was already an old woman. Would I end up the same as her, I wondered, spending all the rest of my life in slavery?

30

Suicide?

I started to feel as though I were no longer alive. I was just a ghost, moving without will from one day to the next. I'd even stopped being able to cry. So it's hardly surprising that I started to think about killing myself. I spent a lot of time in the kitchen, where there were many sharp knives. During the raid on our village in the Nuba Mountains I had seen the raiders stab people in the neck and the heart. So I thought that that must be the easiest way to kill someone. Maybe that was the best way to kill myself too.

One day I took a carving knife and sliced slowly across the end of my index finger, the sharp blade drawing blood easily. I thought about going to my room, lying down on my bed and just stabbing myself with the knife. I wasn't scared about doing it. I just hoped that I'd die very quickly, so I wouldn't be in pain. At the time, killing myself seemed a much better alternative than staying alive. My only worry was that Hanan might discover me before I was dead and rush me off to hospital or something.

As I contemplated taking my own life, I thought about what my life might have been had I never been taken away from the Nuba Mountains. By now I must have been around twenty years old. In the Nuba tribe, we don't keep records of birth dates or even celebrate birthdays. But by counting back the years, I could reach a rough idea of my age. Even if I had gone on to study to be a doctor, I would still have been married off before my fifteenth birthday. That was our tradition. My childhood fianceé, Juba, would have come and claimed me — and then there would have been a big marriage celebration, just like there had been for my sister Kunyant. Juba and I would have built our own *shal* to live in, within shouting distance of the huts of my mother and father and both of my sisters. And who knows? By now we would probably have started our own little family.

I could remember so clearly the happy day when my mother first told me that I was engaged to Juba. I was not even seven years old at the time and all I used to wear was one string of beads around my waist. They were small red and white beads with a big, beautiful red one at the front. One evening, my mother had said that she wanted to take them off me and replace them with a string of black beads.

'But I love these ones, *Umi*, please don't take them,' I'd cried. 'I don't want to wear those horrid black ones.'

'Don't worry, Mende-*cando*,' she'd said. Mende-*cando* was a term of endearment she used for me, meaning something like little Mende in English. 'I only want to re-string them. If I don't, the string will break and then you'll lose them. You'll get them straight back.'

Then she had bent to put the black beads

around me. 'I don't want these black ones. I want my own ones,' I wailed.

'How do you know they're so important to you?' she asked, laughing.

'You gave them to me. So they're very special.'

'No, I didn't,' she said, shaking her head and smiling. 'These beads were given to you by your fiancé, the man who is going to marry you.'

'I'm going to be married, just like Musa and Kunyant?' I exclaimed, in disbelief. 'Is it true, Umi?' My mother nodded her head and I started dancing around our yard with joy. 'Kunyant, Kunyant, one day I'm going to be married, just like you,' I sang at the top of my voice.

'You're so small, you don't know anything. Why're you so happy that you're going to be married?' Kunyant replied, laughing. 'I don't want to be married, even at my age!'

Then my father grabbed me by the hand and pulled me over onto his lap. 'Well, we're not quite ready to lose you to your husband yet,' he chuckled. He spat twice on the top of my head and stroked my hair, which is a traditional Nuba blessing. 'May Allah keep you and bless you so you will grow up happy and be married well.'

'Who is going to marry me, then?' I asked my mother.

'Well, he's a good, brave man. He has big fields and he grows a lot of sorghum. He decided to marry you because he heard what a good family you come from,' my mother said, proudly. 'He heard that your father's father was very strong and brave. But he lives far away, so you won't see him until you're much older. When the time is right, he'll come for you and then you'll be married.'

The contrast of my wonderful childhood memories with my dark, deathly life now in London just made me feel even more hopeless. I thought long and hard about killing myself, and how best to do it so I wouldn't be discovered before I was dead. But there was one thing that stopped me. Hanan was going back to Sudan in a few weeks' time. She had made me a promise that she'd take me with her and that I'd see my family again. I didn't really believe her. I was sure that she was just using this as a way to control me. But of course, part of me wanted to believe that she really was going to take me. This was the hope that got me through each day. I thought that I would wait and see what happened. I wasn't naive. It just gave me something to live for.

At the same time, I began to feel very sick. I started noticing there were clumps of hair all over my pillow each morning. I realised with a shock that my hair was falling out. When I looked in the mirror, I noticed that I was looking exhausted and ill. My face was pinched and yellow, my shoulders hunched like an old woman. I could see that my skin had become dry and scaly like a fish, and it was flaking off.

One night, I woke up with a throbbing pain in my mouth. The toothache was so bad that I couldn't get back to sleep. I wondered what to do. Once, when I was a child in the Nuba Mountains, my mother had had toothache. I'd watched her grind up some salt together with the leaf of a certain tree, and put a wad of it in her mouth. Although I couldn't find the same tree here in London, I knew I could get some salt from the kitchen. I made myself a cotton wool pad with salt on it, and put this in my mouth. Just as I was leaving the kitchen, Hanan came wandering in wearing a dressing gown.

'What are you doing awake at this time of night?' she asked suspiciously.

'I've got toothache. So I'm putting some salt on it.'

'Where's the pain?' Hanan asked, as she got some milk out of the fridge.

'It's in here,' I said, pointing to the back of my mouth, 'and then there's pain all up the side of my face.'

'Well obviously it's in your mouth,' she said irritably. 'I can't see where you're pointing if you stick your finger in there like that. We'll have to take a proper look in the morning.'

The salt stopped the pain for a little while and I managed to get back to sleep. The next morning, I got up and started my work as normal.

'So, how're you feeling? Better?' Hanan asked me, as she came down into the kitchen.

'Yes, I'm feeling better,' I lied.

'That's good,' replied Hanan, clearly relieved. 'It's far too expensive to take you to see a tooth doctor here in London.'

For eight years or so, Rahab had never once taken me to see a doctor, even when I had malaria. So I just accepted that Hanan wasn't going to take me to one either. Shortly after this,

Hanan started preparing for her holidays in Sudan. She spent days shopping for gifts, leaving the children for me to look after. She would come back with armfuls of presents — all done up in fancy wrapping. I was desperate for any sign that she might still be planning to take me with her to Sudan. But she never mentioned it. I became more and more certain that she was planning to leave me behind. I became so angry that I wanted to shout and scream. One morning Hanan was in the living room doing some packing and she called me in to help her. I knelt down next to her and started folding the children's clothes.

'*Yebit*,' she said slowly. 'You know I'm going on holiday next week, back to Sudan. I've decided to go alone for the first week. I'm leaving you here with the children and my husband. When they come out to join me, you're going to stay here. Do you understand?'

I was boiling with so much anger inside that I couldn't speak and there was a long moment's silence before I could reply. Then, quietly but firmly, I said, 'No.'

'Sorry?' she said.

'I said no,' I repeated, surprising myself with my own courage. 'I'm not staying here alone in this house with your husband. I can't do that. It's wrong.'

'What did you say?' she asked, incredulously. 'I really hope you didn't say what I think you did.'

'I said I can't stay alone in this house with your husband,' I replied firmly, my anger making me braver now.

'What!' she exploded at me. 'Are you saying you don't trust my husband! He's an important man in the government. He's a good, decent man. How dare you imply otherwise! The children will be here too. What's your problem?'

'I'm not saying anything against your husband,' I retorted. 'But it's wrong for me to stay here alone with a man. I'm an unmarried woman, and it's not allowed in Islam. That's all.'

Hanan was silent for a few seconds. Back in Khartoum, Rahab had denied that I was a Muslim, saying that Islam wasn't for black people like me. In her mind this had justified her abusing me. But Hanan had never denied me my faith. In fact, Hanan and her husband prided themselves on being very devout Muslims. But I wondered how they could think this, when they treated me, a fellow Muslim, in the way that they did. In my Koran studies at school, I had learned that people are like the teeth of a comb — all created the same and equal. As a Muslim, Hanan knew that she shouldn't go against the rules of Islam where a fellow Muslim was concerned. I was using this against her now and I was feeling more powerful: finally I had found a way to fight back. Or so I thought.

'Yes, of course, I know that,' she said finally. Her tone had changed and she was trying to be persuasive now. 'But it's not just any man, is it? It's my husband. You can trust my husband, you know that. He's very devout and very considerate of these things. You think about it — I'm sure you'll change your mind.'

With that, she dropped the subject. But a week

later, she came to me with a different plan. The whole family would go to Sudan, and I would be sent to stay with one of their friends in London.

'Who is this friend?' I asked her. 'Is he married?'

'Yes,' she said, testily, 'he is married. He has a good Muslim wife and family. So you'll be staying in their home. There. Does that satisfy you?'

'Yes,' I said. 'That should be all right.'

But the day before they were supposed to leave for Sudan, Hanan told me that the plan had changed again. She would still be leaving with the children, but her husband would stay behind for one week. I would have to stay to look after him. After that, he would fly out to join them, and I would go and stay at their friend's house. Now, I would be staying alone in the house for a week with her husband. In Islam, this was the worst possible option.

'Why have you changed your mind?' I asked, in a frightened voice. 'This is even worse than before. You know that I can't stay here alone with a man.'

'There's nothing more to discuss, *yebit*!' she snapped, turning on me. 'I won't hear another word from you on it. My husband has some very important work to do here in London. So he's staying and so are you. And that is the end of it.'

I was so angry and upset. Hanan wasn't taking me back to Sudan with them; I wasn't going to see my family; and now she was leaving me alone in London with her husband. I knew that, in

Islam, it was very wrong for me to be left alone with any man. More to the point, Hanan knew this too. That night, I hardly slept at all. I was consumed with a black despair, because now I knew for sure that I wasn't going to see my family. Since my arrival in London, neither Hanan nor her husband had ever beaten me or abused me physically. But I was still terrified about being left behind, alone in the house with a man: it was against my religion and bad things had happened to me in the past in such situations.

★　★　★

The following day, once I'd finished my work, I went to my room and cried and cried. As I sobbed into my pillow, a memory came into my mind of happier times in my life when I had been so pleased to be left alone with a man — only this time I had felt so safe and secure with him because he was my father. We had been out in the fields together, preparing to plant the crops. In the evening I was lying outside with my head in his lap as we chatted around the fire. As the clouds drifted across the sky, they would cling to the mountain peaks like a blanket.

'Look, Mende,' said my father, pointing, 'the clouds are cuddling the hills.'

'One day, *Ba*, I'd love to touch the clouds,' I told him, dreamily. 'What're they like, hard or soft?'

'Well, a long time ago, the sky was so low that

you could reach up and touch them. But, one day, a greedy woman was making a huge bowl of sorghum porridge. As she was building up the fire, she thought to herself that she would take some of the clouds to eat with the porridge, because they were soft and creamy like butter. She stoked up her fire until the big pot of porridge was bubbling away. But, just as she was about to seize some of the clouds to eat, the sky noticed how big and hot her fire had become. The sky became very afraid, because it feared that all the clouds were going to melt. In fact, the sky was so scared that it rushed away from the earth until it was as far and as high as it is now. So, if it hadn't been for this greedy woman, you could still reach up and touch the sky and feel how soft the clouds are.'

By the time I'd come to the end of this lovely daydream, I'd stopped crying. The memory of my father had cheered me up enough to face the world again. When I came out of my room, the house seemed to be completely deserted. The lounge and the kitchen were messy, so I busied myself with clearing up. At least it gave me something to do. Then I thought I heard a door opening upstairs and the sound of voices. I crept up and peeped around the door to the upstairs lounge. Al Koronky was sitting there alone watching the TV, with the Sunday newspapers spread out on the floor in front of him.

'Where is Hanan?' I asked him, in a shaky voice.

'Didn't you know?' he said. 'She's left for the

airport with the children.'

'They didn't say goodbye to me.'

'No. Why should they have?' he snapped. 'They were late and in a hurry. Now, go and make me some coffee.'

31

Salvation

At the end of that week, Al Koronky left to join Hanan and the family in Sudan. An embassy car came to collect him, and I had to go with him to the airport. Then the driver took me back into London to Koronky's friends' house. Before leaving for Sudan, Hanan had given me strict instructions as to what I could and couldn't do while staying with their friends.

'Do as much work as they ask you to,' Hanan had said. 'Be helpful and do what they tell you to. But the most important thing is that you must stay inside their house and not go out. Whatever you do, you're not allowed to go outside — except when Omer takes you back to clean our house, which he'll do every week. Just stay in their house until we get back from Sudan.'

I was dropped at the house where I would be staying at about seven that evening. An Arab man opened the door with a big smile. 'Welcome, welcome,' he said to me, taking my little bag. 'Come in, come in. You must be Mende?' As soon as I stepped inside, I could feel that there was a happy atmosphere in the house. I immediately felt at home.

'I'm Omer,' said the man, leading me down

the hall. 'Come and meet my wife, Mende. She's called Madina.'

'Hello, you must be Mende,' Madina said, giving me a big hug. 'I've been waiting for you for a week. And now you're finally here. What do you want to drink? Come on. There's tea, coffee, fruit juice or milk. What d'you fancy?'

At first, I was overcome with all their kindness and didn't know what to say. I wanted to go and hide in the kitchen. But I soon realised that Madina and Omer were genuinely good people. They had two daughters, aged five and seven. As their house was small, they gave me their youngest daughter's room while she went to share with her sister. It was lovely, with a big window opening onto the street. I was allowed to sleep late and then get up to have a shower. Soon, I was sleeping in until ten in the morning or later. Then I'd go down and join Madina for breakfast.

After that, if the sun was shining, Madina would suggest a picnic in the park. It was about ten minutes' walk away, along pretty streets lined with brick houses. At first, I was scared to go out because of all Hanan's warnings, but Madina allowed her little girls to run along the street in front of us, laughing and playing. She clearly didn't think they were in any danger. In the park there was a playground and the children loved being pushed on the swings and being whirled around on the roundabout.

That Sunday, Madina took me to a big market in a place called Shepherd's Bush. She wanted to buy presents for all her friends and family back in Sudan. She bought clothes, toys and electrical goods, and she bought me a little white lacy bra. It was very generous of her, but as I'd been running around without one for twenty years or so, I found it far too uncomfortable to wear. She also took me along when we visited her friends, and I would sit there and chat as if I was as free as the rest of them. I was really starting to enjoy myself. I realised that Hanan had lied to me about London. It wasn't a bad or violent place after all. In fact, it seemed very nice and friendly.

But every Saturday, after lunch, Omer would take me back to Koronky's house to do the cleaning. There was one leaky radiator upstairs with a bucket under it. I had to empty this or the water would soak through the ceiling; apart from that there wasn't much cleaning to do, since there was no one there to make the house untidy and dirty. One day, Hanan's children had shown me how to turn on the TV and change the channels. So I'd sit there and watch TV until Omer came to collect me again.

I didn't understand any of the programmes, as they were all in English. But I could watch the pictures. I watched a Saturday afternoon soap opera (I've since found out that it's called 'Family Affairs'). I was intrigued to see what life in England was really like. I was amazed at how many of the characters were shown kissing and hugging on TV. People were even shown in bed together. I was shocked — especially as some of the men seemed to be kissing two different *Hawaja* women. I thought that meant that they must have more than one wife, like the men did back home in the Nuba Mountains.

That first time Omer took me to Koronky's, he locked the front door from the outside. I thought he must be doing this for my own safety, as he knew I was a stranger in London and vulnerable. 'Mende, you mustn't open the door for anyone,' he warned me, before leaving. 'If someone rings the bell, you have to look through the letterbox and check who it is first. It's best only to open the door for me, really.'

By the time the second Saturday came around, Omer must have known I was becoming more confident of myself, as he just handed me the key and said he'd be back to pick me up later. No one was locking me in any more. No one was watching me. They were just treating me like another member of the family.

'You lived with Hanan's sister, Rahab, in Khartoum, didn't you?' Omer asked me, as we ate dinner one evening.

'Yes, I stayed with her for some years, before coming here.'

'That's nice,' Madina said. 'So you know all the family then?'

I nodded. It was clear that they knew nothing about my real situation — that I'd been Rahab's slave for many years and in effect remained so, even though I was now living in London. I didn't want to tell them, either. In spite of their friendliness, I didn't trust them yet. I was worried that they might stop me from going out of the house if they knew that I was a slave. This was my chance to get a little taste of freedom, and I didn't want to give it up for anything. One evening, three weeks into my stay, Madina called me down to have dinner with them, but I was in my room crying. Their kindness was making me more aware than ever how truly miserable my life was. As I hadn't come down for dinner, Madina sent her daughter Rasha to come up and get me.

'Come on, Mende. Dinner,' she said, bursting into my room. But then she noticed my tears. 'Why are you crying, Mende?' she asked, climbing up to sit next to me on the bed.

'I'm not crying, Rasha,' I said, wiping my eyes. 'I just have a headache.'

Then I heard Omer calling from downstairs: 'Come on, you two! Mende, Rasha! Come down for dinner. We're waiting.'

'Daddy, Mende's crying,' Rasha called back.

Omer came upstairs to join us. 'Come on, Mende,' he said gently. 'What's the matter? Why're you crying? Come down and eat with us.'

'It's nothing,' I said, shaking my head. 'I'm not hungry. I don't want to eat anything, that's all.'

'Well, if you don't eat, we're not eating,' said Omer. 'Then we'll all go hungry.' I smiled at him and dried my eyes and then followed them downstairs.

'What's the matter, Mende?' Madina asked me, when I sat down at the dinner table. 'Are you thinking about your family? We all miss our families, so don't cry. Come on. Let's eat, or the food will get cold.'

The next day was a Saturday, so Omer took me over to Koronky's house for the third time. As he didn't have a car, we took the bus. It was maybe a thirty-minute ride to get there and Omer passed the time by chatting to me. Finally, he came around to asking what was really on his mind.

'Mende, why were you crying last night?'

I had been crying because my time at Madina and Omer's had reminded me of my happy, loving childhood.

'Come on, you can tell me,' Omer prompted. 'Has someone been treating you badly? Well have they? Why are you sad?'

'No,' I said quietly. 'No-one's treated me badly.'

'Then why were you crying? Come on, tell me. What's upsetting you?'

'You've all been so kind to me,' I said, looking out of the window, tears welling in my eyes. 'You've been much nicer to me than anyone at the Koronkys' house.'

'Is that why you're crying? Because they've been unkind to you?'

'No,' I lied. 'It's just that I miss my family.'

'Hey, everyone misses their family. I miss mine too. That's no reason to cry. If you work hard here in London you can earn good money and send some of it back to them. That's what I'm doing.'

I nodded.

'What sort of work do you do at Koronky's house anyway?'

'I do everything. I clean the house. I do all the washing and ironing. I do most of the cooking. I do the washing up. I look after the children.'

'You do all of that?' he asked, frowning. 'How

many hours do you work each day?'

'Hours? What do you mean, hours?' I said, shaking my head. 'I just work all the time.'

'What d'you mean, you work all the time?'

'I work all the time.'

'Oh, we're here,' he said, as the bus pulled up at Koronky's house. 'Listen, I'm going to have to go to work now. But I've got a lot of questions I want to ask you later.'

As soon as we had settled into our bus seats for the journey home, he started again. 'So, tell me exactly how long you're made to work each day?'

I was silent for a few moments. Then I said, 'I can't tell you any more.'

'Why not?' he said, surprised.

'Because I don't know if I can trust you.'

'What do you mean?' he said, sounding hurt.

'If I tell you, you might tell Koronky,' I whispered, looking out of the window. 'Or you might tell Madina and then she might tell Hanan.'

'Don't be silly. I won't tell anyone. This is just between you and me. If you tell me, maybe I can help you. If you don't tell me, I can't, can I? You have to trust someone.'

'Look. We've reached your house,' I said with relief, as the bus pulled up at our stop.

'All right, but let's talk again next Saturday. I want you to tell me what's going on.'

Omer worked with Al Koronky at the embassy, so I had a real fear that he would talk to him. But I knew how happy and healthy I'd become in the few weeks that I'd stayed with his family. They'd made me feel so at home that I'd started to put on weight again. I'd been so thin before. The following Saturday, I made a snap decision as we got on the bus: I would answer Omer's questions.

'Listen, Mende, you're just going to have to trust me. I won't tell anyone else and I'll try and help you. I promise.'

'OK,' I said quietly. 'What d'you want to know?'

'Good. Now, exactly how long do you work for each day?'

'All day long. All day long, every day of every week.'

'How can you work all day long? You must be exhausted. Don't they ever give you a day off?'

'No. And yes, I am exhausted.'

'But they can't make you work like that. It's your right to have days off. It's the law.'

'Well they do.'

'OK,' he sighed. 'So how much do they pay you for each hour you work?'

'What?'

'Pay you,' he repeated. 'You know. Your wages. Do they pay you by the hour or the week or how does it work?'

'I don't get paid anything.'

'What d'you mean, you don't get paid anything? That's impossible.'

'Well, they don't pay me anything.'

'Why not? Mende, look. Everyone knows that here in London people cannot be made to work without being paid. And they can't be made to work every hour of every day, without any time off. Do you understand what I mean? In the embassy where we both work, we have women who do the cleaning. They get paid for each hour they work — maybe five or six pounds per hour. And they work set hours each day — say nine to five, or something like that. And they have a set number of days off each month.'

'Well, all I do is work and no one pays me anything,' I mumbled.

'Listen, don't tell Koronky I told you this, but they can't make you work without paying you. You are telling me the truth, aren't you? Do they really pay you nothing at all?'

'I've told you: they don't pay me anything,' I said. I was getting angry now that Omer didn't seem to believe me.

'Well, if that's true, why did you come to London to work for them in the first place? And if they don't pay you, why don't you just leave and get another job?'

I didn't reply. I just stared out of the bus window. 'Look at me, Mende,' he said, exasperated. He grabbed my chin and turned my head around. 'Look, I want you to understand that no-one works in London without being paid. That's the law here.'

I nodded, and then turned back to stare out the window. He doesn't understand, I thought to myself. I knew very well that normal, free people didn't work without being paid. Of course I knew this. And I knew that normal people worked set hours and had days off. But I wasn't 'normal people'. I had always been made to work for no money. I had never known anything else. I was a slave, captured and paid for.

Thinking back on this later, I reckon Omer may have guessed my true situation. He was Sudanese, after all, and slavery isn't exactly rare in Sudan. But perhaps he didn't really want to know. Had he discovered the full truth about me, then he would have been obliged to report it to the police. That would have put Omer in confrontation with one of his senior work colleagues. In effect, it would have been the end of his diplomatic career.

But I was really grateful to Omer. The few weeks that I had spent with his family had shown me that London was a good, friendly place after all. The way his family had treated me, enveloping me in affection, had made me realise that I could be human again. And now, Omer had helped me understand that I was a person with rights — and that people couldn't keep you as a slave in this country. He opened my eyes to my true situation. After talking with him, I decided that I had to try to escape. If I had to go back to my life as a slave, either it would kill me, or I would kill myself. Now was my chance, and I had to seize the opportunity before Koronky and Hanan returned.

I wondered at first if I might ask Omer to help me, but I decided that as he was close to Koronky it would put him in a difficult situation. I needed to try to find someone outside the circle of Hanan and Koronky's colleagues and friends. There must be other Sudanese people living in London, some of whom would be Nuba. In the past weeks, I had already walked to the local shops on my own once or twice to do the shopping for Madina. I decided I would offer to go out again and then try to find help. I prayed to Allah that I would find a friend in my hour of need. The next morning, I offered to do the shopping again for Madina.

'You sure you'll be all right on your own?' she asked, concerned. 'You won't get lost, will you?'

'I'll be fine,' I reassured her. 'I'm not going far.'

'Just be careful of the traffic, OK? Look both ways to check for cars.'

After doing my errands, I hurried to the park. It was a sunny day and there were lots of people around. I took a careful look at any black people I saw, but none looked or sounded Sudanese. The following morning, Madina took me on a long shopping expedition, so it wasn't until the next day that I managed to go out alone again. I headed for the shopping centre to see if I would have better luck there. After half an hour, I spotted a black man looking in a shoe shop window who I thought might be South Sudanese. I went and stood next to him. Plucking up all my courage, I said, 'Assalam alaikum,' which means 'hello' in Arabic.

He turned to me and smiled. 'Hello,' he said in English.

'Do you speak Arabic?' I asked him in Arabic.

'What?' he said, in English, smiling and shrugging his shoulders. 'Sorry?' I smiled apologetically and turned and hurried off. I was embarrassed and angry with myself and I was growing desperate. Why hadn't I learned to speak even a few words of English? I was sure that Madina and Omer would have taught me, had I asked. I was scared to approach anyone else now. I had thought I'd be able to tell a Sudanese person just from their face, but I was mistaken. The following day, I forced myself to try again. After lunch, I told Madina I wanted to go out. It was a grey day and her little girl was in bed with a cold, so I knew that Madina would have to stay at home to look after her.

'Why d'you want to go out today?' Madina asked me, in surprise. 'It's a horrid, cold day.'

'I just want a little fresh air. I won't be long, just a walk to the shops.'

I knew that this was probably my last chance to find help. Koronky and the family were scheduled to return to London in two days' time. For half an hour, I wandered around the shopping centre but I couldn't see anyone who looked Sudanese. I was starting to feel really useless. Maybe my idea was just plain stupid. Maybe I should just give up. On the way back it started to rain, so I stopped in a bus shelter. I glanced over at a nearby garage. There were lots of people washing cars by hand. They were wearing bright yellow overalls and most of them were young black men. They looked like they were enjoying their work.

To one side, others were fitting car tyres, and there I spotted a man who I thought might be South Sudanese. I'd been wrong before, but it was worth a try. I walked in, picking my way between the loose tyres and tools. The man was crouching down, pumping air into a tyre. I went and stood near him, hoping that he would notice me and speak first. But he was concentrating on his job and there was a radio blaring in the background. Finally, I forced myself to speak. '*Assalam alaikum*,' I said quietly, but either he didn't hear me or he didn't understand. I was tempted just to turn around and leave. But instead, I made myself try again. '*Assalam alaikum*,' I said, a little more loudly.

'*Alaikum wassalam*, little sister!' he exclaimed in surprise, craning his head around to get a look at me. 'Where did you appear from?' he continued, in Arabic.

'I'm from Sudan,' I said, my heart in my mouth.

'Hey! I'm also from Sudan.' He grinned. 'But I meant where did you come from just now? You appeared out of thin air!'

'Oh . . . I've just been to the shops.'

'OK,' he nodded, moving around to check another of the tyres. 'So which part of Sudan are you from? The south, yes?'

'I'm from the Nuba Mountains.'

'The Nuba? OK. Well I'm from the south. So, we're like brother and sister really. How long have you been in London? What's your name?'

'My name's Mende,' I said, shyly. 'I've been here for three months.'

'Mende. It's a nice name,' he said, laughing. 'It's much easier than mine. I'm Aluan Akuat Bol. It's a hard one, eh?' he chuckled. 'Where do you live?'

'Oh, I live around here,' I said, being deliberately vague. There was a second's silence, before I asked him, 'Do you know any other Sudanese people in London?'

'Yes. Lots. Are you looking for someone in particular?'

'Do you know any Nuba people?' I asked, trying not to sound as desperate as I felt.

He was silent for a few moments, thinking. Then he broke into a big grin. 'Yes,' he said. 'Yes . . . I do know one Nuba person.'

'Really!'

'Yes,' he chuckled. 'Do you want me to get in touch with him? I've got his number on my mobile. Look, I can call him and you can speak with him if you want,' he added. 'It looks to me like you're dying to find another Nuba person.'

'Well, I am,' I replied, excitedly.

But I knew I would have to be careful. I wouldn't be able to escape just yet, as I didn't want to get Madina and Omer into trouble. I would have to wait until Hanan and Al Koronky were due back before trying anything. Aluan made the call on his mobile. Just as I was giving up hope, I heard someone answer.

'Hello, Babo?' Aluan said. 'Hi. It's me. I've got someone here who wants to speak to you.' He handed me the mobile. 'Go on,' he said, 'take it. He's called Babo.'

My heart leapt. Babo! Babo — the name of my favourite brother. Maybe this was a good sign. 'Hello, Babo,' I whispered nervously into the phone, my hand trembling.

'Hello, little sister,' he answered.

'Your friend told me your name. D'you know mine?'

'No, little sister. What is it?'

I swallowed. I was so excited my mouth felt dry. 'I'm called Mende,' I said. 'And I'm not so little. I'm twenty years old.'

'Well, OK,' he laughed. 'You sound like you're Nuba?'

'Yes. I'm from the Karko tribe.'

'The Karko? Well, we'll have to continue speaking Arabic then. Your tribe's language and mine are too different. So, my Nuba sister, what are you doing with my good friend Aluan?'

I moved away into a corner where I thought I could speak without being overheard. 'I need your help,' I said quietly.

'What sort of help?'

'You have to believe what I'm going to tell you. I need someone to help me escape.' Then I blurted out my story as fast as I could. Once I'd opened the floodgates, I couldn't stop. After I'd finished speaking, there was a stunned silence on the other end of the phone.

'Are you telling me the truth?' Babo finally said. 'You were captured as a child and made a slave? And then sent here to London? And now you want me to help you escape?'

'Yes. It's true. It's all true. You've got to believe me,' I sobbed, breaking down. 'You've got to help me. I don't have anyone else to turn to and I can't stay there any longer.'

'All right,' he said, gently. 'Calm down. I'll do all I can to help you, I promise. But first, we must try and meet. I can't come right now. I'm at work. Give me a phone number so I can call you later and we can arrange it.'

'I don't have a phone number.'

'You don't have a mobile? Or any phone you can use?'

'No.'

'Well, can you give me your address then? You know, the road name or the house number?'

'All I know is that it's somewhere in Willesden Green.'

'You don't know the address?'

'No,' I said. I was starting to feel hopeless again. 'But I do know that the man, my master, does a very important job here in London,' I blurted out, hoping that that might be of some help to Babo. 'He's something powerful in the Sudan embassy.'

'All right. So what's his name?'

'He's called Abdul Mahmoud Al Koronky.'

'Right. I'll try and find out where the house is.'

'How?' I asked, in a worried voice. 'Please don't ask Koronky or anything.'

'Don't worry,' he reassured me. 'Of course I won't. The Sudanese community here in London all know each other. I'll find out one way or another.'

Babo told me that he would try to contact me again as soon as he could. We agreed that if he could find out the phone number, he would try and call me at Koronky's house. If the family were out, I'd pick up the phone and say 'Hello' in my Nuba language, so he'd know it was me. If Hanan or Koronky picked up the phone, he'd say nothing and replace the receiver. Babo also gave me his mobile number, which I wrote down on a scrap of paper. If I found an opportunity to phone him, then I would. The plan wasn't perfect, but it was the best that we could manage in the circumstances.

When I got back to Madina's house, I told her that I'd been looking at mobiles in the shops and I asked her to teach me how to use a phone. We played with her mobile and her normal phone, changing ringing tones and pretending to call each other, until we were both laughing at our own antics. Early the following morning, I had to say goodbye to Madina and Omer and the children. At nine o'clock the embassy driver was coming to collect me and take me back to Koronky's house. I thanked them all tearfully for being so kind and they said they'd miss me very much. The Koronkys were expected back from Sudan that evening. So I spent the whole day back at their house cooking and cleaning and putting fresh linen on the beds. Then at six o'clock I heard the phone ring. Could it be Babo, I wondered, excitedly? I rushed over and picked up the receiver.

'Hello,' I said, nervously. But it was Omer. He told me that Koronky and the family had been delayed for three days, so he would come and pick me up later. I put the receiver down in disappointment. But hardly had I done so when it rang again.

'Hello,' I said again. But there was no answer. 'Hello,' I repeated. Then I remembered our plan. '*Kenwengiero*,' I said, which means 'hello' in my Nuba language.

'Mende,' said a voice, 'is that you?'

'Babo!' I cried. 'Yes, it's me, Mende.'

'Can you talk?'

'Yes, there's no-one here. They're not coming back for another three days now.'

'Listen. I've managed to find the address, telephone number and everything. I've even been over to take a look at the house from the outside. So, are you still sure you want to do this?'

'Yes!' I practically screamed down the receiver at him. 'I have to get out of here.'

'Right. Well, if Koronky and the rest of them are still away, why don't I come and get you now?'

'You can't. Omer is coming to pick me up soon and take me back to his house. If I escape now Omer and Madina will get the blame. They've been so kind to me, it's not fair. I've got to wait until the Koronkys get back.'

'Well, all right. But it's more difficult. If they're coming back in three days' time, that's a Friday. Right. I'll come to the house on the Monday. That's this Monday, the eleventh of September. It's the first day that I've got free. It'll give me time to organise a car too. This is what we'll do. Take the rubbish out to the front of the house. Check that they're not watching you. Then run up the drive as fast as you can and don't look back. I'll be waiting for you, just around the end of the drive. You've got that? You understand? I'll be there waiting for you from three to three-thirty in the afternoon.'

'All right,' I replied, nervously.

'So, I'll see you then, yes?' said Babo, reassuringly. 'And remember. Don't pack a bag or do anything that makes it look suspicious. Just come exactly as you are.'

'Yes. Oh, Babo? Thank you, Babo. Thank you.'

'That's all right,' he said quietly, 'but it's not over yet. Just you be strong and brave. We'll get you out of there. Oh, one other thing. There's another Nuba — he's called Monir Sheikaldin — I've asked him to help me rescue you. He just wants to have a quick chat with you too. I'll try and get him to call you right now, as there's no one there. All right?'

A few minutes later, the phone rang again. It was Mr Sheikaldin. I repeated my story for him and then he gave me his mobile number too.

'Look, Mende, if you have any problems, just try to call us,' he reassured me. 'You know how to use the telephone? You can call me or Babo at any time — if you're scared or worried about anything.'

As I put the receiver down, I felt happy and scared and excited all at the same time. I then spent three more days at Omer's house before being taken back to the Koronkys'. The family arrived home that evening. I had cooked dinner, and soon I was changing the twins' nappies and cleaning up after them all again. Hanan had brought nothing back from Sudan for me — not even any news of my family. It was as if they'd never been away. Hanan told me that Rahab and her family were well, but that didn't really interest me any more. I did ask her about Nanu, the Nuba girl who had replaced me as their slave.

'She's called Nanu?' Hanan asked. 'Oh, she's

348

fine, I think. I didn't really notice.'

That night and the next I hardly slept at all. I kept running over the escape plan again and again in my mind. What could go wrong? What if there was no rubbish to take out to the bins? What if Hanan was watching me from the upstairs window? What if they spotted me running up the drive? What if, when I reached the road, Babo wasn't there? I was excited and frightened all at the same time. But nothing was going to stop me now.

I thought about my family. How were they surviving? The raid must have made things much harder for them. I wondered if they had enough to eat. I thought about how I might earn some money in London after I'd escaped. About how I might use this to buy a flight back to Sudan. I imagined taking a bus from Khartoum down to Dilling town. I imagined travelling up into the Nuba Mountains. I imagined running through the village, searching for my mother and father. I imagined the first sight of them. The tearful hugs. How we'd sit around the fire and tell each other about all the time that had passed since we had last sat down as a loving family together.

★　★　★

The morning of Monday, the eleventh of September, I was up early doing my chores, but I was dismayed when Al Koronky didn't leave for work at his normal time and stayed around the house all morning. It was a Monday, so why wasn't he going in to the embassy? 'Oh no!' I thought to myself. 'He's not leaving. How am I going to get out of the house?' When I'd thought over the escape plan, I had imagined myself at home with just Hanan and the twins. I had worried that the front door would be locked from the inside, but if that was the case I would look for an excuse to get let out — like putting the rubbish out the front or something. What I hadn't planned for was the possibility that Al Koronky might actually be at home at the time of my escape.

But now Al Koronky was here as well and I didn't know what to do. There was a huge stack of ironing and for once I was thankful for it. It would give me something to occupy myself with until three o'clock came around. I kept running over the escape plan in my mind and I was becoming more and more nervous. Every five minutes I caught myself glancing up at the clock on the wall. I kept messing up the ironing. At three I went into the dining room to hang out some wet washing. I shut the door behind me and peeped out from behind the curtains. I wanted to check if Babo was there or not, but I couldn't see past the trees. I went to my room. I was sweating and faint with anxiety. I didn't know how I was going to get out of the house without being caught. I looked around the room at my few possessions. Uran, my little toy 'cat', was lying on my pillow. On impulse, I snatched her up and stuffed her inside my knickers. There was no way I was leaving her behind. Then I heard Hanan calling me from the kitchen.

'*Yebit*, I'm going to fetch the kids from

school,' she told me. 'I'm leaving the twins here with you.'

I nodded, trying to avoid her eyes. I felt sure she knew that I was up to something. She went and shouted up the stairs to Koronky: 'Come on, darling! I'm ready.'

'I'm just coming,' he shouted back down.

Then Hanan went and unlocked the front door and came back to get her shoes from the cupboard under the stairs. 'Oh God,' I thought to myself, 'they are going to leave at exactly the same time that I'm supposed to meet Babo!' I realised that I had to make a run for it now, while the door was unlocked and I still had the chance to escape. I grabbed the sack of rubbish and practically ran towards the door, my body shaking all over. As I hurried past Hanan, who was sitting in the hall tying her shoelaces, I could hear Al Koronky coming down the stairs behind me.

I threw the rubbish in the bin and turned around to look back at the house. It seemed my luck was holding. No one had come out yet. I forced myself to move. I turned and started running up the driveway — all the time looking back over my shoulder and expecting to see one of them rushing after me.

I felt wild with terror. As I approached the road, a new fear took hold of me. What if Babo wasn't there? What if he wasn't there! Oh please Allah, make him be there! Make him be there! And then I caught sight of a tall black man across the road, waving at me frantically.

'Come on! Come on!' he mouthed at me.

'Run, Mende! Run!' I rushed headlong across the road and fell straight into his arms.

'Quickly! Quickly!' I screamed at him. 'They're coming! They're coming! We have to go now! Now! You have to hide me!'

We ran off down the street, Babo leading me by the hand. He took me to a small green, where we hid behind a broad, spreading tree. I was beside myself with fear and I couldn't stop crying.

'We're too close,' I wailed. 'We're too close. They'll find us. They'll come and get me. We have to get away.'

'It's OK. It's OK,' said Babo soothingly, wrapping his arms around me. 'Don't worry. I won't let them get you. Just stay hidden while I make a call. We've got a car waiting.'

I heard Babo explaining exactly where we were on his mobile phone and, seconds later, a car drew up besides us. I was bundled into the back and with a squeal of tyres we were off. I huddled down besides Babo, trying to stay out of sight.

'Are they after us? Are they after us? Please. Look out the window. See if they're following us. I'm afraid. I'm afraid. I'm afraid.'

'Don't worry, Mende,' he said, laughing. 'It's all right. No-one's following us.'

'Hello, Mende,' I then heard a calm voice say from the driver's seat. 'I'm Monir. You must listen to us and calm down. We've rescued you. You're safe with us. We'll protect you. No one can come and get you now.'

'Listen to Monir, Mende,' said Babo, gently. 'There's nothing to worry about now. You're

352

safe. We're taking you to a lawyer. She's going to help you get permission to stay here in England. And after that, we're going to take you to Monir's house. You'll be staying with him and his wife and family to start off with. All right? You're free now.'

At first, I couldn't take any of this in. I just kept thinking that by now Koronky would have found out that I'd escaped, and that he'd be after me. I was terrified that they'd try to recapture me. As far as I was concerned, Koronky had absolute power. He was the government and he was the law. I may have been Rahab's slave still, but it was Koronky that I feared, now that I had escaped. I couldn't believe that I could ever get away from him.

Here I was in this strange city in a foreign country, so very far from home, and I didn't speak the language, and the only people I knew were the two Nuba men in the car with me. But Babo had said that I was free. And Monir had told me that I was safe and that no one could come and get me again. These were my people, Nuba people, and I knew that I could trust them. I knew that they would tell me the truth. So maybe my years as a slave were finally, finally over. Maybe I was truly free, after all.

32

Desperately Seeking Asylum

It is now over two years since I escaped. In that time, London has become my new home and the place where I have tasted my first years of freedom. How has it been for me? To me freedom is so precious, and I would not give it up for all the world. I have realised that for those who live in the West, freedom is so often something they take for granted. It has always been there for them. It is their unnoticed, unrecognised, constant companion and friend. But for those of us who come from countries like Sudan, freedom is wonderful and precious. And for those like me who were enslaved, it remains a uniquely beautiful, special experience. Even now, two years after my escape, I am still amazed when I hear people openly criticise the British government. Or when people hold demonstrations on the streets of London. Or expose politicians in the press. I'm still so surprised that no one gets arrested, punished or imprisoned.

But for me, this freedom is also a terrifying thing. I was captured when I was still a child. I spent my teenage years and my early adulthood in slavery. For all that time, I had no freedom. I was a non-person. I didn't really exist. I had no doctor, no dentist, no school, no friends, no family, no money, no bank account, no taxes to pay, and nothing to buy or sell. I had no diary, no papers to file, no phone calls to make or take, no letters to send or receive, and no bills to pay. I had no decisions to make about my own life, everything was decided for me: when to get up; what clothes I had to wear; when to start work; when to eat; when to sleep. In short, I learned nothing that a normal person learns when going through the transition to adulthood. After I escaped, I realised that *I just didn't know how to do any of these things*. I was faced with all this freedom, but with it came so much that was unknown and so much responsibility. After my escape, I had to start deciding every single thing in my life, and I just didn't know how to do so. Faced with so many decisions, I realised how frightening freedom can be.

I had to start learning even the most basic things from scratch. I had to learn how to use money — the small weekly allowance that the British government gives to asylum seekers. I had to learn what a bank account was, how to pay money in and get money out again. I had to be taught to understand the very concept of money itself — that I should not give all my money away to the first person who came along and asked me to loan it to them. I had to learn how to cook for myself, and how to eat three regular meals a day (a lesson I'm still learning). I had to learn how to try to make friends. Ever since my capture, everyone I'd met had been a master, a master's family, or their circle of friends. Or they'd been slaves like me. Since my childhood, I'd never had the opportunity to make my own friends. Up until now, I had taught myself not to grow dependent on, or close to, anyone. Gradually, I realised that I didn't really understand the concept of friendship any more: that a friend is someone you don't have to hide things from and that you can trust with your deepest secrets and your fears. That a good friend will never turn on you and beat you for no reason. That they will never insult you just for the fun of it. That they will always treat you as their equal.

I had to learn basic social etiquette too. I had to learn that hiding behind doors to eavesdrop on other people's conversations isn't a good thing to do. This was a habit that I'd learned first in Khartoum — it was the only way I could find out what was going on and what my masters might have planned for me. But it isn't a nice thing to do to my friends in London. I had to learn to sit at a table with others and eat dinner with them. I had to learn to stop clearing the table as soon as they had put down their knives and forks. I had to learn to stop rushing out to the kitchen to do the washing up, a place where I felt so much more at home. One of the most difficult things for me still is to be in a restaurant being served by others. It just doesn't feel right. Recently, I was having dinner with a British politician who wanted to hear my story. She had taken me to her private club in London's Green Park area. As soon as we'd finished the first course, I just couldn't help myself from getting up to clear the table.

'I'm just going to take the dishes out,' I told her, with a sheepish grin.

'You go right ahead, my dear,' she boomed at me. 'The staff around here look like they could use a little help. I think the kitchen's over there,' she added, pointing towards a doorway.

I scooped up all the empty plates and dishes and carried them out towards the kitchen. As I went, I bumped into one of the waiting staff. She was a black girl, and looked like she was from Africa too. 'What're you doing?' she asked me in surprise, looking at my arm full of dirty plates. 'Oh . . . you want the kitchen? It's just over there, through that door. Oh, and thanks . . . ' she shouted after me, as I disappeared into the kitchen with the dishes, ' . . . but there's no need to do the washing up too!'

I had to learn how to walk safely on the street without getting run over. I had to learn how to use a bus to travel from A to B. Even now, I still haven't mastered the London public transport system. I haven't plucked up the courage to use the underground yet. I know it is the quickest way to get around, but to me it feels like descending into a grave when I walk down those steps into the neon-lit dark of a station. I prefer using buses. They may be slow, but at least they travel above ground in the daylight. Yet even the buses aren't without their problems. Recently, I went to jump on a number 38 bus to travel home, but it pulled away just as I was stepping on to it; I was dragged down the street for a hundred yards or so, hanging onto the rail for dear life with my feet bumping along the road. I was screaming for the bus to stop and all the passengers were staring out the window at me in shock. Even though it was October, I was still wearing sandals, as I've never really got used to proper shoes. When the bus driver finally realised what had happened and stopped, my feet were all cut up and bruised.

As I sat there hunched on the roadside and sobbing my eyes out, two black men on the bus started having an argument. One of them was shouting at me for being so stupid and getting on the bus when it was moving and holding all the passengers up. The other one started to defend me, saying I hadn't done it on purpose and that I was hurt. I thought for a moment that they were going to have a fight. But just then the police turned up in a car with a flashing blue light and a wailing siren. Two policemen in crisp uniforms came over to me. I was scared. In Sudan, the police are often feared by the public. I wondered if they were going to arrest me or beat me. I still hadn't got used to the idea that the police in England are there to protect and help people and uphold the law. They crouched down beside me and asked me in a kindly way if I was all right First, they checked to see if I was seriously hurt and if I needed an ambulance. When they were satisfied that I'd only suffered small cuts and bruises, they asked me if I was able to find my own way home.

'Where d'you live, love?' one of the two officers asked me.

'In Hackney,' I told him.

'OK . . . But whereabouts in Hackney? I'm

going to need to take your name and address as we have to make an incident report.'

'I don't know exactly the road or number . . . I just know how to get there by walking,' I told them.

They looked at me with a mixture of bemusement and disbelief. 'You don't know your own address?'

'No,' I said. How was I going to explain this to them, I wondered? How was I going to explain that I didn't know the road name or number because that's not how I viewed the world around me? How was I going to explain that I knew it was ten minutes' walk down the hill from the bus stop where I get off? That I knew it was the yellow house with the blue door and the red steps? That I knew it was around the corner from the children's school, midway down the street, on the opposite side to the tyre fitting shop? Eventually, I settled the matter by telling the policemen the name of the English school that I went to and the part of London it was in. That seemed to satisfy them. They made sure I got onto another 38 bus safely and waved me off, smiling to themselves and shaking their heads. What did they think of me, I wondered? What did they think of this little girl from the African bush trying to find her way around the biggest city in Europe?

But most difficult of all, I had to learn how not to be afraid any more. The day that I escaped, I was terrified that those who had held me captive for so long would come after me. I was petrified that they were following our car, that they were pursuing me, and that I would be grabbed and captured and forced back into an even worse situation than before. If they did recapture me, I dreaded to think how I would be punished for escaping. I had spent so many years convinced that those who had held me captive and treated me as their slave held ultimate, unlimited power over me.

Of course, these were my own, deep-seated fears, and everyone kept telling me that no-one could recapture me on the streets of England. It just wasn't possible. But it took some convincing before I was able to believe that England was a free country and that the authorities there would protect powerless people like me from those who I had believed were all-powerful. Gradually, I learned how not to be scared: how not to fear taking the bus to school on my own; how not to fear walking to the shop alone to buy some milk; how not to fear being left alone in the house for a few hours watching TV. They may have been only my own fears inside my own head, but to me they were very, very real.

The very day of my escape, phone calls were made to the house of Monir Sheikaldin, the person who had rescued me, from a woman in Sudan. I wasn't told this at the time, as he tried to protect me from all this. She was very angry, and she demanded to speak with me. When he denied that I was there, she became threatening. She said that she'd find my family and have them all thrown into prison. There were several calls like this, and then a man from the Sudanese embassy in London started calling. All this culminated in a number of Sudanese govern-ment ministers intervening directly to try to pressurise those who had helped me escape to stop shielding me. Then, the family that I was staying with started to receive anonymous phone calls from Sudan. 'We know where your family live,' the man would say, menacingly, 'and we know how to find them.' All of this was reported to the British police. But these phone calls have continued, even until today.

★ ★ ★

Months after my escape, Monir, the man who had rescued me, received a phone call from my brother, Babo. He did not tell me this immediately, as he could tell that Babo was being pressurised to call me and that he could not speak freely. Instead, he asked Babo to call at a later date, from a safe place where they could talk openly. I can't reveal where this place is, for obvious reasons. But first my brother, then my sister Kunyant, and then my father and my mother all managed to contact me and speak by phone. It's impossible to describe how wonderful it was to talk to them again after so many years of loss and separation. At first, I cried and cried and cried. But eventually my mother made me laugh, by telling me that my accent had changed so much she could hardly understand my Nuba any more. My father just asked me to come home, as all he wanted in the world was to see me again.

But it was a bitter-sweet experience. My

brother told me that, following my escape, the first the family knew that I was alive was when my mother, father and brother were tracked down in the Nuba Mountains and forced to go to Khartoum. They were told that I was in England and that I had been kidnapped and sold to Christian extremists. They were told that I had been converted from Islam to Christianity and that I was in grave danger. They were told that my name had been changed from Mende to Caroline, a good Christian name. They were told all these things and made to feel very scared. They only realised the truth when I managed to speak to them on the phone and tell them that I had escaped and that I was finally free.

I explained to my parents that everything they had been told was untrue: that far from being kidnapped in London, I had escaped into freedom; that far from being converted to Christianity, I could now practise my Islamic faith freely for the first time in many years; that far from being in grave danger, I was safer than I ever had been during my years of beatings and abuse and enslavement. My parents were so relieved to hear this. They could tell from my voice that I was happy. I could tell that my mother and father were getting old. My mother's hearing was very bad as she'd been savagely beaten around the head during the raid. My father sounded not as strong as he used to be. But they hadn't lost their spirit or their pride, and I could tell that they still loved me dearly. My father was angry when I told him the truth, because he realised that he'd been tricked.

So, the nightmare of my years in slavery didn't end as soon as I escaped. It was just the nature of my suffering that changed. After escaping, I wasn't worried so much for my own future or security any more. I had become far more worried for the safety of my family back in Sudan, and for those who had helped rescue me and enabled me to be free. Or at least that's how things were until very recently. But subsequent events shook to the core my belief that my future was safe and secure. Over the past two years, I had become convinced that England is a free country, one that respects human rights and safeguards the vulnerable. I had believed that the English authorities would protect me. That belief was to be badly shaken.

*   *   *

The day of my escape, I made an application for asylum here in the UK. Prior to my escape, I had no idea that this was what I would have to do. I'd never heard of the concept of asylum before, or had any understanding of what it meant. I'd just hoped that once I'd escaped, I might somehow work and earn enough money in London to pay for a flight back to Sudan. Then I might sneak back into the Nuba Mountains without anyone noticing me, find my family and disappear. Two years after my escape, my asylum application had still not been decided. Everyone around me — my friends, my lawyers, supporters, journalists — were so confident that it would be successful. No one ever thought about what we

363

would do if it were turned down. No one had ever contemplated that possibility — least of all me. After the first publication of my book, in Germany, the pressure mounted on the British government to make their decision on my asylum claim. We were all confidently expecting to have something to celebrate.

It was a rainy Thursday when I heard the news that would send me into a complete panic, that would drive me to the edge of despair and beyond. I had just finished school and I was on the bus home. I had a call on my mobile. I looked at the number and could tell it was Damien, the British journalist whom I'd met on the day of my escape and who had helped me write my book. Over the past two years, this man had become my close friend. He had helped me so much, in so many ways. I had my own special name for him, 'Corba'. In Nuba, this means 'no man can do what he does'. But as soon as I heard his voice, I knew that something was badly wrong. He was always so full of energy and optimism and hope for a better world. But now, he sounded drained and exhausted: it struck me that he sounded almost as if he were frightened.

'Mende, where are you? Are you OK? You're on your way home from school, right? I have to see you. Now. You have to come here, immediately. D'you understand?'

'Why? What's wrong! Please, tell me. I know something is wrong . . . '

'Look, just get over here, now. I'll tell you when you get here. It's going to be OK . . . '

'No! Tell me now! What's happened? Oh my

364

God! What's happened?'

'OK. Listen to me. They have turned down your asylum claim. I don't know why or how they can have done this. I've only just found out, and God knows we're going to make them pay for this. But you have to come to see me, now. I don't think even Alison, your lawyer, knows this yet. We have to start preparing your answers . . . Don't worry . . . '

'Oh my God! They're going to send me back to Sudan! No! They can't. Oh my God! When? When will they try to do this? Oh my God . . . '

The rest of that journey is all a blur to me. When I reached Damien's house, I was in such a state I collapsed in despair. Damien explained to me that he'd only just received the news by telephone and that he hadn't seen the documents yet. They were being sent over by courier from my old home. It seems the Home Office had managed to send them to the wrong address, despite the fact that they'd been informed of the new address many months ago; he wasn't sure if even my lawyers had seen them yet. The problem was that I only had ten days in which to mount an appeal against the decision, he explained. Without this, they would try to deport me. Because the documents had been posted to the wrong address, we now had barely a handful of days left in which to make the appeal deadline. I'd have to be strong, he explained, because we'd have a lot of work to do getting it ready over the next few days.

'Oh my God. They can't send me back. They can't. They'll kill me! Oh my God . . . They can't send me back . . . ' I was in shock and I just kept repeating this over and over again.

'Listen. Don't worry. No one's sending you back to Sudan. They can't, Mende. You have the right to appeal. And there're so many people who won't let that happen. There's Alison, your asylum lawyer. There's your publishers. There's all the journalists who've written about you and broadcast your story. There's all the politicians behind you. And there's me.'

The first thing he had done, he explained, was alert my publishers to the news of my asylum refusal, so that they in turn could contact the world's media about it. Then he had got on to the rest of my support network — politicians, my legal team and human rights charities — all of whom would help defend me. He was in the middle of writing a briefing for all these people about what had happened, but he needed some space in which to work, he explained. So he asked his partner to look after me for a while. She's a lovely African girl called Eva, and she did her best to comfort me, and let me cry as much as I needed to. She told me I should stay there with them that night as I shouldn't be on my own. And anyway, Damien would probably need me there, she said, as things were moving quickly now. A little later, I heard a ring at the front door. A large brown envelope had arrived by courier. I watched anxiously as Damien opened it. As he started reading, his face fell and then his jaw dropped to the floor.

'The bastards, the bastards!' He just kept repeating it, over and over again. 'How the hell

366

can they write such bullshit and think they can get away with it? I mean, how *can* they?' Eventually he turned to face me. 'Mende. D'you want to know what it says?'

'Yes,' I answered, in a scared voice.

'Firstly, it says that slavery is not persecution — persecution is another way of saying serious suffering. So they're trying to say that during the last ten years of your life you did not suffer enough to qualify for asylum here in the UK. I mean, unbelievable! How could you have suffered any more than you did? They say that although there is slavery in Sudan, the Sudan government is not involved. Yeah. Really. Like anyone who's investigated this says they are, but the British government says they aren't. Smart. They say that Sudan is such a large country that the Sudanese government would not notice if you were sent back. I mean, Jesus! Are these people just plain stupid? It's a big country, so they won't notice you. Oh yeah, so what happens when she arrives back at the airport, morons? Oh, and it says that although the Nuba have suffered in the war because the government forces have attacked them, there's a ceasefire now in the Nuba Mountains, so it's safe for you to go home. Oh well, that's all right then, isn't it? I mean, it's not as if there's a record of ceasefires being broken in Sudan or anything, is it? Or that they haven't already broken this one. For God's sake! Whoever wrote this is a total moron. Mende, don't worry. This is so messed up there's no way they'll get away with it. Look, they're even stupid enough to get your country wrong, and talk about returning you to Somalia, not Sudan. Morons! Complete morons! Don't worry. Alison will tear them apart. And the media will crucify them. They'll look so stupid, they'll have to beg you to stay.'

'But I *am* worried, Damien. I'm so worried.' I was worried because I could see that he was so concerned. I could tell that beneath his anger, Damien was scared for me now. And that made me terrified.

'Yes. I know you're worried. I'm worried too. But all we can do is start answering this bullshit. So, come and sit here next to me and let's start to draft your response. So, tell me first, what do you say to the British Home Office when they say that slavery doesn't count as suffering?'

'The British Government say they do not believe that I have suffered enough persecution either in Sudan or the UK to justify my asylum claim,' we wrote down. 'How could I possibly have suffered more than I have done over the past ten years? Things could only have been any worse for me if they had killed me. In my asylum ruling, the British government accepts that there is slavery in the war zones and that slaves are sent to North Sudan — yet they are refusing to give me asylum when I was captured and kept as a slave in exactly the way they describe. The British government accept that the Nuba people suffer death and injury because the Sudan government attack the Nuba people, yet they propose to return me to the Nuba Mountains. How can I possibly be safe there? The British government say that if I am sent back to Sudan I will not be noticed by the Sudanese government. How can they possibly say this when I have written a book exposing the role that regime plays in slavery? As soon as I arrive at the airport they would know about it, seize me and then I would disappear.'

We read back over what we had written so far. When I was satisfied it was what I wanted to say, we continued. 'The British government say there is no evidence that the Sudanese government were involved in my capture and enslavement. How can they say this when I and other captured children were taken to Sudanese government army camps; and when I was sent to the UK to work for a Sudanese diplomat? The British government say that my asylum claim is not based upon suffering due to my race, religion or nationality. How can they possibly say this, when I was enslaved and oppressed by Arabs because I am black, a Nuba person? The British government say there are no reasons to believe that I will be killed if I am sent back to Sudan. The Sudanese government kills ands tortures its own people — and I am one of the few Sudanese who have stood up and exposed the government's role in war-driven slavery in Sudan. How can they possibly say my life would not be in danger if I were sent back?'

We then read the statement through from beginning to end, to make sure that it said exactly what I wanted it to say. Then Damien suggested I make a general statement at the end to sum up my feelings. 'Since my escape,' we wrote, 'I believed that Britain was a democratic country that respected human rights, justice and freedom. For the first time in my life, I had started to feel safe and secure in this country. I cannot believe that the British government will now send me back to face the horrors that for certain await me in Sudan. I am shocked and shaken to the core by this asylum decision.'

Once the news of my asylum refusal had reached the world's media, along with my statement, it provoked a storm of protest. Front page stories around the world condemned the British government's decision. The *Guardian* published a major investigation into the story. The *Voice* newspaper started a 'Let Mende Stay' campaign. Film crews from German TV, Sky, the BBC and elsewhere all wanted to speak to me. Amnesty International and Anti-Slavery International came out in support of my asylum claim. Baroness Cox led a cross-party group of MPs to lobby the government to reverse its decision, and MPs' letters flooded into the Home Office.

For the next few days, my life became one exhausting round of TV, radio and newspaper interviews. All the journalists wanted to ask me the same questions. How can the British government decide to send you back to Sudan? What will happen to you if they do so? How do you feel now they have refused your asylum claim? I talked a lot. I cried a lot. I felt my world was falling apart. Partly, I felt scared about all this criticism, all this trouble that I was causing the British government. But everyone I trusted told me that there was no other way. The British government had to be made to understand that unless they reversed their decision, they would sink under a storm of media protest. They had to realise that if they did attempt to deport me, it would cost them very dear.

The reaction from around the world to the news of my asylum refusal was amazing. I had letters and e-mails of support from so many people, and reading these helped me to find the courage and the strength to fight the decision to deport me.

One fifteen-year-old boy wrote from Germany: 'Dear Mende, I think that on our earth there are too many people who are chased, killed or bullied by others. I wish that all people could live <u>together</u> and not fight each other. My girlfriend and I heard about your sad story . . . I hope that you and those who support you are strong enough to let you live in England. Good luck and best wishes. Yours, Tim.'

A German couple wrote from Munich: 'Dear Mende, We are shocked about the British intention to send you back to Sudan. If you feel it would be helpful for you, we are willing to adopt you and give you the German nationality. As a German we are sure you would be protected from deportation. If there is a chance for you in this course of action and if you are interested in it, please contact us. We will react very quickly. All the best for you and kindly regards, Angelika & Thomas Kaubisch.'

As well as Amnesty International and Anti-Slavery International, Germany's Society for Threatened Peoples came out supporting my fight for asylum. A campaign to e-mail protests to the Home Office was launched, and these began flooding in. Candlelight vigils were held outside the British Embassy in Berlin. People were deeply moved by my story and wanted to help. I in turn was deeply touched by the hundreds of messages of support sent to me. I was especially moved by the family who offered to adopt me. It was so good to know there were such kind people in the world, but how could they adopt me, I wondered? I wasn't a child any more. I was an adult in my early twenties. My lawyers looked into this, just to see if it was possible. But the more they explored it, the more it seemed that under the European-wide asylum laws, I would have to stay and fight my case here in the UK. If I tried to go to Germany, the government there would be duty bound to return me to the UK, the country where I first claimed asylum.

A few days after my asylum refusal, I by chance met another girl whose asylum had also been turned down. She was from Somalia, an African country not far from Sudan. She was a Muslim, like me, and she looked about my age. Her country is infamous for being the most anarchic and war-torn in the whole of Africa. She told me that she had been waiting seven months for her appeal, and that she still had no date for the hearing. During those seven months of fear and uncertainty and dread, she felt she was going to go mad. 'You're so lucky,' she told me. 'At least you have many people supporting you. Powerful people helping you win your asylum. The media doing stories

372

about you. Friends to talk to about all this. There's no one helping me or supporting me like that. I feel so alone sometimes. And so afraid.'

★　★　★

'They're not sending you back to Sudan, Mende,' said Alison Stanley, my asylum lawyer, when I went to see her a few days later. 'Don't worry. It'll be over my dead body.'

I liked this woman. She had a kind, friendly way with me, but I was sure she could be tough as hell when she needed to be. And I'd been told by lots of people that she was the best asylum lawyer in Britain. If anyone could win my appeal, Alison Stanley at Bindman & Partners could. I had come to meet her to discuss the ongoing campaign for my asylum. A week previously, Alison had completed my appeal and succeeded in filing it before the deadline. This meant I was now safe for now; the appeal would have to come before the courts and be lost before the British government couldn't carry out their decision to deport me. In reality this meant that I would probably remain in the UK at least until the New Year, because such cases usually took a number of months to come to court. But each day that I had to live under such uncertainty and stress was taking a horrible toll on me. I felt exhausted, nervous and very, very low.

'You know, Mende, I think it's just a cock-up,' Alison continued.

'A what?' I asked.

'Oh. Yes. Sorry,' she said, laughing. 'Yes, that's not a word you should learn from me or use. It's very rude.'

'What does it mean?'

'A cock-up? Well, it means a very big mistake. I'm trying to explain to you — I'm not doing very well though — that I think they have just made a big mistake. I don't think they have decided to send you back because you are a difficult, high-profile case or anything. In fact, quite the reverse. I think the person who made this decision didn't have any idea about your case. It's such a sloppy, badly worded and badly written document, it's shocking really.'

'So, it's a cock-out,' I said, smiling at her.

'No. No. Not cock-out. Cock-up. But you're not allowed to use that word. You can't have your asylum lawyer teaching you bad language, can you? Now, listen to me. I don't want you to get your hopes up too much, but I met the head of the whole asylum section a couple of days ago. I had a word with him and asked him to reconsider your asylum ruling. I told him that it was clearly a mistake. Funnily enough, he hadn't even heard of your case, which is shocking considering it's been all over the media. But that supports the cock-up theory — sorry, the big mistake theory. Anyway, the point is he's agreed to reconsider it. I'm confident they will change their mind, Mende. They've clearly made a very big, very stupid mistake. And with your book being published and all the media coverage over your asylum refusal, they'll realise that. So, I hope you may have some good news in a few weeks' time.'

Thus, two years after my escape, it seemed that my nightmare was far from over and that I was still struggling to be free. Part of me wondered what I had done in life to deserve so much suffering. And part of me kept wondering when my suffering would ever end.

★ ★ ★

My asylum claim was initially refused on 17 October 2002. A little over a month later, on 23 December 2002, I was at last recognised as a refugee by the British government, and granted asylum and permanent residency in the United Kingdom.

Epilogue

Truly Free?

I chose to speak out, and to write this book because I know that there are so many other women, girls and boys still enslaved in Sudan. A few of them I know — Asha, Katuna, Nanu — remain my friends. How could I not speak out if, by doing so, there is at least a chance that the scourge of slavery would be removed from my long-suffering country? Perhaps my motives are best expressed in a TV interview I recorded with Damien Lewis in London three days after I escaped. It contains everything I want to say. It was an emotional, tearful interview, which I hope the words alone can convey:

Now that you have escaped, how does it feel to be free?

Despite the fact that I've escaped, I still can't believe it's true. I just keep fearing they'll come and capture me again, and take me back there. I can't really believe that I'm free, even though I'm living it and experiencing it. I feel like this is a dream and the reality will arrive when I am still enslaved. And I'm frightened that something will happen to my family — that they'll take revenge on them for what I've done.

What do you want to say to those people who believed they had the right to keep you in slavery for so many years?

I would say to them that there should be justice and kindness and equality between all people, all colours, between black and white, and between all religions. We are all Allah's creation and we are all created the same. There is no justification to treat people with injustice, with cruelty. And I want them to stop causing this misery and cruelty to all those people who are still slaves in Sudan.

What would you say to the people of the world about slavery in Sudan today?

I'd say that there is slavery going on, right now, today. I am an example and I am the living proof and it happened to me, personally. It happened to me in Sudan and then in London. And I know there are lots of other people still enslaved in Sudan. I want people to realise this and that they need to do something to help stop it.

Now you are free, what are your hopes for the future?

All I can think about right now is how to convince myself that I am really, truly free. Until then, I can't even think about the future. I just want to experience this feeling of freedom for a while. Then later, I might think about what my life might bring.

You have just escaped and it's been a very traumatic time. What gives you the strength and bravery to talk for hours about these difficult, terrible years?

I get this strength because I now know that there are kind people in the world, here in

England. Here, people are free and there is justice. I have been enclosed in kindness from all the people I have met since my escape — which has given me back some of my confidence. And I also have my beliefs inside me, which have kept me strong.

Is there anything you would like to add?

I just want to say that I miss my parents and I hope they are all right. I want to say that I want all the others who are still in slavery and misery to be set free too. How can I really feel free, when I know that they all remain enslaved?

Just one last question. Look, if we could fly you back into the Nuba Mountains, if it were possible, would you be willing to go? Would you be willing to go with me and a film crew, back to your home?

Is it possible? Is it really possible? Of course I would go. Would you go with me? If you would go I would go. I would love nothing more in the world. I'd love nothing more than to see my family again and to see my home. That's my dream.

It remains my dream. Not only to see my parents, but to take them on the Haj, the great pilgrimage to Mecca, in Saudi Arabia, Islam's holiest shrine. It is the duty of all Muslims, wherever possible, to make the Haj once in their lifetime, and I should like to enable my father and mother to do so. But I will have to be patient. And patience is a virtue I learned to possess in abundance when I spent all those years in slavery.

I still feel my life has a long way to go before it

will really make sense to me, before I will really understand where this journey from slavery to freedom is ultimately taking me. And what do I want from life myself? At the moment, I go to school and learn English. I fly around the world speaking out against slavery at international conferences.

I often feel happy and fulfilled and free, too. Happy that my time is my own, that I am studying and may one day qualify to be a nurse and care for people. Happy that one day I might meet the man of my dreams and have children of my own. For me, that would be one way to rebuild the sense of family, identity and security that the years in slavery and exile have taken from me.

Maybe my story will have a happy ending, after all. *Inshallah* — God willing.

Afterword

Mende Nazer escaped on 11 September 2000 — on a sunny day on the streets of a leafy North London suburb. I first heard about her plight a few days earlier from a Nuba friend. He wanted help in rescuing her: in particular, a journalist to witness the rescue so it was 'on the record'. That's where I came in. Today, as I write this two years later, Mende Nazer is a young, vivacious, highly intelligent woman, with hope and belief in the future. Mende doesn't know her exact age, as the Nuba people keep no record of birth dates and don't celebrate birthdays. But counting back the years from the day of her capture, she must be somewhere in her mid twenties. Yet that first time I saw her on the day of her rescue, she was a hunched, petrified, trembling shadow of a human being. It is almost impossible to believe the change that two years of freedom in England have wrought in her.

Mende has never given up the childhood dream she shared with her father: she hopes she might train as a nurse and then a doctor. Her greatest wish now is to be able to see her family again. Sometime in the future, she also hopes to get married and have children of her own. She hopes that will give her back the sense of having a loving, close family around her — something that was stolen from her at the age of twelve in the slave raid. The circumcision that Mende suffered whilst a child is of the most severe kind possible, called infibulation. She has been advised that she will face real risks during childbirth as a result — both personally and in terms of her baby dying. It is hard to believe how such suffering continues into adulthood.

Perhaps equally hard to believe is the reality of the slave trade in Sudan today: today, not three hundred years ago, when we British were the masters of this trade in human misery. But today, a full fifty years after the UN Universal Declaration of Human Rights stated that all human beings are equal and that no person shall be a slave of another. I first witnessed this modern-day slave trade when I went to Sudan in 1996 to produce a report for Channel 4 television. I travelled into South Sudan clandestinely as the guest of a tiny charity. I was at first sceptical. I simply couldn't believe that at the end of the twentieth century, black Africans were still being traded as so much cattle. Yet the reality on the ground was far worse than I could have possibly imagined: I witnessed scenes of indescribable horror. These people were not only being bought and sold: they were being seized in brutal slave raids, where hundreds were slaughtered, raped, tortured and abused. Whole villages were being burned to the ground, and people incinerated alive inside their huts. I had stumbled into a veritable living nightmare.

Since then, I have reported on slavery in Sudan from many areas, including the Nuba Mountains, for broadcasters all over the world. I have filmed and interviewed hundreds of escaped slaves and some of the Arab slave traders themselves. It is always the same, horrific story. Arab tribes are formed into militias, armed with AK47 machine guns, and told to wage Jihad, or Holy War, against the black tribes of the Nuba Mountains and the south. As their reward for doing so, the Arab tribes get to keep the booty of war — including cattle, goats, and human beings as slaves. In the raids they mount on the villages, they take only the women and children alive: it has proven too difficult to break the will of grown men and turn them into slaves. Young boys are sold as cattle herders; young girls like Mende as domestic slaves; the women are often sold into sexual slavery. After decades of civil war, Sudan is one of the most under-developed countries on earth: the going price of a slave today is less than 150 dollars.

Stories like Mende's have been documented literally in their thousands by organisations like the UN, Human Rights Watch and Anti-Slavery International. A recent report by the US Bureau of African Affairs found that 'slavery in Sudan is characterised by violent capture and abductions, subjection to forced labour with no pay, denial of a victim's freedom of movement and choice, prohibition of the use of native language, and the denial of contact with the victim's family'. That one sentence could well be used to sum up Mende's own story. The crucial difference is that in Mende's case the story did not stop at the borders of Sudan; she was sent to a European country that offered her the chance to escape. But for Nanu, the little girl who replaced Mende as a slave in Khartoum, there are no such opportunities. Who will help her to be free, and the thousands more like her still enslaved in Sudan?

Until recently, the present regime in Sudan, the National Islamic Front (NIF), denied that slavery existed. Although it is a signatory to the main international conventions that outlaw slavery, and has its own, domestic law doing the same, the NIF turned a blind eye to what was happening in its own country. But in 1999, international pressure forced the NIF into creating the Committee for the Elimination of Abduction of Women and Children (CEAWC). This organisation is tasked with eliminating 'abductions' in Sudan and reuniting all abductees with their families. It is at least a recognition that the problem of slavery exists — despite NIF insistence on characterising the problem as 'abduction' rather than 'slavery'.

Recently, I met the Director of CEAWC in London, and he assured me that CEAWC is doing everything in its power to use legal remedies to end all slavery in Sudan. Sound intentions require results to back them up. A sceptical world community might be more convinced if it started seeing actual prosecutions in Sudan of those responsible for the slave trade. So far, it seems, there have been none. Moreover, the NIF has refused to accept responsibility for the acts committed by the Arab militias under its de facto authority, or done anything to curb their excesses. In fact, the Arab militias appear to act with impunity. At best, the regime can be said to be turning a blind eye to slavery within its borders. At worst, its attitude is seen by many as giving a licence to continue these abuses.

And what of the role of Mahmoud Al Koronky and the Sudan embassy in London, in Mende's case in particular? Mr Al Koronky's status at the Sudanese embassy in London during the period covered by this book should not be exaggerated. His official position was as the press attaché to the embassy. He was only made the acting chargé d'affaires for a much-reduced diplomatic mission during the period of the cooling of UK-Sudanese diplomatic relations — in the direct aftermath of the US cruise missile strikes on Khartoum (see Chapter 20). Since Mende's escape, Mr Al Koronky and his family have returned to Sudan, as have the other embassy figures mentioned in this book. At the time of writing, he is reportedly no longer in the Sudanese diplomatic service and is taking 'an extended holiday'.

It is also clear that the worst abuses suffered by Mende took place in the Sudan, not in London with the Al Koronkys. Mende believes that this is largely because by the time she arrived in London she had learned exactly how to behave so as not to attract punishment. However, she still suffered in the UK to such an extent that she was willing to contemplate suicide and to take the very real risk of trying to escape.

Deception appears to have been used in Khartoum in order for Mende to come to the

UK. When Mende was first told she was to be sent to London, Mr Al Koronky had a visa application for her turned down by the British authorities. This was because, prior to Mende's arrival, another young woman had been brought to the UK from the Sudan to work in his household, and she too had run away and claimed British asylum. Her asylum claim is ongoing, and her lawyers are in contact with Mende's asylum lawyers. This explains why Mende was first told that she was being sent to the UK and then the whole issue was forgotten for several months before she did eventually get sent to London. It also explains why Mende was ordered to tell the British authorities that she was going to work for one Ali Bashir Gadalla — a man whom she has never in her life met or even seen — when she was really going to the Al Koronkys. A visa had to be secured in the name of Ali Bashir Gadalla because one had been refused to the Al Koronkys.

Mende's fight to win her asylum claim and her battle to be allowed to speak out has been a long and tortuous one. It was not helped by an article published in the *Sunday Telegraph* newspaper, shortly after her escape. Entitled, 'Sudan diplomat 'kept slave girl in London home' ', it constituted an extraordinarily inept and irre-sponsible piece of journalism. Just weeks after Mende's escape, it was written and published without Mende's permission and without the journalist having met with or even spoken to Mende. Consequently, it contained several inaccuracies. It stated that Mende was sick and in need of hospital treatment immediately after her escape, and carried the implication that she suffered sexual abuse in the Al Koronky household. Neither point was true. It also carried what looked like a quote from Mende, even though the journalist had never spoken with her. And although the journalist had been in contact with some of the Sudanese who helped Mende in her escape, they made the point that it was far too early for Mende to speak with anyone from the press. Although the *Sunday Telegraph* journalist never made contact with Mende, she did, it appears, talk to Mrs Al Koronky, who is quoted extensively in the article. Mrs Al Koronky claimed that Mende was a housemaid who was treated like a member of the family and had been paid some money (two hundred pounds). 'We even gave her the same food as us and offered to have her educated,' she is quoted as saying in the article. 'I am really shocked and haven't slept since she escaped,' Mrs Al Koronky continued.

It beggars belief that a reputable newspaper could publish such an article against the interests of a vulnerable asylum seeker — in particular when the journalist had no access to her in order to verify the story. Following publication, Al Koronky sued the *Sunday Telegraph* for libel. Mende was then advised by her asylum lawyers that she unfortunately had little choice but to assist the *Sunday Telegraph* in their defence, because the outcome of the libel case might adversely affect her asylum claim. Doing this proved particularly unpleasant for her. In spite of

Mende's assistance, the libel case was eventually settled before trial, a joint statement being read out in open court to the effect that the whole story as published by the *Sunday Telegraph* was untrue. Once again, Mende was not contacted about this statement in open court or consulted over it. Had she been consulted over the original newspaper story and the statement in open court, she would have had an opportunity to correct the inaccuracies contained in both. In the final analysis, Mende was in effect cast as the Al Koronkys' au pair, her story of abduction and slavery in Sudan and then London presented as being nothing but a tissue of lies.

Of course, Mende's story did not stop the day she stepped into freedom on the streets of London. In particular, her fear for the safety and well-being of her family back in Sudan bears heavily on her mind and for very good reasons. Attempts have been made to intimidate and pressurise her family in Sudan, although it is not clear exactly by whom. After her escape, Mende managed to make contact with her family. I was a witness to the first time that she talked to members of her family after the many years of forced separation, and it was a heart-breaking scene. All her family did survive the raid, although her mother was badly injured. But her best friend, Kehko, with whom she used to walk to school, was killed.

Mende studied English while awaiting the result of her asylum application and achieved very good results in her exams. She was invariably top of the class. Increasingly, her story attracted media and political attention. In recognition of her bravery in speaking out in her book — first published in Germany — the Spanish Coalition Against Racism (CECRA) granted Mende its 2002 International Human Rights Award.

Since this book was first published in Germany, a number of people have asked me how Mende and I went about writing it — a white Englishman in his late thirties and a black Nuba woman in her early twenties. In July 2001, Mende and I left London and travelled to Wiltshire, in the West Country, where a friend of mine, Roger Hammond, offered us the peace and tranquillity of his country retreat in which to work. It is a grand Georgian castle set in stunning grounds. Before leaving London, I had thought long and hard about how to get the best out of the writing ahead of us. Mende still only spoke basic English after a year living as a free person in London. I spoke almost no Arabic, and my Nuba was non-existent. At first, I considered the idea of working with an English-Arabic translator, but I knew that so much of Mende's story was going to be deeply personal, difficult material to talk about. I knew that the key to her being able to tell me about her story from the heart lay in the closeness that would develop between the two of us. She would need to trust me with her most difficult, painful memories and fears. I knew that having a translator sat between us would make that impossible.

I talked this over with Mende. We agreed that

working slowly, in English, using an English-Arabic dictionary where necessary, we could make ourselves understood. We then toured the bookshops of London, buying up anything we could find on Sudan, the Nuba Mountains, and slavery. All of this would help us with the writing. I remember one particular day when, having found Leni Riefenstahl's photo-book on the Nuba people, Mende spent a whole journey home on the number 38 bus looking through the pages of that book in wonder. She was so happy . . . and so sad at being able to see scenes from her home again. 'That's just like my village,' she'd say, stabbing a finger at a picture on the page. 'That man looks just like my dad. Oh lovely, lovely!' Then she'd bend down and lightly kiss the photograph on the page. When we finally got down to our castle retreat to start our work, I found that I had a whole library of material in the back of the car with us to help with the writing.

We started in July and we didn't finish until September. We worked side by side at a desk, me typing the story into my laptop as she talked. I would always ask her the same questions: 'What did you see? What did you hear? What did you say? What did you smell? How did you feel?' Whenever we did have problems making ourselves understood in English, I'd ask her to draw what she was talking about. Or sometimes, I might draw a picture to clarify things, and ask her: 'So, was it like this?' We filled a whole A4 notepad full of sketches — ranging from a picture of the gourd school lunch box her father made for her to a ground plan of her master's house in Khartoum. At times, we even got up and acted out scenes together so that I might get a better idea of how the Nuba wrestling worked or how her Khartoum master threw Mende down onto the kitchen table and cut her leg open.

And we took lots of long walks in the countryside around the castle. These were not just breaks from the intensity of the writing. They were also the first opportunity for Mende since she was captured to set foot in forests and hills again — places so reminiscent of her childhood. It was during these strolls that many of the memories of her childhood came back to her — like the wonderful scene when her father tells Mende about what the clouds are made of. I always carried a notebook with me, so we could capture these memories as we walked. 'Come on, Mende,' I'd say. 'Sit down here. Let's write that down. It's a lovely little story and we should put it in the book.'

I was struck not so much by the horror of Mende's story — as a journalist, I have been to Sudan many times before and reported so many terrible stories of escaped slaves — but was more surprised by the depth of the detail in which Mende remembered things, especially from her early childhood. Before we started writing, I had no idea that the first part of the book would paint such a joyful picture of a happy, loving childhood, or that it would portray the richness and vibrancy of the Nuba culture so fully. I can remember saying to Mende, 'How do you remember things in such detail? I can hardly remember anything from my childhood.' The answer, of course, is that she comes from an oral tradition. Her tribe never wrote anything down, but relied on their memories and their skill at storytelling for a sense of who they are, their identity and their place in the world. Even now, Mende hardly ever writes anything down. I keep trying to get her to write a daily diary and to note down the time and date of appointments, but with little success.

Much of what we wrote about Mende had never told anyone before — in particular, the terrible ways in which she suffered. Prior to her escape, there was no-one she could have told these things to. There were tears and trauma during the writing of the most difficult parts: but as Mende herself recognised, perhaps talking about all this was the first step on the road towards healing all the hurt and the pain. At the end of those three months, we had produced a 300,000-word monolith. The final book is a little over 100,000 words. In the next four months, the book went through an intensive stage of creative writing, involving six or seven different redrafts until it was finally complete. During all of this time, Mende was actually staying in my house as a guest of my partner and myself (her situation in the asylum accommodation where she had been staying had become unbearably bad). This meant that she was always on hand during the period of the redrafting, if I was ever unsure of anything. I read through the last redrafts with Mende from cover to cover, making sure that every word and nuance in the story was as intended.

Of course, no story is ever complete: Mende's has been through a creative process of selection, condensation and story writing, such that it may be read in an accessible, compelling form. Names have been changed and locations altered, for obvious security reasons. Some scenes and parts of the narrative have been part-fictionalised in order to protect identities, and to aid the narrative flow of the story. But the only times that I have significantly added any material are, for example, where factual clarification was absolutely necessary (for example, Chapter 20 — Revenge, where I add in some facts and figures on the numbers killed in the US cruise missile strike on the Al Shifa plant in Khartoum). The final product — *Slave* — remains an incredibly detailed account of Mende's life story. In it I hope I have captured the voice of a young Nuba child and then woman in a way that is authentic, compelling and real.

Acknowledgements

So many people helped me to tell my story in this book and then in my fight for my right to asylum in the UK. No list can ever do justice to all those who did so, but I would like to give special thanks to the following.

My literary agent Felicity Bryan, a real fighter and a visionary, for her unshakeable belief in me and my story and her tenacity in getting this book published; to her colleagues, Michele Topham and Carole Robinson, for their unyielding commitment to getting my story told, and Ruth West, for organising such an effective campaign on my behalf and for being such a very, very good friend. I am grateful to my lawyer Alison Stanley, of Bindman & Partners, for her dogged determination to win my asylum case, and Geoffrey Bindman, of the same law firm, a man of tenacity and principle. Baroness Caroline Cox, a Peer and Deputy Speaker of the House of Lords, gave me tea at the House of Lords and her unstinting support at the highest political levels. David Leigh of the *Guardian* newspaper contributed trenchant articles during the darkest hours of my fight for asylum; Shirin Aguiar of *The Voice* newspaper launched the 'Let Mende Stay' campaign to fight against my threatened deportation, while Darius Barzagan, David Lloyn and several others helped support my asylum claim at the BBC, and Marianne Velmans first saw the potential of my life story as a book.

My deep appreciation to Roger Hammond for inviting me into his home and letting me work on the book in the peace and tranquillity of his Wiltshire castle; Mrs Christine Edwards and her late husband Derek, for making me so welcome in their home and family — you have become like a second mother to me; Mrs Jess Wilcocks, for being like a grandmother to me and inviting me to her 90th birthday party; Nelly and Joe, from Geneva, for reading my story and then taking me into their hearts and their home; Christina Barrett, for teaching me how to live and survive in London and travel around that huge, frenetic city; Amel Mohammed, my fellow asylum seeker and very dear friend; Waris Dirie, author of *Desert Flower* and a fellow African sister who has supported me and my book so vocally; Mitchel Woolf and Rosanna Mesquita for their legal help and advice; Sarah Woodhouse, a wonderful neighbour, for all her help and legal advice; Peter Von Felbert, my photographer and now close friend, and Emma Mills at the Foreign & Commonwealth office for taking my concerns over my family so seriously.

Special thanks, too, to Mike Schwarz, also of Bindman & Partners, for helping me in my on-going legal battles and fight for justice; Amnesty International, Anti-Slavery International, the NCADC and Germany's Society for Threatened Peoples — for their tireless campaigning on my behalf; Carlos Nuñez, of the Spanish Coalition Against Racism (CECRA), for my recent Award and all his subsequent support

396

and help; Fred Mulder and Fenella Rouse, for their warm words and friendship; everyone at Andrew Nurnberg Associates, who secured publication of my book all across Europe; Hans-Peter Ubleis at my German publisher, Droemer, for having the bravery and fortitude to first publish my story; Carolin Graehl, my editor at Droemer, for her empathy and soft touch during the editorial process; Barbara Plueck-hahn, of the Droemer publicity department, for the tireless press campaign she mounted in Germany to fight against my deportation; and all the other staff at Droemer who believed in me and my story.

I thank Kate Darnton and her team at Public Affairs, my American publisher, for having faith in my story; Ursula Mackenzie and her team at Time Warner Books, my British publisher, for their determination that my story should be told in the UK; and Martin Soames at law firm DLA for his skilled legal support. I would like to especially thank Elaine Pearson for taking me to Geneva to speak to the UN on my first ever trip abroad with my new British travel papers; Jo Jacobs and Sally Matta, for befriending me and helping me try to be a woman; Hannah Lewis, for trust and laughter and gentle help; and Mike Mawhinney, Sean O'Connor, John Miles and Alex Morgan, for the time they volunteered to film and edit my story. I would also like to extend my thanks to the many people who have helped me so much but whom I cannot, for obvious reasons, name here (you know who you are); and finally I would like to thank the people of Germany, Spain, Italy, the UK and elsewhere who read my book and then went out of their way to lend their support to my fight to remain safely in Britain. Together, you have made me believe again that there are good, kind people in the world.

Mende Nazer,
London 2003

Helpful Addresses

Anti-Slavery International
Thomas Clarkson House
The Stableyard
Broomgrove Road
London SW9 9TL
email: info@antislavery.org

Human Rights Watch
2nd Floor, 2–12 Pentonville Road
London N1 9HF
Tel: 020 7713 1995
www.hrwuk@hrw.org

www.sudanslaves.org

We do hope that you have enjoyed reading this large print book.

Did you know that all of our titles are available for purchase?

We publish a wide range of high quality large print books including:
Romances, Mysteries, Classics
General Fiction
Non Fiction and Westerns

Special interest titles available in large print are:
The Little Oxford Dictionary
Music Book
Song Book
Hymn Book
Service Book

Also available from us courtesy of Oxford University Press:
Young Readers' Dictionary
(large print edition)
Young Readers' Thesaurus
(large print edition)

For further information or a free brochure, please contact us at:
Ulverscroft Large Print Books Ltd.,
The Green, Bradgate Road, Anstey,
Leicester, LE7 7FU, England.
Tel: (00 44) 0116 236 4325
Fax: (00 44) 0116 234 0205

Other titles published by
The House of Ulverscroft:

THE LAST OF THE GENTLEMEN ADVENTURERS

Edward Beauclerk Maurice

In 1930, sixteen-year-old Edward Beauclerk Maurice was faced with a stark choice: follow his mother and siblings to New Zealand, or pursue an uncertain future as an apprentice fur trader among the Eskimos. He decided to sign up for five years of Arctic life. With no telephone, no radio communication and only one annual visit from the supply ship, he found life in Baffin Land isolated and harsh. The Innuit taught him to build igloos, hunt polar bears and survive ferocious storms. After three years, he was sent to his own outpost, where, alone, he had to save the community from illness and starvation. This is the story of a young man determined to triumph over every circumstance.

THE STORYTELLER'S DAUGHTER

Saira Shah

Saira Shah grew up in Britain, but she was always told she came from somewhere else: a fairytale land of orchards and gardens. The country was Afghanistan, the storyteller her father. Then, aged twenty-one, Saira set out to find the truth about her family's homeland. Instead of finding a paradise, she was plunged into a country at war. The journey spanned more than fifteen years. Whether extricating herself from an arranged marriage, walking through minefields with the mujahidin, or slipping clandestinely into the Taliban's Kabul, Saira learnt the bitter limits of the stories she loved. But she discovered the reality of a country more complex and challenging than anything she could have imagined.

FORGET YOU HAD A DAUGHTER

Sandra Gregory, Michael Tierney

Sandra Gregory was living a life in Bangkok that many only dream of — until illness, unemployment and political unrest turned it into a nightmare. Desperate to get home, she agreed to smuggle an addict's personal supply of heroin. She didn't even make it on to the plane. In this memoir, she tells of the events leading up to her arrest, the horrific conditions in Lard Yao prison, her trial and how it feels to be sentenced to death. Four and a half years later, she was transferred to the British prison system and an equally harsh regime. Following relentless campaigning by her parents, she was pardoned by the King of Thailand and released in 2000.

ALMOST THERE

Nuala O'Faolain

In 1996, a small Irish press approached
Nuala O'Faolain, then a writer for the IRISH
TIMES, to publish a collection of her opinion
columns. She offered to write an introduction
to explain the life experience that had shaped
her views. The book became an international
bestseller and launched a new life for its
author. In ALMOST THERE, she begins her
story from the moment her life began to
change, in all manner of ways — subtle,
radical, predictable and unforeseen. It is a
provocative meditation on the 'crucible of
middle age'. It is also a story of good fortune
chasing out bad. Intelligent, thoughtful,
hilarious, fierce, moving, generous, it is full of
surprises.

SOPHIE'S STORY

Vince Smith

In 1990, while Vince Smith was working as a senior keeper at Chester Zoo, a newborn chimpanzee in his care was abandoned by her mother. Named Sophie, the baby chimp was taken home and hand-reared by Vince and his wife. Six months later another new baby arrived: Oliver, their son. This is an enthralling account of Sophie's life: her early years in the English countryside with Vince and his family; her traumatic removal from the family she adored into a captive zoo world; her repatriation to Africa and eventual reunion with her human foster family; and, finally, her integration into a semi-wild group of chimpanzees.

EMMA'S WAR

Deborah Scroggins

Emma McCune's passion for Africa, her unstinting commitment to the children of the Sudan, and her striking beauty and glamour set her apart from other aid workers from the moment she arrived in southern Sudan. But no one was prepared for her decision to marry a local warlord — a man who seemed to embody everything she was working against — and to throw herself into his violent quest to take over southern Sudan's rebel movement. Deborah Scroggins - who met McCune in the Sudan — charts the process by which McCune's romantic delusions led to her descent into the hell of Africa's longest running civil war.